Developing Responsive Web Applications with AJAX and jQuery

Design and develop your very own responsive web applications using Java, jQuery, and AJAX

Sandeep Kumar Patel

[PACKT] open source *
PUBLISHING   community experience distilled

BIRMINGHAM - MUMBAI

Mohammad Amzad Hossain has 7 years of experience building large-scale complex websites and web applications. He works as a Branch Manager in Sourcetop Inc. where he leads an offshore team in Dhaka, Bangladesh. His day-to-day life requires him to plan, analyze, guide, and provide solutions for complex requirements. In his free time, he digs into recent trends in web development and follows hundreds of RSS that help him to keep up in the fast-track world of development. He has a BSc degree in Computer Science Engineering.

Jake Kronika, a software developer and UI architect with over 20 years of experience, brings to bear extensive proficiency implementing both server-side and user interface (UI) solutions including multiple responsive web applications to date.

He began his career early in life using online tools for static content and rapidly progressed to building dynamic applications incorporating databases and server-side scripting languages. He has been a Senior User Interface Software Engineer at ADP Dealer Services in Seattle, WA, USA from 2011. Prior to this, he occupied numerous senior-level positions in the UI space in Chicago, IL. He has also balanced considerable freelance work under a sole proprietorship named Gridline Design & Development, accessible at `http://gridlined.com/`, online since 1999.

Over the past several years, particularly as the HTML, CSS, and JavaScript portions of websites have experienced rapid evolution, he has continually sought out and digested new technological knowledge through reading, personal and client projects, and other means. Some of his favorite current tools include Node.js and AngularJS, Less/Sass, and Git VCS.

Prior to this book, he was a technical reviewer for the following Packt Publishing titles:

- *Django JavaScript Integration: AJAX and jQuery, Jonathan Hayward*, in January 2011
- *jQuery UI 1.8: The User Interface Library for jQuery, Dan Wellman*, in August 2011
- *jQuery Tools UI Library*, *Alex Libby*, in February 2012

Credits

Author
Sandeep Kumar Patel

Reviewers
Fernando Doglio
Md. Zahid Hasan
Mohammad Amzad Hossain
Jake Kronika

Commissioning Editor
Julian Ursell

Acquisition Editor
Mohammad Rizvi

Content Development Editor
Balaji Naidu

Technical Editors
Venu Manthena
Mrunmayee Patil

Copy Editors
Roshni Banerjee
Sarang Chari
Janbal Dharmaraj
Gladson Monteiro
Deepa Nambiar
Karuna Narayanan
Adithi Shetty

Project Coordinator
Aaron S. Lazar

Proofreaders
Simran Bhogal
Paul Hindle

Indexers
Hemangini Bari
Rekha Nair
Priya Subramani

Graphics
Abhinash Sahu

Production Coordinator
Shantanu Zagade

Cover Work
Shantanu Zagade

About the Author

Sandeep Kumar Patel is a senior web developer and the founder of
`www.tutorialsavvy.com`, a widely-read programming blog since 2012. He has
more than 4 years of experience in object-oriented JavaScript and JSON-based web
application development. He is GATE 2005 Information Technology (IT) qualified
and has a Master's degree from VIT University, Vellore. At present, he holds the
position of Web Developer in SAP Labs, India. You can find out more about him
from his LinkedIn profile (`http://www.linkedin.com/in/techblogger`).
He has received the DZone Most Valuable Blogger (MVB) award for technical
publications related to web technologies. His article can be viewed at
`http://www.dzone.com/users/sandeepgiet`. He has also received the Java
Code Geek (JCG) badge for a technical article published in JCG. His article can be
viewed at `http://www.javacodegeeks.com/author/sandeep-kumar-patel/`.

About the Reviewers

Fernando Doglio has been working as a web developer for the past 10 years. During that time, he fell in love with the Web and has had the opportunity of working with most of the leading technologies such as PHP, Ruby on Rails, MySQL, Node.js, AngularJS, AJAX, REST APIs, and others.

In his spare time, he likes to tinker and learn new things, which is why his GitHub account keeps getting new repos every month. He's also a big open source supporter and tries to win the support of new people with the help of his site: `http://www.lookingforpullrequests.com/`. He can be contacted on Twitter at `@deleteman123`.

When not programming, he can be seen spending time with his family.

Md. Zahid Hasan is a professional web developer. He got his BSc and MSc in Information and Communication Engineering from University of Rajshahi (RU), Rajshahi. Now, he is working as a Lecturer in the department of Computer Science and Engineering at Green University of Bangladesh. He previously worked as a Software Developer at SEleven IT Limited for 2 years in Bangladesh.

He has a wide range of technical skills, Internet knowledge, and experience across the spectrum of online development in the service of building and improving online properties for multiple clients. He enjoys creating site architecture and infrastructure, backend development using open source tools such as Linux, Apache, MySQL, and PHP (LAMP), and frontend development with CSS and HTML/XHTML.

Mohammad Amzad Hossain has 7 years of experience building large-scale complex websites and web applications. He works as a Branch Manager in Sourcetop Inc. where he leads an offshore team in Dhaka, Bangladesh. His day-to-day life requires him to plan, analyze, guide, and provide solutions for complex requirements. In his free time, he digs into recent trends in web development and follows hundreds of RSS that help him to keep up in the fast-track world of development. He has a BSc degree in Computer Science Engineering.

Jake Kronika, a software developer and UI architect with over 20 years of experience, brings to bear extensive proficiency implementing both server-side and user interface (UI) solutions including multiple responsive web applications to date.

He began his career early in life using online tools for static content and rapidly progressed to building dynamic applications incorporating databases and server-side scripting languages. He has been a Senior User Interface Software Engineer at ADP Dealer Services in Seattle, WA, USA from 2011. Prior to this, he occupied numerous senior-level positions in the UI space in Chicago, IL. He has also balanced considerable freelance work under a sole proprietorship named Gridline Design & Development, accessible at `http://gridlined.com/`, online since 1999.

Over the past several years, particularly as the HTML, CSS, and JavaScript portions of websites have experienced rapid evolution, he has continually sought out and digested new technological knowledge through reading, personal and client projects, and other means. Some of his favorite current tools include Node.js and AngularJS, Less/Sass, and Git VCS.

Prior to this book, he was a technical reviewer for the following Packt Publishing titles:

- *Django JavaScript Integration: AJAX and jQuery, Jonathan Hayward,* in January 2011
- *jQuery UI 1.8: The User Interface Library for jQuery, Dan Wellman,* in August 2011
- *jQuery Tools UI Library, Alex Libby*, in February 2012

www.PacktPub.com

Support files, eBooks, discount offers, and more

You might want to visit www.PacktPub.com for support files and downloads related to your book.

Did you know that Packt offers eBook versions of every book published, with PDF and ePub files available? You can upgrade to the eBook version at www.PacktPub.com and as a print book customer, you are entitled to a discount on the eBook copy. Get in touch with us at service@packtpub.com for more details.

At www.PacktPub.com, you can also read a collection of free technical articles, sign up for a range of free newsletters and receive exclusive discounts and offers on Packt books and eBooks.

PACKTLIB

http://PacktLib.PacktPub.com

Do you need instant solutions to your IT questions? PacktLib is Packt's online digital book library. Here, you can access, read and search across Packt's entire library of books.

Why subscribe?

- Fully searchable across every book published by Packt
- Copy and paste, print and bookmark content
- On demand and accessible via web browser

Free access for Packt account holders

If you have an account with Packt at www.PacktPub.com, you can use this to access PacktLib today and view nine entirely free books. Simply use your login credentials for immediate access.

Table of Contents

Preface

Welcome to *Developing Responsive Web Applications with AJAX and jQuery*. If you want to learn and understand responsive layout development or social application integration using AJAX and jQuery, then this book is for you. It covers a systematic approach for building a responsive web application.

All the key features of a responsive application are explained with the detailed code. It also explains how to debug and test a responsive web application during development.

What this book covers

Chapter 1, Introduction to a Responsive Web Application, introduces you to the responsiveness of an application and lists the key benefits of a responsive application for a commercial site.

Chapter 2, Creating a Responsive Layout for a Web Application, explains how to develop a layout that will support different screen sizes to render using Bootstrap 3.

Chapter 3, Adding Dynamic Visuals to a Web Application, explains how to make a jQuery AJAX call for JSON data and render content in different parts of the web application.

Chapter 4, Twitter Integration, demonstrates how to integrate the Twitter4J library to incorporate different features such as tweets and posts from the web application.

Chapter 5, Facebook Integration, demonstrates how to integrate the Facebook SDK to add the Facebook login and Like features in the web application.

Chapter 6, Google+ Integration, shows how to integrate the Google+ login and +1 feature into the web application.

Chapter 7, Linking Dynamic Content from External Websites, explains how to integrate the YouTube API to embed a recommended video into a web application.

Chapter 8, Integrating E-Commerce or Shopping Applications with Your Website, illustrates the integration of the PayPal payment API into the application. Also, it introduces the integration of the Shopify API into the application.

Chapter 9, Integrating the Google Currency Converter with Your Web Application, explains how to integrate the Google Currency API to help a user see the amount in a different currency.

Chapter 10, Debugging and Testing, introduces the different available online and offline tools to test a responsive application during development.

What you need for this book

The following list of tools and libraries are required for this book:

- Eclipse IDE for Java EE Developers
- Apache Tomcat 7.0
- Bootstrap 3.0
- jQuery 2.1.0

Who this book is for

This book is for Java web developers who want to create responsive web applications. This book is also helpful for those who want to learn about the integration of social applications into existing web applications. Finally, the book is for everyone interested in better understanding AJAX-based responsive web application development.

Conventions

In this book, you will find a number of styles of text that distinguish between different kinds of information. Here are some examples of these styles, and an explanation of their meaning.

Code words in text, database table names, folder names, filenames, file extensions, pathnames, dummy URLs, user input, and Twitter handles are shown as follows: "The `data-toggle` attribute has the value for the effect property such as collapse."

A block of code is set as follows:

```
<div class="navbar-collapse collapse" id="ts-top-menu">
  <ul class="nav navbar-nav">
    <li class="active"><a href="#">Category 1</a></li>
    <li><a href="#">Category 2</a></li>
    <li><a href="#">Category 3</a></li>
  </ul>
</div>
```

When we wish to draw your attention to a particular part of a code block, the relevant lines or items are set in bold:

```
<!DOCTYPE html>
<html>
<head>
<link rel="stylesheet" href="asset/css/bootstrap.min.css">
<title>Responsive product Store</title>
</head>
<body>
    <div class="container-fluid"></div>
</body>
</html>
```

New terms and **important words** are shown in bold. Words that you see on the screen, in menus or dialog boxes for example, appear in the text like this: "The **Arguments** option is for passing additional arguments."

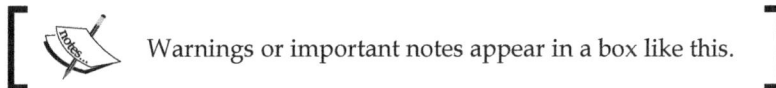

> Warnings or important notes appear in a box like this.

> Tips and tricks appear like this.

Reader feedback

Feedback from our readers is always welcome. Let us know what you think about this book — what you liked or may have disliked. Reader feedback is important for us to develop titles that you really get the most out of.

To send us general feedback, simply send an e-mail to feedback@packtpub.com, and mention the book title via the subject of your message.

If there is a topic that you have expertise in and you are interested in either writing or contributing to a book, see our author guide on www.packtpub.com/authors.

Customer support

Now that you are the proud owner of a Packt book, we have a number of things to help you to get the most from your purchase.

Downloading the example code

You can download the example code files for all Packt books you have purchased from your account at http://www.packtpub.com. If you purchased this book elsewhere, you can visit http://www.packtpub.com/support and register to have the files e-mailed directly to you.

Errata

Although we have taken every care to ensure the accuracy of our content, mistakes do happen. If you find a mistake in one of our books — maybe a mistake in the text or the code — we would be grateful if you would report this to us. By doing so, you can save other readers from frustration and help us improve subsequent versions of this book. If you find any errata, please report them by visiting http://www.packtpub.com/submit-errata, selecting your book, clicking on the **errata submission form** link, and entering the details of your errata. Once your errata are verified, your submission will be accepted and the errata will be uploaded on our website, or added to any list of existing errata, under the Errata section of that title. Any existing errata can be viewed by selecting your title from http://www.packtpub.com/support.

Piracy

Piracy of copyright material on the Internet is an ongoing problem across all media. At Packt, we take the protection of our copyright and licenses very seriously. If you come across any illegal copies of our works, in any form, on the Internet, please provide us with the location address or website name immediately so that we can pursue a remedy.

Please contact us at copyright@packtpub.com with a link to the suspected pirated material.

We appreciate your help in protecting our authors, and our ability to bring you valuable content.

Questions

You can contact us at questions@packtpub.com if you are having a problem with any aspect of the book, and we will do our best to address it.

1
Introduction to a Responsive Web Application

In this chapter, we be introduced to **responsive web design** followed by an understanding of technology stack that made responsive web application development possible.

The current trend of technology revolution has led us to a point where we can see many wireless devices with different screen size, resolution, and processing capabilities. It is really challenging and difficult to create different versions of web applications for each and every device type. To address this challenge, it needs a design solution that can address these problems. Responsive web design provides the platform and flexibility where we can write code once and publish the application everywhere.

Designing a website to look good at one particular resolution was the standard and that standard was adequate for almost all purposes. Now, more and more people are viewing web content on smartphones and tablets. The most successful websites must have content designed to fit on any size screen or any type of device. Designing content in this manner is also known as responsive web design. We need to give all users, regardless of their access platform, a seamless experience, and responsive web design offers a cost-efficient way of achieving that. Responsive web content can dynamically change size, fonts, and colors to match whatever device your customers might be using.

The most important dimensions of a responsive design are as follows:

- An adaptive grid-based layout that must be responsive enough to the client-side environment. There are two different approaches for an adaptive layout: the first one is a fixed layout and the other one is a fluid layout. Fluid layouts are always proportional to the screen size.

- Fluid images must maintain the aspect ratio. To maintain the aspect ratio, we can go for two approaches, either setting the max-height to 100 percent or max-width of 100 percent. This makes the images overflow in either direction. The other way of handling the images is to clip a portion of the image, though it is not recommended.

- The new CSS3 media queries make the browser more intelligent. Now, browsers can make the decision to load the appropriate CSS at runtime. This makes them adaptable to the client environment.

> Responsive design is made possible through the use of three core ingredients: a flexible grid-based layout, flexible images and media, and CSS media queries.

Benefits of a responsive design

The most important benefits of responsive web application are as follows:

- Pleasant user experience in each type of device

- Reduced development cost compared to developing different applications for each device type

- Reduced cost on advertising and marketing compared to maintaining campaigns for every application for each device

- Better indexing in search engines and improved search engine optimization (SEO)

- Increased conversion rates and lead generation as SEO is increased (visibility of a web application in search engines)

Responsive web design uses a single code base, but in reality, different devices have to be accounted for. While a desktop version can display a lot of content at once, for smaller screens, you need to know exactly what content truly matters. To create a great experience for all users, you need to consider that people will use different devices in different circumstances and with different goals. With a responsive web design, more effort and time will be involved to get the right user experience for your target audience.

If you look into different applications present online such as blogs and sports applications, then you will notice that the end user behaviors are similar and follow a common pattern. To provide the same experience for the end users, the layout and other elements in the application must be designed for customization. This needs more effort and time in developing the layout and the code.

Server- versus client-side detection

Addressing the issue of developing applications for different media types and devices can be solved in two ways. The first one is the server-side detection where middleware is responsible for reading the request header sent by the browser and redirects the request to the appropriate version of the application. This requires you to develop a different version of the application. It means an e-commerce site must have a separate code base for each type of device.

The second one is the client-side detection. It should be done by the browser and apply relative CSS based on the device or screen type. With this idea, the responsive design is born. The real benefit is that one has to maintain a single code base for this.

The technology stack

The following diagram shows the building blocks for responsive web application development. Each block in the diagram represents a technology that enables responsive web application development.

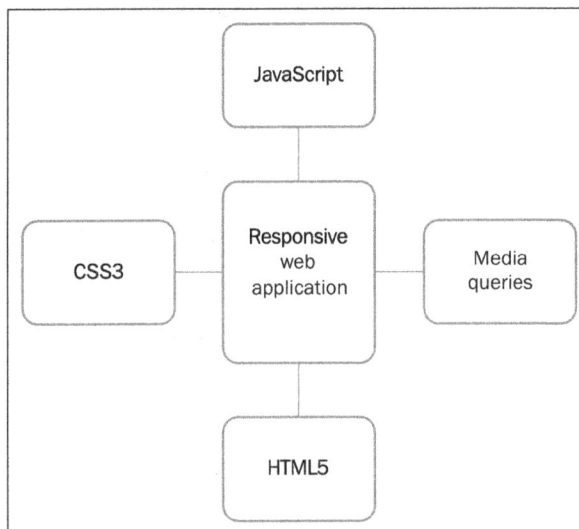

HTML5

HTML5 is the latest version of HTML, released by the W3C foundation with more modern features included such as more semantics and usability features. This helps in responsive web application development with more ease and less effort. Some of the key points that highlight why HTML5 is a better candidate than other versions of HTML are as follows:

- Inclusion of new HTML5 elements such as video and audio as native reduces the use of an additional third-party plugin
- Enhanced existing elements such as form element reduce the need for an additional amount of code to be written
- Inclusion of Canvas and SVG for graphic rendering and drawing adds additional capabilities

CSS3 and media queries

Features such as media type detection and layout manipulation of media queries are useful to build a responsive layout. Some of the key points of CSS3 are as follows:

- CSS3 animations and transitions reduce the need for JavaScript processing, favoring, instead, a native implementation that can vastly improve performance on mobile devices where processing power can be quite limited, while falling back gracefully to immediate changes in browsers that do not support them.
- Support of new measuring units such as rem helps in building a logical relationship among elements' dimensions present inside a page.
- Ultimately, the vw and vh units will greatly enhance the ability of a developer to size elements relative to the viewport.
- FlexBox provides numerous benefits with direction-based alignment and element ordering inside a layout. For a responsive design, this means that a default ideal order can be established via the document order to provide greater SEO benefits, while different ordering can be provided based on viewport size, device orientation type, and so on, to display content in the best format for a given use case.

JavaScript

JavaScript brings the capability of feature detection for the browser. It helps in choosing the right component for the end user and makes the browser responsive to its environment.

Some of the key points about JavaScript are as follows:

- Browser feature detection helps you to find features that are supported by the browser. This helps in helps you to execute the appropriate code in the application.
- Rendering behavior of the site can be altered using JavaScript.

Measuring responsiveness

There are many parameters for measuring the responsiveness of an application. Layout, content, and navigation are the three most important parameters for a responsive web application development. The following diagram shows the three different building blocks of a responsive web application:

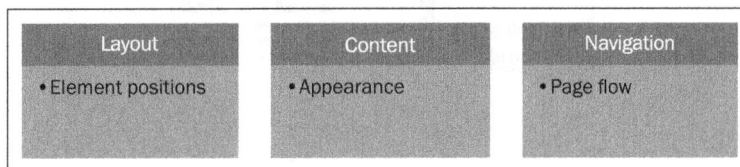

- **Layout**: While developing a responsive web application for all kinds of devices, the layout should be developed based on the available size. Based on the breakpoints for each device size, the layout gets altered. This includes show and hide of a section in the layout.
- **Content**: For small screens, the available viewing space is very small. While developing a responsive web application, the text content must be responsive. It includes the typography, images, and other media elements present inside the page.
- **Navigation**: For touch-enabled devices, the navigational elements will be different to those on medium devices. How these navigational items are to be presented to the end user is really a design challenge. It should be rendered seamless to the end user while navigating in any devices.

Devices and screens

If you look at the gadget market for handheld devices, you can find a wide range of devices with different screen sizes. If you ask me what the optimal size for a device screen is, I probably could not answer you without knowing the purpose. Each and every device is good for a specific use. So, the optimal size of a screen is directly dependent on the end user.

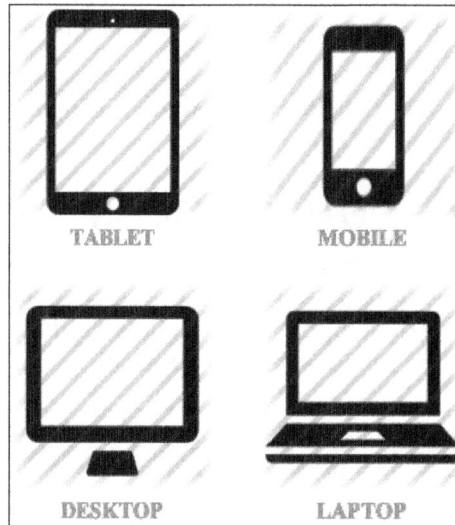

A wide screen with good graphics and pixel density may be the best fit for a gaming end user. For a regular end user, a small device is a good fit. The web application design must support all these screen sizes. The usability and the user experience must be equivalent to all types of screens. Also, it is much more important when it comes to an e-commerce site. If the end user is browsing the site on a mobile device and the e-commerce device is only designed for a desktop, then it does not generate the same pleasant experience that will lose the leads.

The soul of an e-commerce site is lead generation and it is only possible when the application will provide seamless access to the end user irrespective of the browsing device. This clearly requires the application to be responsive to its environment or adapt itself based on the screen or device.

Media types

All these devices (desktops, tablets, mobiles, and laptops) fall in one of the following media types. The following figure shows all the media types listed in the W3C specification:

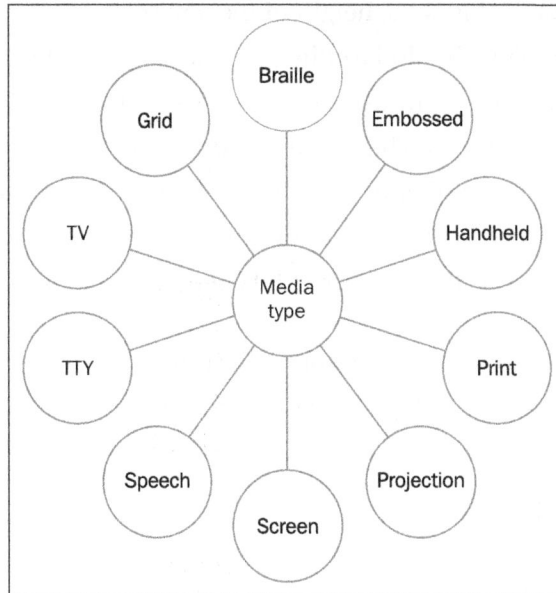

- **Braille**: This is used for braille tactile feedback devices.
- **Embossed**: This is used for paged braille printers.
- **Handheld**: This is used for handheld devices. Smartphones and tablets do not fall to this.
- **Print**: This is used for paged material and for documents viewed on screen in the print preview mode.
- **Projection**: This is used for projected presentations, for example, projectors.
- **Screen**: This is used primarily for color computer screens and smartphones.
- **Speech**: This is used for speech synthesizers.
- **TTY**: This is used for media using a fixed-pitch character grid. It includes teletypes, terminals, or portable devices with limited display capabilities.
- **TV**: This is used for television type devices. It includes low resolution, color, limited-scrollability screens, and audio.
- **Grid**: This is used for visual and tactile media types.

Available expressions for media queries to filter the CSS rules are as follows:

- `width`: This is the width of the current window
- `height`: This is the height of the current window
- `device-width`: This is the width of the device

- device-height: This is the height of the device
- orientation: This should be either landscape or portrait
- aspect-ratio: This is the aspect ratio of the current window
- device-aspect-ratio: This is the aspect ratio of the device
- color: This is the number of color bits per color component
- color-index: This is the number of available colors on the device
- monochrome: This is the number of bits per pixel in a monochrome frame buffer
- resolution: This is the resolution of the device
- scan: This should be either progressive or interlace

Media queries

Media queries are one of the best features of CSS3. Using this feature, we can decide which style sheet should be applied on the web page at runtime.

Media queries can be used as external or internal style sheets. An external style sheet is easier to organize; it is not downloaded by browsers that don't support it, but it uses an extra HTTP request. An internal style sheet, on the other hand, does not require an extra HTTP request, but the whole style sheet is downloaded for browsers even if they do not support media queries, and it can be harder to organize.

The following code is an example of an external media queries call:

```
<link rel="stylesheet" type="text/CSS" media="screen and (max-device-width: 480px) " href="abc.css" />
```

The following code is an example of internal media queries:

```
body {
    background: gray;
}
@media all and (max-width: 480px){
body{
    background: blue;
    }
}
```

Role of media queries

CSS3 provides a new set of features called media queries for responsive web application development. These media queries are helpful for conditional CSS3 used on a page based on the media type, device width, and other parameters. Generally, the following parameters help in applying the correct CSS3 to the web page:

- Height and width of the device refers to the size of the device
- Height and width of the browser refers to the viewable area
- Screen resolution refers to the pixel and color depth of the screen
- Orientation of the device refers to the portrait or landscape mode

Using media queries, the layout can be designed in the following two ways:

- **The adaptive layout**: This is based on a pretty simple idea: instead of using percentage, we will give our layout fixed sizes. The layout will adapt those sizes depending of the width of the browser/viewport, thus creating a layout with different breakpoints.
- **The responsive layout**: This is a mix between fluid and adaptive layouts. It will use the relative units of the fluid layout and the breakpoints of the adaptive one.

Responsive frameworks

There are many frameworks available from different vendors for responsive web application development. Some of the popular libraries are explored in the following sections.

Bootstrap

Some of the key points about the Bootstrap framework are as follows:

- Twitter's Bootstrap library is the most popular responsive framework.
- It is based on mobile-first design strategy. The source code of the projects is available in the SASS and LESS format.
- Bootstrap 3, SASS, and LESS really helps in customizing modules needed for the project.
- There are many resources and plugins available on the Internet for the Bootstrap framework.
- You can get more information from `http://getbootstrap.com/`.

The Foundation framework

Some of the key points about the Foundation framework are as follows:

- Foundation framework is yet another popular responsive framework by ZURB foundation
- Foundation Version 5 follows mobile-first design strategy (designing your site or app for the small device first, and then expanding that to include larger displays and more full-featured devices)
- The major benefit of Foundation framework is that the rem unit is used for its sizing of fonts and positioning
- You can get more information from `http://foundation.zurb.com/`

The Cascade framework

Some of the key points about the Cascade framework are as follows:

- The Cascade framework is lightweight and modular.
- The code packages in the Cascade framework are done based on their features.
- For example, for coloring purpose, there is a color module to be invoked and used. All features of Cascade framework support Internet Explorer from IE6 upwards or degrade gracefully.

- The whole library comes under four different modules: grid, typography, icons, and components. It has also some reusable web page templates in a different section.

- You can get more information from `http://www.cascade-framework.com/`.

The Pure CSS framework

Some of the key points about the Pure CSS framework are as follows:

- Pure CSS is a lightweight responsive framework by Yahoo Inc.

- The Pure CSS library is very tiny in size, and is about 4.4 KB minified and compressed version. This library targets mobile devices.

- The core of this library is `Normalize.css`. The Normalize library provides layout and styling of the HTML elements.

- You can get more information from `http://purecss.io/`.

The Gumby framework

Some of the key points about the Gumby framework are as follows:

- The Gumby framework is incredibly customizable

- It's as easy as download, tweak, and deploy

- Gumby is built on the SASS authoring framework

- Most eye-catching features in Grid modules such as Basic Grid, Hybrid Grid, Nested Grid, Sematic Grids, Tiles, and Fancy tiles are part of the Gumby framework

- You can get more information from `http://gumbyframework.com/`

Bootstrap 3 for a responsive design

There are many components and utilities available for responsive web application development in Bootstrap. Bootstrap features are available in the following three different modules:

- **CSS**: This module has a lot of standard classes to use and is easily extendable for customization

- **Component**: This module has all the reusable built-in components

- **JavaScript**: This module has the jQuery plugin in Bootstrap style

Some important features that we are going to use in our web application development are presented in the following diagram:

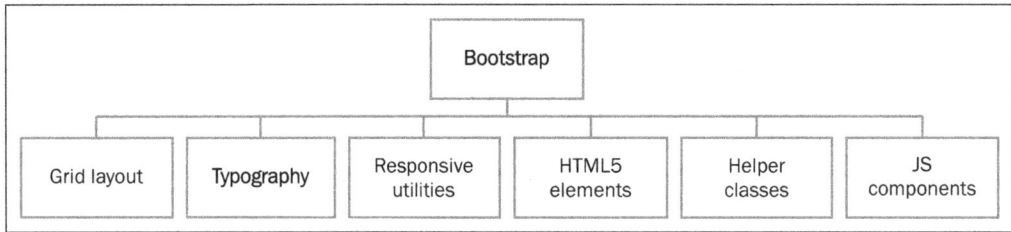

```
                          ┌─────────────┐
                          │  Bootstrap  │
                          └──────┬──────┘
   ┌───────────┬──────────┬──────┼───────────┬──────────┬──────────────┐
┌──┴──────┐┌───┴──────┐┌──┴──────┐┌──┴──────┐┌──┴──────┐┌──┴──────────┐
│  Grid   ││          ││Responsive││  HTML5  ││  Helper ││     JS      │
│ layout  ││Typography││ utilities││ elements││ classes ││ components  │
└─────────┘└──────────┘└─────────┘└─────────┘└─────────┘└─────────────┘
```

- **Grid layout**: This module has different grid classes for xs, sm, md, and lg type devices. The details of these grid classes are listed as follows:
    ◦ xs stands for extra small devices. For example, a phone's screen resolution is less than 768 pixels.
    ◦ xm stands for small devices. For example, a tablet's screen resolution is greater than or equal to 768 pixels.
    ◦ md stands for medium devices. For example, a desktop's screen resolution is greater than or equal to 992 pixels.
    ◦ lg stands for large devices. For example, a desktop's screen resolution is greater than or equal to 1200 pixels.

- **Typography**: This module has different classes based on the font size requirements.

- **Responsive utilities**: This module contains classes for conditional classes based on the types of devices.

- **HTML5 elements**: This module has default style classes for all HTML5 elements.

- **Helper classes**: This module has classes for frequently used alignment and positioning issues.

- **JS components**: This module has additional components such as carousel, tooltip, popover, and so on.

What are we building?

We are going to use the Bootstrap 3 framework for responsive web application development. In the following chapters, we will build an e-commerce web application that will be responsive in design.

The plan is as follows:

- Building the layout for the application
- Populating the content in the layout
- Integrating the application with social media sites
- Integrating a payment system with the Add to Cart feature
- Building a currency converter
- Debugging and testing the web application for responsiveness

Summary

In this chapter, we have learned about the need for a responsive web application and what challenges it brings to a web developer. We have also learned about the latest responsive libraries available for development. We have understood how a responsive layout can increase the user experience. In the following chapter, we will learn to develop a responsive layout using CSS3.

2

Creating a Responsive Layout for a Web Application

In this chapter, we will set up our Java-based web project and develop the layout required to create our responsive web application. The process of developing the layout follows a step-wise approach. Initially, we will draw a wireframe for the layout, and then, we will prepare code for each section using Bootstrap 3 classes. Later on in this chapter, we will verify the layout with different screen sizes using some tools.

Required software and tools

We need the following software to be installed to develop the responsive web application:

- An Eclipse Java EE IDE of Juno/Kepler version for web developers (http://www.eclipse.org)
- Apache Tomcat 7
- Opera Mobile emulator
- The draw.io online tool
- The Mozilla Firefox browser
- The Google Chrome browser

Setting up a Java-based web project

In this section, we will set up a Java-based web project in Eclipse. To do this, we have to create a new dynamic web project. The following screenshot shows the window to create a new web project. In Eclipse, click on the **File** button and choose **New** to list the different project types present in Eclipse.

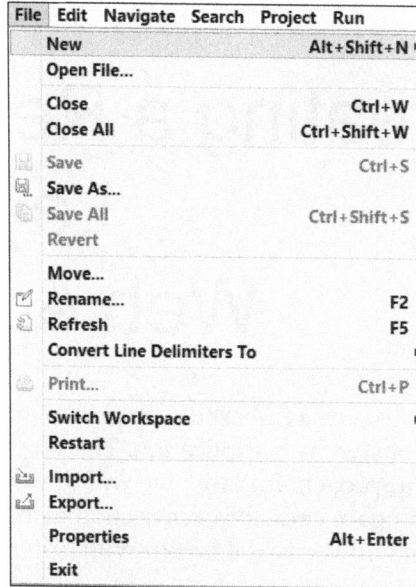

File	Edit	Navigate	Search	Project	Run	
New						Alt+Shift+N ▶
Open File...						
Close						Ctrl+W
Close All						Ctrl+Shift+W
Save						Ctrl+S
Save As...						
Save All						Ctrl+Shift+S
Revert						
Move...						
Rename...						F2
Refresh						F5
Convert Line Delimiters To						▶
Print...						Ctrl+P
Switch Workspace						▶
Restart						
Import...						
Export...						
Properties						Alt+Enter
Exit						

The different available project types present are shown in the following screenshot. When this window appears, choose the **Dynamic Web Project** option.

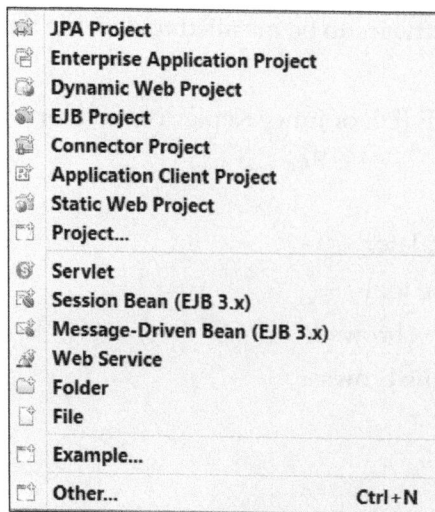

- **JPA Project**
- **Enterprise Application Project**
- **Dynamic Web Project**
- **EJB Project**
- **Connector Project**
- **Application Client Project**
- **Static Web Project**
- **Project...**
- **Servlet**
- **Session Bean (EJB 3.x)**
- **Message-Driven Bean (EJB 3.x)**
- **Web Service**
- **Folder**
- **File**
- **Example...**
- **Other...**   Ctrl+N

When you have chosen the **Dynamic Web Project** option, a **New Dynamic Web Project** window will open asking for **Project name**, as shown in the following screenshot:

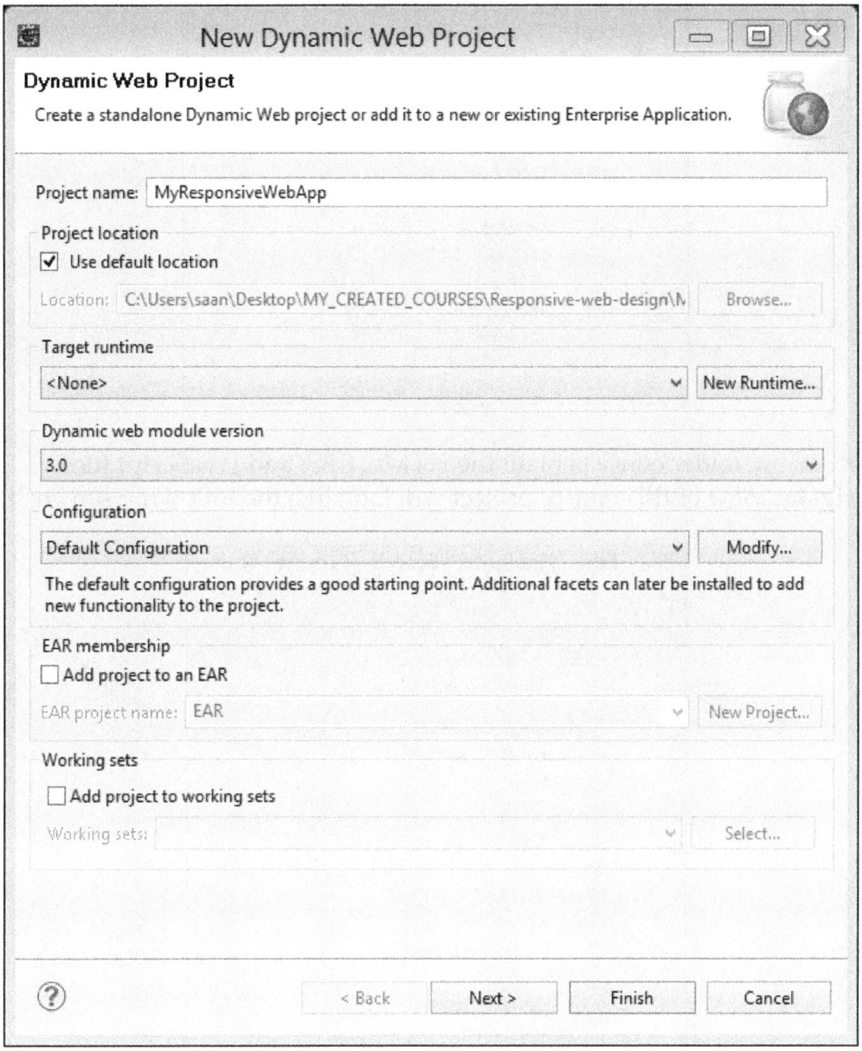

For our application, we will name the project MyResponsiveWebApp. The project structure will look like the following screenshot:

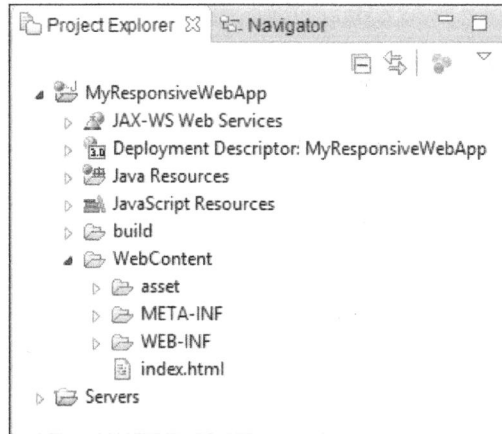

The WebContent folder consists of all the HTML, CSS, and JavaScript files. The **Navigator** view of this empty project will look like the following screenshot:

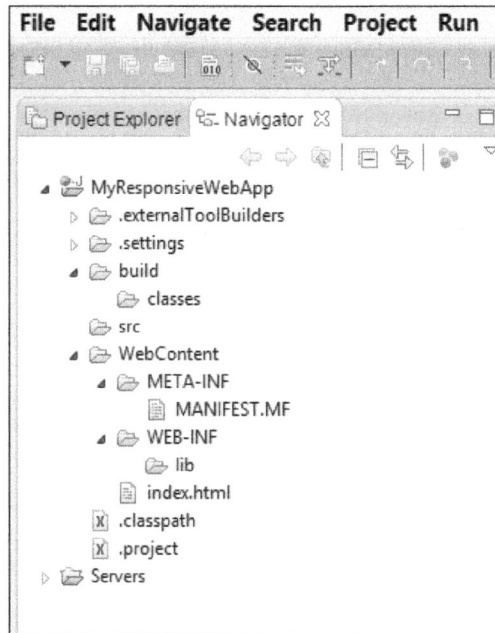

Configuring Bootstrap 3

In this section, we will configure the Bootstrap 3 library in our web project. Download the Bootstrap 3 library from `http://getbootstrap.com/getting-started/#download`. Bootstrap 3 has three different folders in its distribution package. They are explained as follows:

- `js`: This folder contains all the scripts required for the Bootstrap 3 library
- `fonts`: This folder contains all the font-related files including the **Glyph** icons
- `css`: This folder contains all the style sheet-related files with Bootstrap's default theme

The following figure shows the structure of the Bootstrap 3 library:

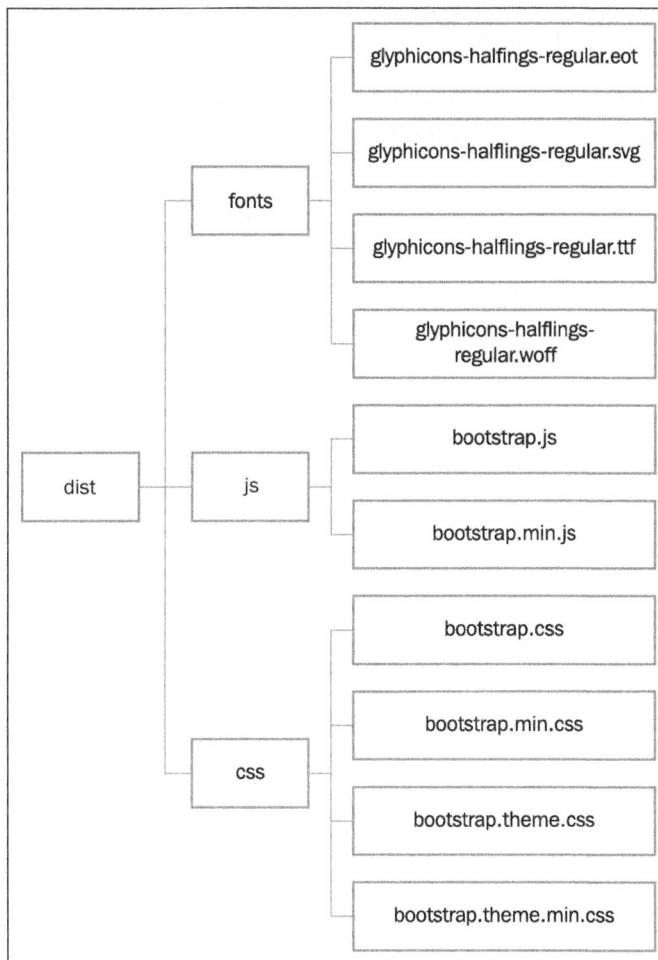

```
dist ─┬─ fonts ─┬─ glyphicons-halfings-regular.eot
      │         ├─ glyphicons-halflings-regular.svg
      │         ├─ glyphicons-halflings-regular.ttf
      │         └─ glyphicons-halflings-regular.woff
      │
      ├─ js ────┬─ bootstrap.js
      │         └─ bootstrap.min.js
      │
      └─ css ───┬─ bootstrap.css
                ├─ bootstrap.min.css
                ├─ bootstrap.theme.css
                └─ bootstrap.theme.min.css
```

The details of each file present inside these folders are given as follows:

- The `fonts` folder contains the `glyphicons-halflings-regular.eot`, `glyphicons-halflings-regular.svg`, `glyphicons-halflings-regular.woff`, and `glyphicons-halflings-regular.ttf` files containing all icons used in Bootstrap 3.

- The `js` folder contains the `bootstrap.js` and `bootstrap.min.js` script files. The `bootstrap.js` file is the uncompressed version, while `bootstarp.min.js` file is the compressed file.

- The `css` folder contains the `bootstrap.css`, `bootstrap.min.css`, `bootstrap.theme.css`, and `bootstrap.theme.min.css` style sheet files. The `bootstrap.css` file is the uncompressed version, while the `bootstrap.min.css` file is compressed file. The `bootstrap.theme.css` file contains the default Bootstrap styles in the uncompressed format. The `bootstrap.theme.min.css` file contains default Bootstrap styles in the compressed format.

To configure Bootstrap 3 in the project, we need to put the `css`, `js`, and `fonts` folders inside the `WebContent` folder and add the corresponding files, as shown in the following screenshot:

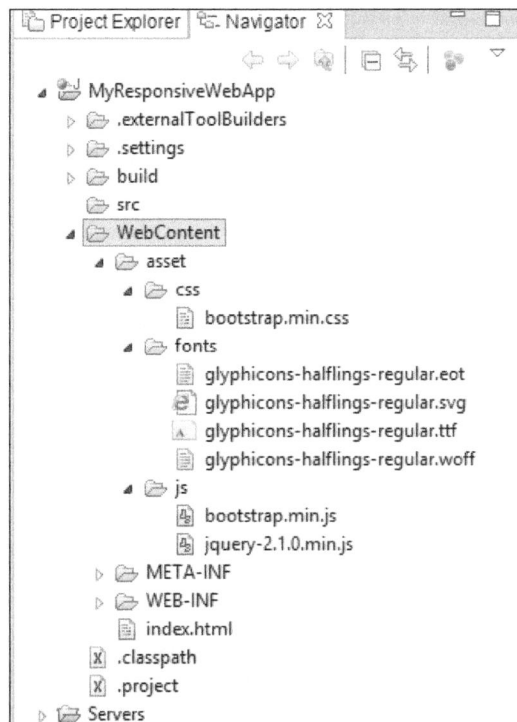

Creating a wireframe for a web application

In this section, we will create a wireframe for our web application. An online tool called **draw-io** is used to draw the wireframe. You can check out the tool at `https://www.draw.io/`. The following screenshot shows the prototype of the drawing created using the draw.io tool:

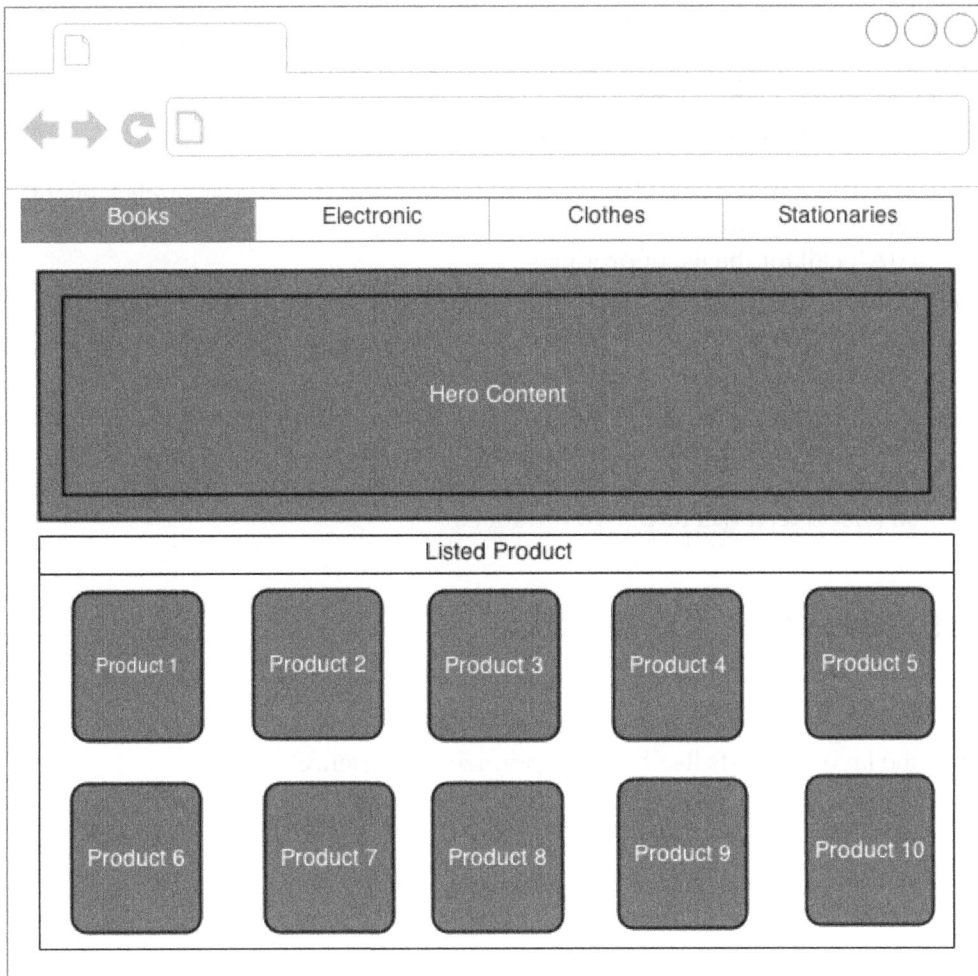

- The first row is about the product categories (the menu). For example, a product store can have books, electronics, and stationary sections.

- The second row is about the hero content. The hero section can have a carousel that can contain different product offers or important announcements.

- The third row is to display all the listed products for any selected category. Each product can have an image, pricing, and social links. The listed products are in a grid format. Each row in a grid may contain N number of products depending on the screen's size.

The interaction of these components is explained as follows:

- The first row is the navbar containing all product categories. A click event will be associated with each product category. The click event will make an AJAX call for the list of products.

- The second row is a hero section. This section will display the product of the day. For example, it may be a big image or a carousel highlighting an important announcement or an offer.

- The third row will render all the listed products from the previous response (the hero section). The number of products listed in the grid row depends on the screen size. For example, a bigger screen will have five products and a smaller screen will have two products.

Responsive layouts

A responsive layout has many benefits, which are as follows:

- **Scaling based on the screen size**: Based on the screen size of the client, the layout adjusts itself for an optimized experience

- **Single code file based**: A single HTML file is always easy to maintain than multiple versions of the file

- **Similar user experience**: A similar user experience is maintained in all types of devices

- **Lead generation**: This will increase proportionally as per better user experience

Creating a layout for large and small devices

Based on the wireframe, we have a flat design for large devices. In our application, the important component is the list of products where products are shown as grids in the row and column format. Based on the device's screen size, the number of products per row will change. For example, a device with a large screen can show four products in a row and a device with a small screen can show three products per row. The layout of the page is a fluid layout and will change based on the screen's size.

Developing the layout

In this section, we will realize the previously discussed wireframe with real code. From the preceding section, it is evident that we need to develop three sections, mentioned as follows:

- The menu section
- The hero section
- The list of products section

Before going into the development of each section, we need to understand the containers provided by Bootstrap. The following section discusses the Bootstrap containers.

Bootstrap 3 containers

Bootstrap provides fixed- and fluid-width containers. The CSS classes, `.container` and `.container-fluid`, are used to set up the base layout.

An example of the `.container` class is as follows:

```
<!DOCTYPE html>
<html>
<head>
<link rel="stylesheet" href="../asset/css/bootstrap.min.css">
<title>Responsive product Store</title>
</head>
<body>
    <div class="container"></div>
</body>
</html>
```

The following screenshot shows Chrome's development toolbar's layout that has a fixed width:

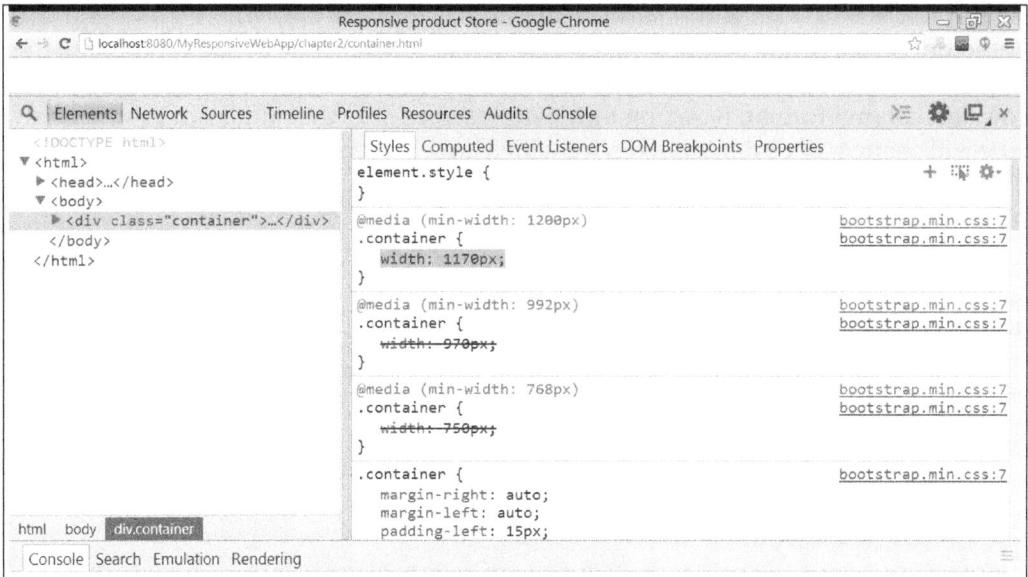

An example of the `.container-fluid` class is as follows:

```
<!DOCTYPE html>
<html>
<head>
<link rel="stylesheet" href="asset/css/bootstrap.min.css">
<title>Responsive product Store</title>
</head>
<body>
    <div class="container-fluid"></div>
</body>
</html>
```

The following screenshot shows Chrome's development toolbar's layout that has no width:

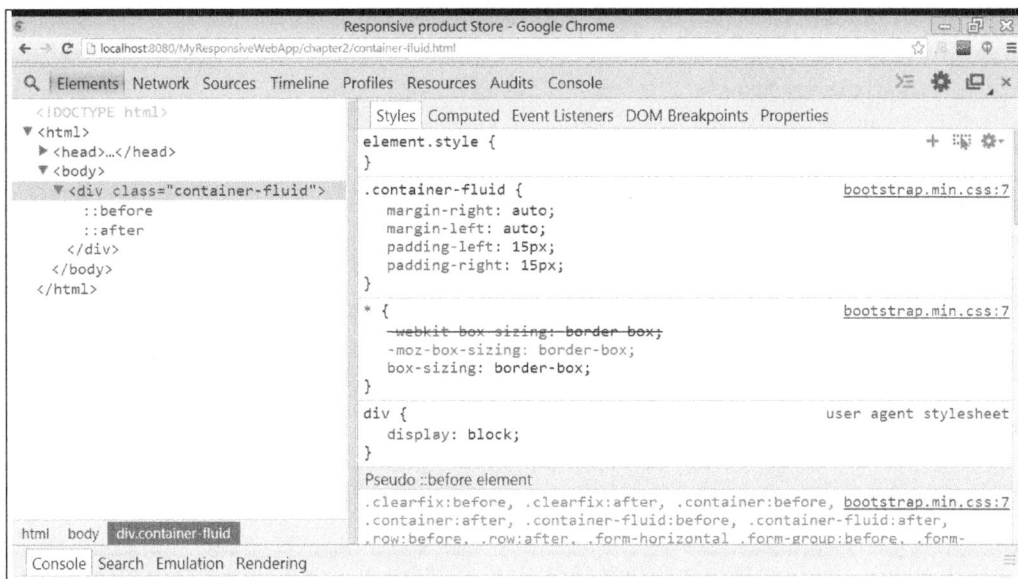

Developing a row

In Bootstrap 3, the `.row` class is used to create a row. There can be many rows in a single page. All the rows' classes must be enclosed inside a `container` class, shown as follows:

```html
<!DOCTYPE html>
<html>

<head>
  <link rel="stylesheet" href="asset/css/bootstrap.min.css">
  <title>Responsive product Store</title>
</head>
```

```
<body>
  <div class="container">
    <div class="row">
        Row1
    </div>
    <div class="row">
        Row2
    </div>
    <div class="row">
        Row3
    </div>
  </div>
<script src="asset/js/jquery-2.1.0.min.js"></script>
<script src="asset/js/bootstrap.min.js"></script>
</body>

</html>
```

The following screenshot shows the three different rows created in the browser:

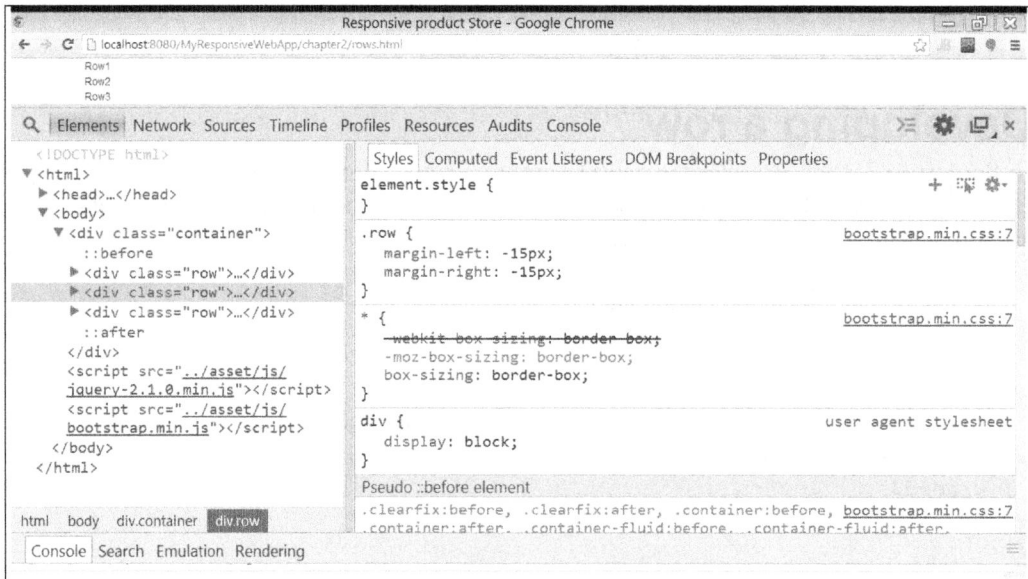

Developing the menu section

Based on the wireframe, a menu is similar to the navbar. The nav element is used to create the navbar element in Bootstrap 3. Each menu item is nested in the li tag, inside an **unordered list (ul)**, shown as follows:

```
<!DOCTYPE html>
<html>

<head>
  <link rel="stylesheet" href="../asset/css/bootstrap.min.css">
  <title>Responsive product Store</title>
</head>

<body>
  <div class="container">
    <nav class="navbar navbar-inverse navbar-static-top"
role="navigation">
      <div class="container-fluid">
        <div class="navbar-header">
          <button type="button" class="navbar-toggle collapsed" data-
toggle="collapse" data-target="#ts-top-menu">
              <span class="sr-only">
                  Navigation buttons
              </span>
        <span class="icon-bar"></span>
        <span class="icon-bar"></span>
        <span class="icon-bar"></span>
          </button>
          <a class="navbar-brand" href="#">PRODUCTS</a>
        </div>
        <!-- Collect the nav links, forms, and other content for
toggling -->
        <div class="navbar-collapse collapse" id="ts-top-menu">
          <ul class="nav navbar-nav">
              <li class="active"><a href="#">Category 1</a>
              </li>
              <li><a href="#">Category 2</a>
              </li>
              <li><a href="#">Category 3</a>
              </li>
          </ul>
      </div>
      </div>
    </nav>
```

```
    </div>
<script src="asset/js/jquery-2.1.0.min.js"></script>
<script src="asset/js/bootstrap.min.js"></script>
</body>

</html>
```

The navbar will be rendered in the browser, shown as follows:

For a smaller screen size, it will be rendered as shown in the following screenshot. It has a button to expand the detailed menu list. This view is really helpful for small screens due to the space constraint in the monitor. The following screenshot is taken in Chrome in a smaller screen size:

The expanded version for the preceding navbar looks like the following screenshot. The property to expand and collapse is due to the `data-toggle` and `data-target` attributes, which are explained as follows:

- The `data-toggle` attribute has the value for the property of the effect, such as collapse

- The `data-target` attribute has the value for the target DOM element that will expand and collapse on click event

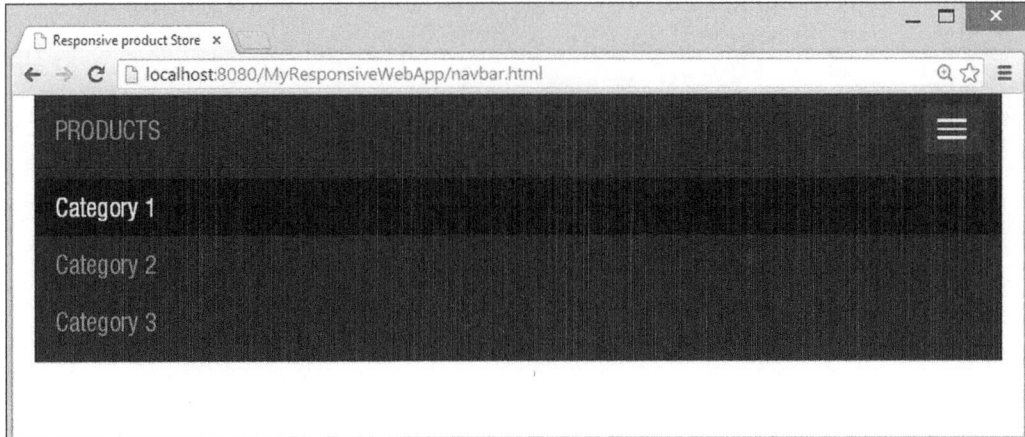

Developing the hero section

Based on the wireframe, developing the hero section will be the main focus area. To the represent the hero section, Bootstrap has a `.jumbotron` class.

The code of the `jumbotron` class is shown as follows:

```
<!DOCTYPE html>
<html>

<head>
  <link rel="stylesheet" href="asset/css/bootstrap.min.css">
  <title>Responsive product Store</title>
</head>

<body>
  <div class="container">
    <div class="jumbotron">
```

```
        <h1>Hero Section</h1>
    </div>
  </div>
<script src="asset/js/jquery-2.1.0.min.js"></script>
<script src="asset/js/bootstrap.min.js"></script>
</body>

</html>
```

The jumbotron class renders in browser, as shown in the following screenshot:

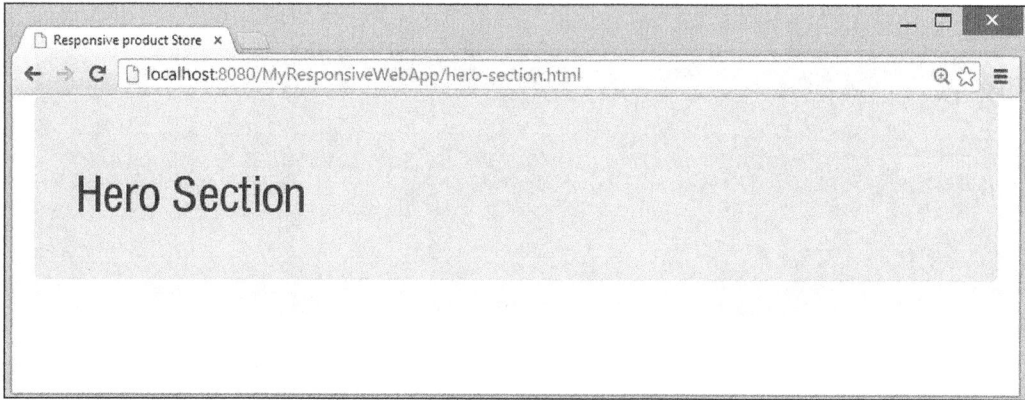

Developing the list of products section

Based on the wireframe, this section will display the list of products.
The ts-product class is the css class to represent each product. To align
products in a row inside a grid, we have used a container class called
.ts-product-container. The display:inline-block style sheet
property is used to put each product in a row.

To display the list of products in a grid, we have created another style sheet
called ts-responsive-web-style.css, as shown in the following code:

```
.ts-product-container{
    text-align:center;
}
.ts-product-container .ts-product{
    display: inline-block;
    height: 250px;
    margin: 10px 40px;
```

```
    width: 200px;
    background: #eee;
    font-weight: bold;
}
```

The HTML code for the list of products is shown in the following code:

```
<!DOCTYPE html>
<html>

<head>
  <link rel="stylesheet" href="asset/css/bootstrap.min.css">
  <link rel="stylesheet" href="asset/css/ts-responsive-web-style.css">
  <title>Responsive product Store</title>
</head>

<body>
  <div class="container">
    <div class="panel-body ts-product-container">
      <div class="ts-product panel panel-default">
        <div class="panel-body">
          <h3>product</h3>
        </div>
      </div>
      <div class="ts-product panel panel-default">
        <div class="panel-body">
          <h3>product</h3>
        </div>
      </div>
      <div class="ts-product panel panel-default">
        <div class="panel-body">
          <h3>product</h3>
        </div>
      </div>
      <div class="ts-product panel panel-default">
        <div class="panel-body">
          <h3>product</h3>
        </div>
      </div>
      <div class="ts-product panel panel-default">
        <div class="panel-body">
          <h3>product</h3>
        </div>
      </div>
      <div class="ts-product panel panel-default">
```

```html
      <div class="panel-body">
        <h3>product</h3>
      </div>
  </div>
  <div class="ts-product panel panel-default">
      <div class="panel-body">
        <h3>product</h3>
      </div>
  </div>
<div class="ts-product panel panel-default">
      <div class="panel-body">
        <h3>product</h3>
      </div>
  </div>
    <div class="ts-product panel panel-default">
      <div class="panel-body">
        <h3>product</h3>
      </div>
  </div>
  <div class="ts-product panel panel-default">
      <div class="panel-body">
        <h3>product</h3>
      </div>
  </div>
  <div class="ts-product panel panel-default">
      <div class="panel-body">
        <h3>product</h3>
      </div>
  </div>
  <div class="ts-product panel panel-default">
      <div class="panel-body">
        <h3>product</h3>
      </div>
  </div>
  <div class="ts-product panel panel-default">
      <div class="panel-body">
        <h3>product</h3>
      </div>
  </div>
  <div class="ts-product panel panel-default">
      <div class="panel-body">
        <h3>product</h3>
      </div>
  </div>
```

```
<div class="ts-product panel panel-default">
   <div class="panel-body">
     <h3>product</h3>
   </div>
</div>
<div class="ts-product panel panel-default">
   <div class="panel-body">
     <h3>product</h3>
   </div>
</div>
<div class="ts-product panel panel-default">
   <div class="panel-body">
     <h3>product</h3>
   </div>
</div>
<div class="ts-product panel panel-default">
   <div class="panel-body">
     <h3>product</h3>
   </div>
</div>
<div class="ts-product panel panel-default">
   <div class="panel-body">
     <h3>product</h3>
   </div>
</div>
<div class="ts-product panel panel-default">
   <div class="panel-body">
     <h3>product</h3>
   </div>
</div>
<div class="ts-product panel panel-default">
   <div class="panel-body">
     <h3>product</h3>
   </div>
</div>
<div class="ts-product panel panel-default">
   <div class="panel-body">
     <h3>product</h3>
   </div>
</div>
<div class="ts-product panel panel-default">
   <div class="panel-body">
```

```
            <h3>product</h3>
         </div>
      </div>
   </div>
</div>
<script src="../asset/js/jquery-2.1.0.min.js"></script>
<script src="../asset/js/bootstrap.min.js"></script>
</body>

</html>
```

The list of products will be rendered as shown in the following screenshot:

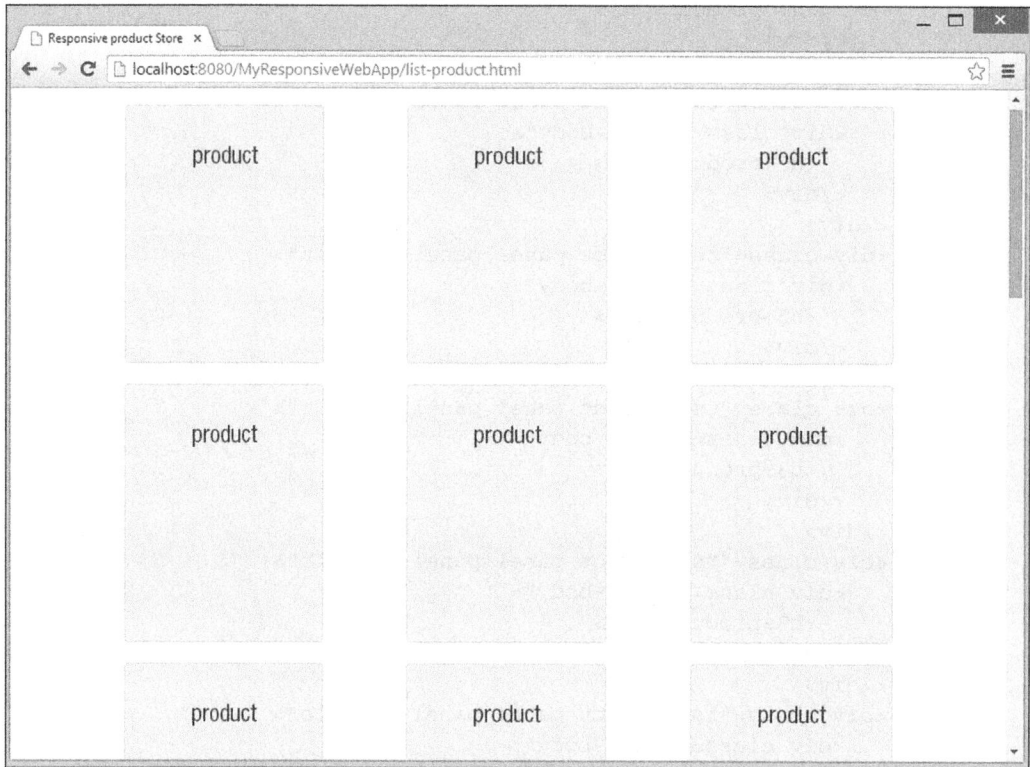

> The `.container` and `.container-fluid` classes are for proper alignment and padding. All the `.row` elements must be inside these containers. For more details, you can look at the Bootstrap 3 documentation.

The combined layout

In the previous sections of this chapter, we have seen how the individual components are laid out. In this section, we will combine all the previous sections into a single code file. You can see we have used the `bootstrap.min.css` file, which is the default style for Bootstrap, and `ts-responsive-web-style.css` containing the application-specific style. The whole code for the layout development is combined in the `index.html` file, shown as follows:

```html
<!DOCTYPE html>
<html>
<head>
<link rel="stylesheet" href="asset/css/bootstrap.min.css">
<link rel="stylesheet" href="asset/css/ts-responsive-web-style.css">
<title>Responsive product Store</title>
</head>
<body>
<div class="container">
<div class="row">
 <nav class="navbar navbar-inverse navbar-static-top"
role="navigation">
      <div class="container-fluid">
        <div class="navbar-header">
          <button type="button" class="navbar-toggle collapsed" data-
toggle="collapse" data-target="#ts-top-menu">
            <span class="sr-only">Navigation buttons</span>
            <span class="icon-bar"></span>
            <span class="icon-bar"></span>
            <span class="icon-bar"></span>
          </button>
          <a class="navbar-brand" href="#">PRODUCTS</a>
        </div>
        <!-- Collect the nav links, forms, and other content for
toggling -->
        <div class="navbar-collapse collapse" id="ts-top-menu">
          <ul class="nav navbar-nav">
            <li class="active"><a href="#">Category 1</a></li>
            <li><a href="#">Category 2</a></li>
            <li><a href="#">Category 3</a></li>
          </ul>
        </div>
      </div>
 </nav>
</div>
<div class="row">
```

```
            <div class="jumbotron">
               <h1>Hero Section</h1>
            </div>
      </div>
      <div class="row">
       <div class="panel-body ts-product-container">
            <div class="ts-product panel panel-default">
               <div class="panel-body">
                    <h3>product</h3>
               </div>
            </div>
            <div class="ts-product panel panel-default">
               <div class="panel-body">
               <h3>product</h3>
               </div>
            </div>
            <div class="ts-product panel panel-default">
               <div class="panel-body">
               <h3>product</h3>
               </div>
            </div>
            <div class="ts-product panel panel-default">
               <div class="panel-body">
               <h3>product</h3>
               </div>
            </div>
            <div class="ts-product panel panel-default">
               <div class="panel-body">
               <h3>product</h3>
               </div>
            </div>
            <div class="ts-product panel panel-default">
               <div class="panel-body">
               <h3>product</h3>
               </div>
            </div>
            <div class="ts-product panel panel-default">
               <div class="panel-body">
               <h3>product</h3>
               </div>
            </div>
           <div class="ts-product panel panel-default">
               <div class="panel-body">
               <h3>product</h3>
```

```
      </div>
   </div>
    <div class="ts-product panel panel-default">
      <div class="panel-body">
      <h3>product</h3>
      </div>
   </div>
   <div class="ts-product panel panel-default">
      <div class="panel-body">
      <h3>product</h3>
      </div>
   </div>
   <div class="ts-product panel panel-default">
      <div class="panel-body">
      <h3>product</h3>
      </div>
   </div>
   <div class="ts-product panel panel-default">
      <div class="panel-body">
      <h3>product</h3>
      </div>
   </div>
   <div class="ts-product panel panel-default">
      <div class="panel-body">
      <h3>product</h3>
      </div>
   </div>
   <div class="ts-product panel panel-default">
      <div class="panel-body">
      <h3>product</h3>
      </div>
   </div>
   <div class="ts-product panel panel-default">
      <div class="panel-body">
      <h3>product</h3>
      </div>
   </div>
   <div class="ts-product panel panel-default">
      <div class="panel-body">
      <h3>product</h3>
      </div>
   </div>
   <div class="ts-product panel panel-default">
      <div class="panel-body">
```

```
          <h3>product</h3>
          </div>
      </div>
      <div class="ts-product panel panel-default">
          <div class="panel-body">
          <h3>product</h3>
          </div>
      </div>
      <div class="ts-product panel panel-default">
          <div class="panel-body">
          <h3>product</h3>
          </div>
      </div>
      <div class="ts-product panel panel-default">
          <div class="panel-body">
          <h3>product</h3>
          </div>
      </div>
      <div class="ts-product panel panel-default">
          <div class="panel-body">
          <h3>product</h3>
          </div>
      </div>
      <div class="ts-product panel panel-default">
          <div class="panel-body">
          <h3>product</h3>
          </div>
      </div>
      <div class="ts-product panel panel-default">
          <div class="panel-body">
          <h3>product</h3>
          </div>
      </div>
      <div class="ts-product panel panel-default">
          <div class="panel-body">
          <h3>product</h3>
          </div>
      </div>
</div>
</div>
</div>
<script src="asset/js/jquery-2.1.0.min.js"></script>
<script src="asset/js/bootstrap.min.js"></script>
</body>
</html>
```

Verifying the layout

In this section, we will test our layout in different screen sizes. Also, we will test our layout in the **Opera Mobile emulator**.

The Opera Mobile emulator

The Opera Mobile emulator provides the bridge between the real devices during the development. It can be downloaded from `http://www.opera.com/developer/mobile-emulator`.

The initial window of the emulator has different sections:

- The window listing different devices, for example, HTC, Samsung, Sony Ericson, Motorola, and Nokia, as shown in the following screenshot:

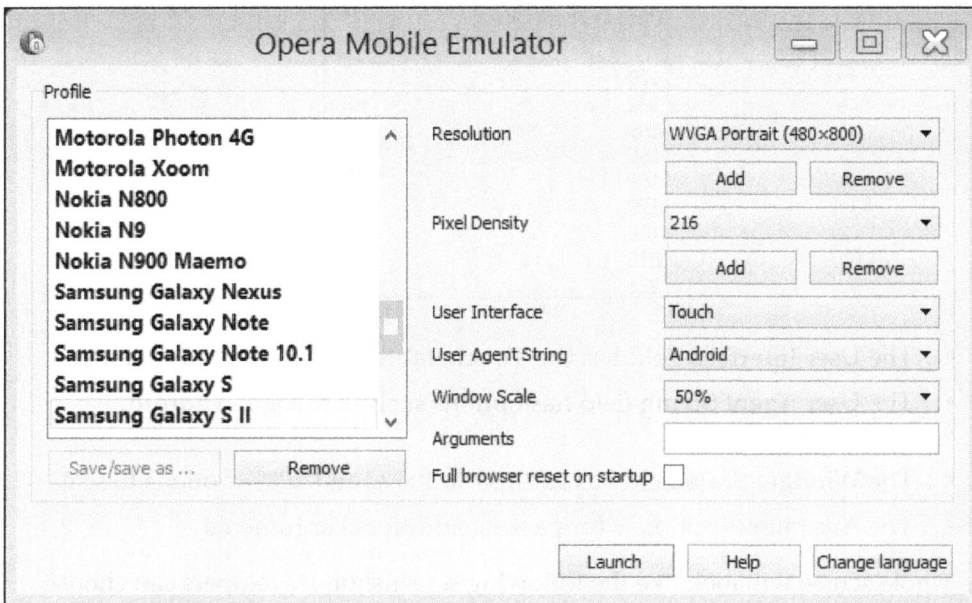

- The **Profile** section has the list of devices that can be selected and used for testing

- The **Resolution** field represents the width and height of the screen, as shown in the following screenshot:

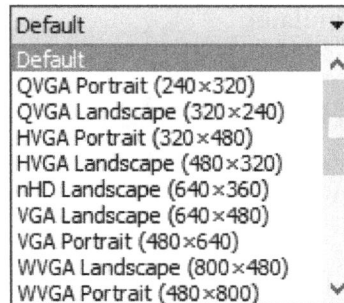

```
Default                          ▼
Default                          ∧
QVGA Portrait (240×320)
QVGA Landscape (320×240)
HVGA Portrait (320×480)
HVGA Landscape (480×320)
nHD Landscape (640×360)
VGA Landscape (640×480)
VGA Portrait (480×640)
WVGA Landscape (800×480)
WVGA Portrait (480×800)          ∨
```

- The **Pixel Density** field represents the pixels per inch on the device's screen

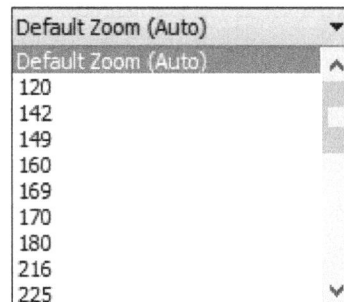

```
Default Zoom (Auto)              ▼
Default Zoom (Auto)              ∧
120
142
149
160
169
170
180
216
225                              ∨
```

- The **User Interface** field has the **Touch**, **tablet**, and **keyboard** options
- The **User Agent String** field has options such as **Meego**, **Android**, and **Desktop**
- The **Window Scale** field has **25%**, **50%**, **100%**, and **200%** options to scale
- The **Arguments** option is for passing additional arguments

The whole screen will look like the following screenshot. Developers can choose different options and configure the testing window screen. These options are really helpful to test the application on a different emulated device.

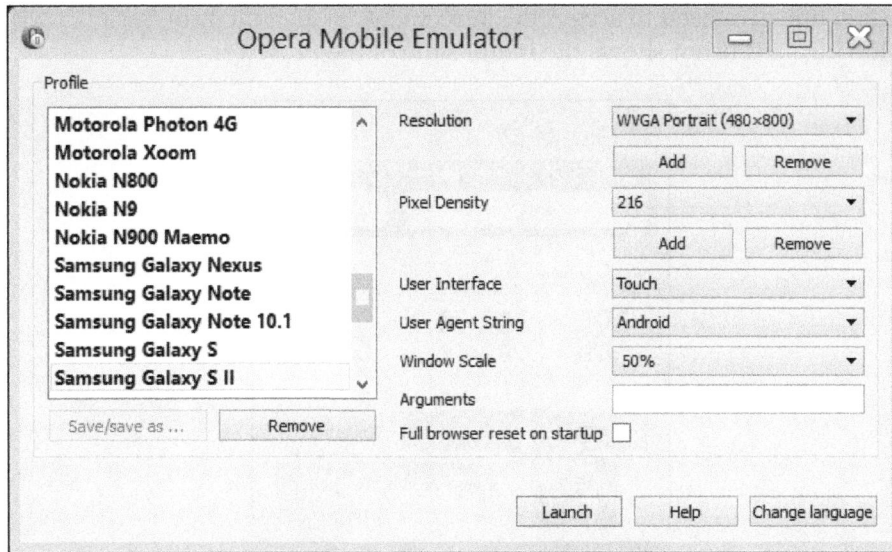

The emulator will open in a new window. The following screenshot shows the home page for the emulator:

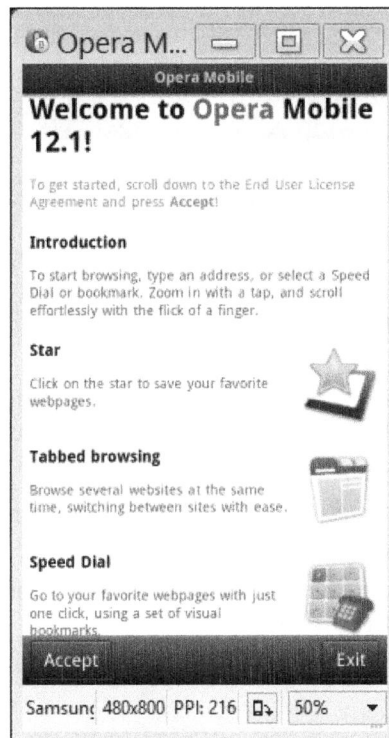

For the first time, we need to accept the agreement to open the browser. The following screenshot shows the initial state of the browser:

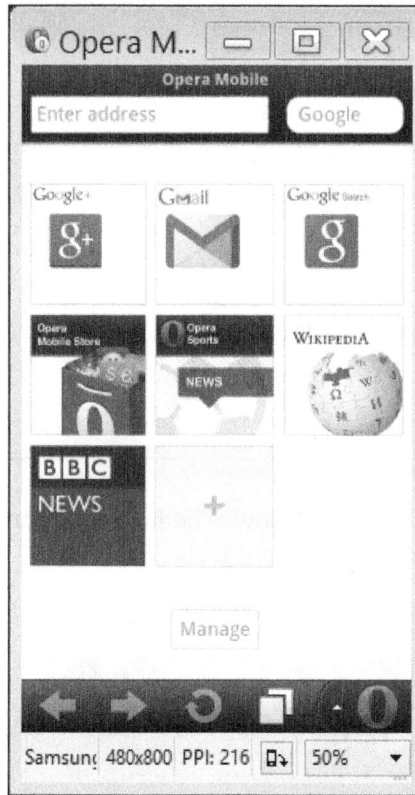

The Opera browser has many different options, which are as follows:

- **The address bar**: This element is for passing the URL of the application for browsing.
- **The forward and backward button**: This element is in the footer section. These buttons are used to navigate forward and backward in the browser history.
- **The refresh button**: This element is present in the footer. This button is used to reload a page in the browser.
- **The full screen option**: This element is also present in the footer. It can be used for full size of the screen for the emulator.

The different menu options present inside the Opera emulator are as follows:

- **Bookmarks**: This is used to bookmark different URLs
- **History**: This contains all the browsed pages
- **Start Page**: This has the initial page containing a list of quick dial pages
- **Saved Pages**: This has all the saved pages
- **Downloads**: This has the list of the downloaded files
- **Settings**: This can change the browser settings such as privacy and proxy settings
- **Find in Page**: This is used to find text in the current page
- **Help**: This has additional help for the browser
- **Exit**: This is to exit the browser

The following screenshot shows the menu options that we discussed in the preceding section:

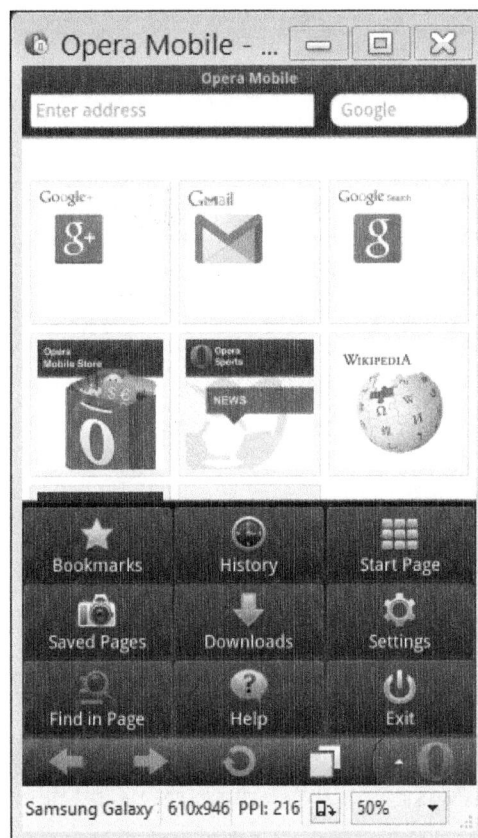

The following screenshot shows the Samsung Galaxy S II Version of the emulator. This emulator represents the following:

- The number of products and as the screen size is very small, the number of products is three in a single row
- Each product has the property to be displayed with the `inline-block` value

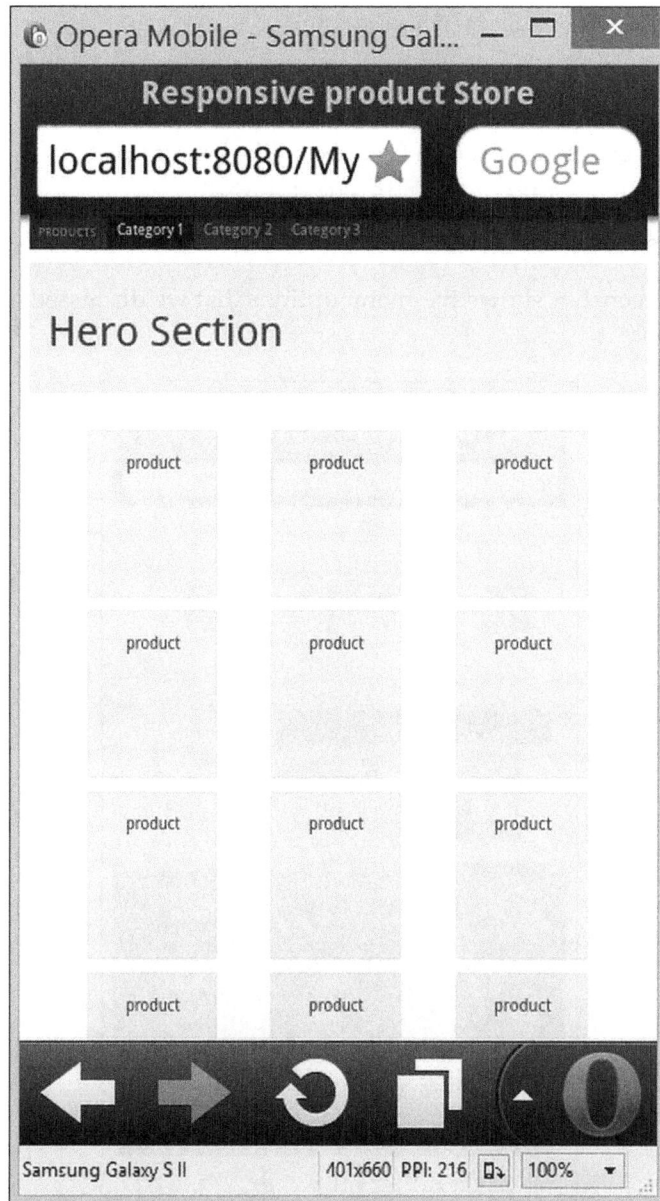

The final layout will look like the following screenshot:

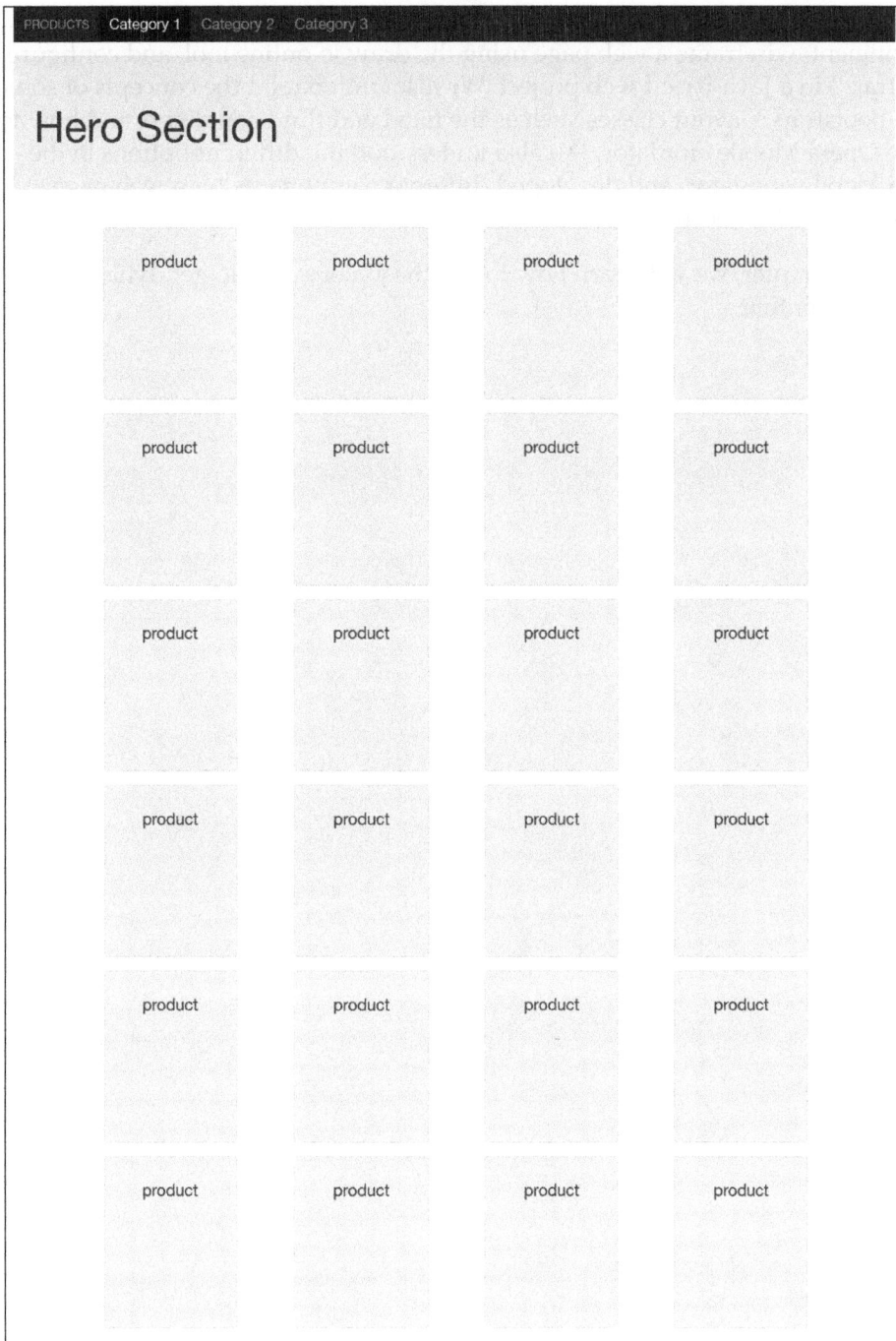

Summary

In this chapter, we learned to set up a Java-based web project in the Eclipse Juno environment, wireframe a web page using the draw.io online tool, and configure Bootstrap 3 in a Java-based web project. We also understood the concepts of some of the Bootstrap 3 layout classes such as the fixed and fluid containers and how to set the Opera Mobile emulator. We also understood the different options in the Opera Mobile emulator, and developed different components for a web page such as the navbar, hero section, and product list.

In the next chapter, we will learn how to use the jQuery calls to get dynamic and responsive content.

3
Adding Dynamic Visuals to a Web Application

In this chapter, we will learn how to create servlets returning JSON data followed by understanding the concepts of jQuery AJAX and promising and templating a library to render data in our page. In the later section of this chapter, we will learn how to create a carousel for the hero section.

Building a JSON servlet

In this section, we will develop a Java servlet that will return a list of products as a JSON array. Before building the servlet, we need to create a Java class named Product. This class is known as a **Plain Old Java Object** (**POJO**) as it does not implement any interface or extend any other classes. This class will have many different properties that we are going to use to store the corresponding values.

Creating a POJO class

The value object of the Product class has all properties related to a product. The different fields of a product are:

- **Title**: This field contains the title of the product and is of the type string. The getTitle() and setTitle() methods are two getter and setter methods.
- **Cost**: This field contains the pricing of the product and is of the type integer. The getCost() and setCost() methods are two getter and setter methods.
- **Description**: This field contains the information about the product and is of the type string. The getDescription() and setDescription() methods are the two getter and setter methods.

- **URL**: This field contains the URI of the product image and is of the type `string`. The `getUrl()` and `setUrl()` methods are two getter and setter methods.

- **Type**: This field contains the type of the product and is of the type `string`. The `getType()` and `setType()` methods are two getter and setter methods.

The following code shows the implementation of all the preceding fields in the `Product` Java class:

```
package com.packt.product.obj;

public class Product {

    private String title;
    private int cost;
    private String description;
    private String url;
    private String type;

    public String getTitle() {
        return title;
    }
    public void setTitle(String title) {
        this.title = title;
    }
    public int getCost() {
        return cost;
    }
    public void setCost(int i) {
        this.cost = i;
    }
    public String getDescription() {
        return description;
    }
    public void setDescription(String description) {
        this.description = description;
    }
    public String getUrl() {
        return url;
    }
    public void setUrl(String url) {
        this.url = url;
    }
    public String getType() {
        return type;
    }
```

```
    }
    public void setType(String type) {
        this.type = type;
    }
}
```

Creating a product store

Also, we need to create a list of products for our application. For the purpose of this book, we have used the names of some of the Packt Publishing books and videos. The getAllListedBook() and getAllListedVideo() methods are the two methods that return list of the hardcoded products. It should be noted that in a real-world application, these methods would tie into a database to retrieve the appropriate records instead of having a hardcoded values.cerateStaticJSON() method that takes the list of products and returns its JSON equivalent string. The conversion of POJO to JSON is done by the GSON library. All these methods are written in the ProductStore class, as shown in the following code:

```
package com.packt.product.store;

import java.util.ArrayList;
import java.util.List;
import com.google.gson.Gson;
import com.google.gson.GsonBuilder;
import com.packt.product.obj.Product;

public class ProductStore {

    public static List<Product> getAllListedBook() {
        List<Product> listProduct = new ArrayList<Product>();

        Product product2 = new Product();
        product2.setTitle("Buddy press theme development");
        product2.setCost(12);
        product2.setDescription("Lorem ipsum dollar.Lorem ipsum
dollar.Lorem ipsum dollar.");
        product2.setUrl("asset/image/books/2.png");
        product2.setType("book");

        Product product3 = new Product();
        product3.setTitle("Master Web Application Development with
AngularJS");
        product3.setCost(14);
```

```
        product3.setDescription("Lorem ipsum dollar.Lorem ipsum
dollar.Lorem ipsum dollar.");
        product3.setUrl("asset/image/books/3.png");
        product3.setType("book");

        Product product4 = new Product();
        product4.setTitle("Instant GSON");
        product4.setCost(10);
        product4.setDescription("Lorem ipsum dollar.Lorem ipsum
dollar.Lorem ipsum dollar.");
        product4.setUrl("asset/image/books/4.png");
        product4.setType("book");

        Product product5 = new Product();
        product5.setTitle("jQuery UI Cookbook");
        product5.setCost(17);
        product5.setDescription("Lorem ipsum dollar.Lorem ipsum
dollar.Lorem ipsum dollar.");
        product5.setUrl("asset/image/books/5.png");
        product5.setType("book");

        Product product6 = new Product();
        product6.setTitle("Learning IPython For Interactive Computing
And Data Visualization");
        product6.setCost(13);
        product6.setDescription("Lorem ipsum dollar.Lorem ipsum
dollar.Lorem ipsum dollar.");
        product6.setUrl("asset/image/books/6.png");

        listProduct.add(product2);
        listProduct.add(product3);
        listProduct.add(product4);
        listProduct.add(product5);
        listProduct.add(product6);

        return listProduct;
    }
    public static List<Product> getAllListedVideo() {
        List<Product> listProduct = new ArrayList<Product>();

        Product product1 = new Product();
        product1.setTitle("Fast Track to Adobe Captivate 6");
        product1.setCost(12);
        product1.setDescription("Lorem ipsum dollar.Lorem ipsum
dollar.Lorem ipsum dollar.");
```

```
        product1.setUrl("asset/image/video/2.png");
        product1.setType("video");

        Product product2 = new Product();
        product2.setTitle("Cassandra Administration");
        product2.setCost(14);
        product2.setDescription("Lorem ipsum dollar.Lorem ipsum
dollar.Lorem ipsum dollar.");
        product2.setUrl("asset/image/video/3.png");
        product2.setType("video");

        Product product3 = new Product();
        product3.setTitle("Play! Framework For Web Application
Development");
        product3.setCost(10);
        product3.setDescription("Lorem ipsum dollar.Lorem ipsum
dollar.Lorem ipsum dollar.");
        product3.setUrl("asset/image/video/4.png");
        product3.setType("video");

        Product product4 = new Product();
        product4.setTitle("Getting Started With magneto");
        product4.setCost(17);
        product4.setDescription("Lorem ipsum dollar.Lorem ipsum
dollar.Lorem ipsum dollar.");
        product4.setUrl("asset/image/video/5.png");
        product4.setType("video");

        Product product5 = new Product();
        product5.setTitle("Building a Network Application With Node");
        product5.setCost(13);
        product5.setDescription("Lorem ipsum dollar.Lorem ipsum
dollar.Lorem ipsum dollar.");
        product5.setUrl("asset/image/video/6.png");
        product5.setType("video");

        Product product6 = new Product();
        product6.setTitle("Oracle Apex Technique");
        product6.setCost(13);
        product6.setDescription("Lorem ipsum dollar.Lorem ipsum
dollar.Lorem ipsum dollar.");
        product6.setUrl("asset/image/video/7.png");
        product6.setType("video");

        listProduct.add(product1);
```

```
        listProduct.add(product2);
        listProduct.add(product3);
        listProduct.add(product4);
        listProduct.add(product5);
        listProduct.add(product6);

        return listProduct;
    }

public static String cerateStaticJSON(List<Product> listOfProduct) {
    Gson gson = new GsonBuilder().setPrettyPrinting().create();
    String json = gson.toJson(listOfProduct);
    return json;
    }
}
```

Converting from POJO to JSON

In this section, we will convert our product list (that is a Java POJO array) to a JSON array. We have used a GSON library from Google to covert the Java POJO objects into a JSON string, as described in the following figure:

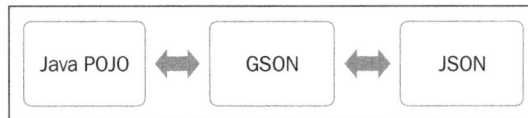

Some key points about JSON conversion in GSON are as follows:

- A GSON object needs to be instantiated using a `new` keyword with `GsonBuilder` and a `create` method
- Using the `toJson()` method, a Java POJO object is converted to its equivalent JSON string

Creating the servlet

Now, the main servlet, `ProductServlet`, which reads the request parameter type, calls the appropriate method, and sends the response in the JSON string, is shown as follows:

```
package com.packt.product.data;

import java.io.IOException;
import java.io.PrintWriter;
```

```
import java.util.List;
import javax.servlet.ServletException;
import javax.servlet.annotation.WebServlet;
import javax.servlet.http.HttpServlet;
import javax.servlet.http.HttpServletRequest;
import javax.servlet.http.HttpServletResponse;
import com.packt.product.obj.Product;
import com.packt.product.store.ProductStore;

@WebServlet("/ProductServlet")
public class ProductServlet extends HttpServlet {
    private static final long serialVersionUID = 1L;
    public ProductServlet() {
        super();
    }
    protected void doGet(HttpServletRequest request,
HttpServletResponse response) throws ServletException, IOException {

String type = request.getParameter("type");
    List<Product>  listOfProduct = null;

    if("book".equalsIgnoreCase(type)){
      listOfProduct = ProductStore.getAllListedBook();
    }else if("video".equalsIgnoreCase(type)){
      listOfProduct = ProductStore.getAllListedVideo();
    }
String productJsonString = ProductStore.cerateStaticJSON(listOfProdu
ct);
response.setContentType("application/json");
    PrintWriter out = response.getWriter();
    out.write(productJsonString);
    }
}
```

Some of the key points about `ProductServlet` are as follows:

- `ProductServlet` reads the type parameter from the URL and based on the type, it calls the `ProductStore` method to get the list of products.
- If the type is `book`, then it calls the `getAllListedBook()` method and if the type is `video`, it calls the `getAllListedVideo()` method.
- Finally, the `createStaticJSON()` method is called with a list of projects as Java object to get converted into a JSON string. The generated JSON string is then passed back as a response to the client using the `PrintWriter` method.

All these servlet calls are the GET method by default, from the client. The following screenshot shows the JSON data returned for the type book as a parameter in the URL string:

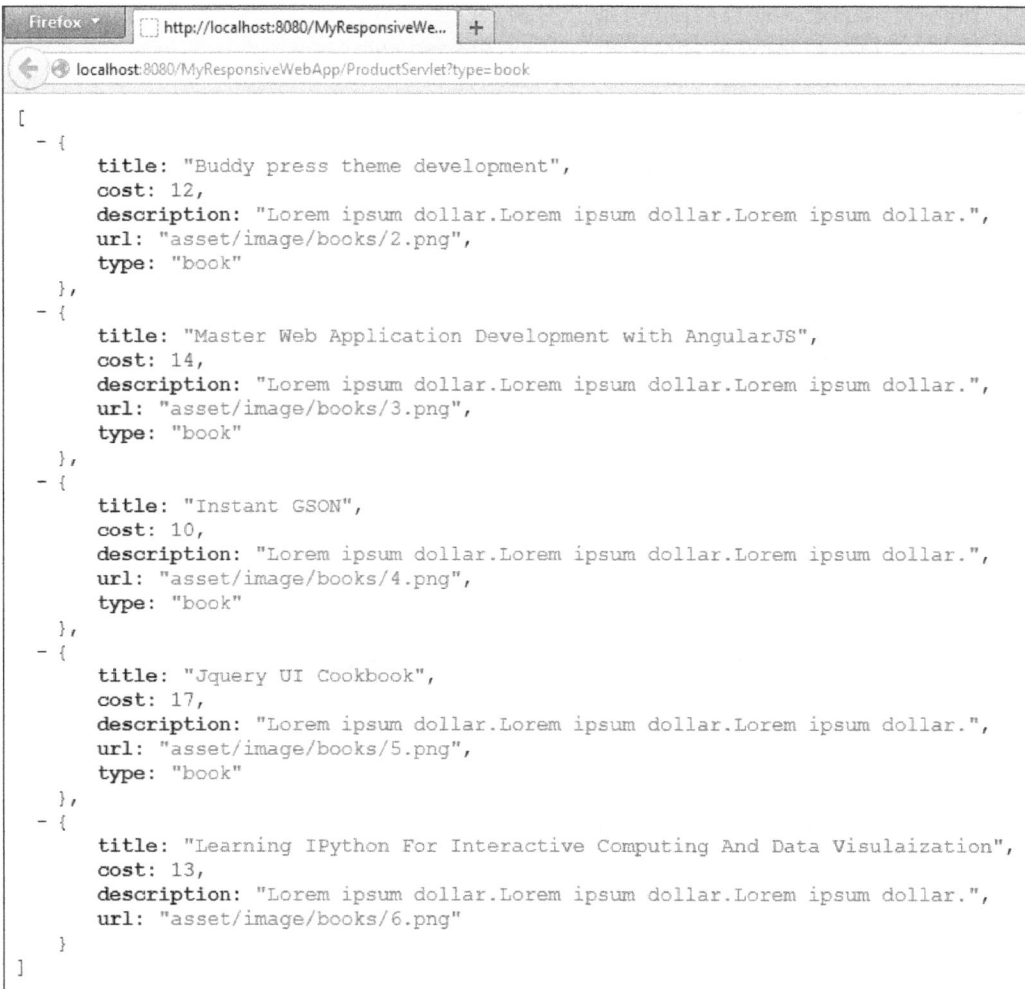

```
Firefox ▼      http://localhost:8080/MyResponsiveWe...   +

     localhost:8080/MyResponsiveWebApp/ProductServlet?type=book

[
  - {
        title: "Buddy press theme development",
        cost: 12,
        description: "Lorem ipsum dollar.Lorem ipsum dollar.Lorem ipsum dollar.",
        url: "asset/image/books/2.png",
        type: "book"
  },
  - {
        title: "Master Web Application Development with AngularJS",
        cost: 14,
        description: "Lorem ipsum dollar.Lorem ipsum dollar.Lorem ipsum dollar.",
        url: "asset/image/books/3.png",
        type: "book"
  },
  - {
        title: "Instant GSON",
        cost: 10,
        description: "Lorem ipsum dollar.Lorem ipsum dollar.Lorem ipsum dollar.",
        url: "asset/image/books/4.png",
        type: "book"
  },
  - {
        title: "Jquery UI Cookbook",
        cost: 17,
        description: "Lorem ipsum dollar.Lorem ipsum dollar.Lorem ipsum dollar.",
        url: "asset/image/books/5.png",
        type: "book"
  },
  - {
        title: "Learning IPython For Interactive Computing And Data Visulaization",
        cost: 13,
        description: "Lorem ipsum dollar.Lorem ipsum dollar.Lorem ipsum dollar.",
        url: "asset/image/books/6.png"
  }
]
```

The following screenshot shows the JSON array for type `video` as a parameter in the URL string. The JSON array is an array of objects where each object represents a JSON string that is equivalent to the object of a `Product` class.

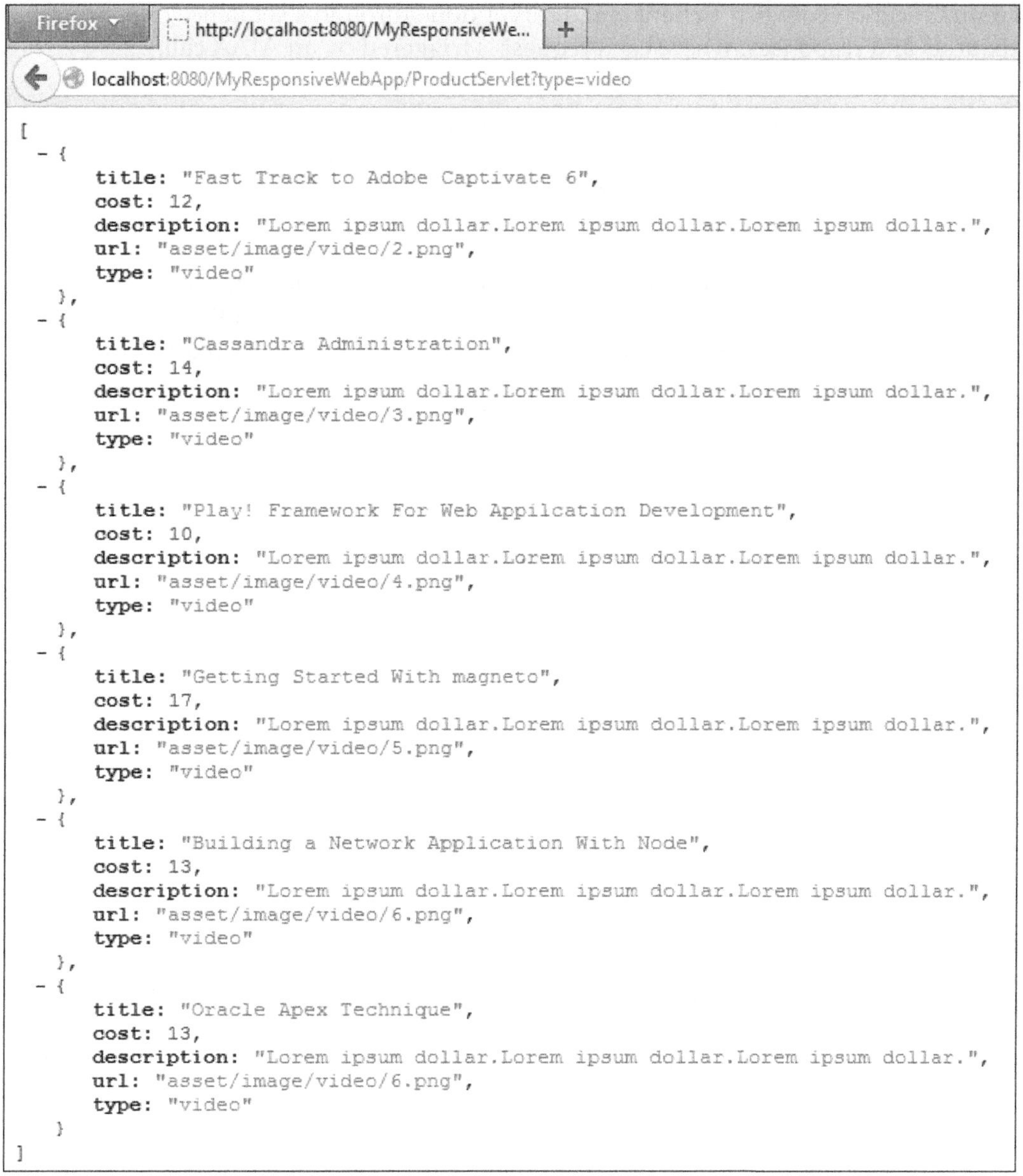

Building a jQuery AJAX method

In this section, we will learn to develop a jQuery AJAX method in order to make server calls. The following figure shows the block diagram of a typical communication between a client and a server done through a sequence of requests and responses, where each request is triggered by an AJAX call:

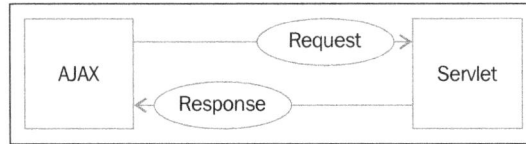

jQuery provides an AJAX method `$.ajax()` to call the remote data. For our application, we will call our servlet `ProductServlet` to download the product list in the JSON format. The AJAX method makes an `XMLHttpRequest` request to the servlet to get the data.

The syntax for the AJAX method is shown as follows:

```
$.ajax(<url>,{configuration properties})
```

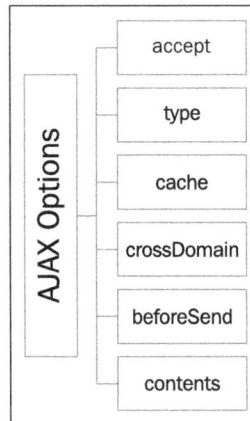

Some of the configuration properties are described as follows:

- **accepts**: This field represents the request method to use, such as GET or POST. By default, if the parameter type is not specified, the call is assumed to be a GET method request.
- **beforeSend**: This field can be a function attached to it and uses a preprocessing of requests before making the final call to the server resource.
- **cache**: This field takes a Boolean value and represents the caching of resources in the browser.

- **crossDomain**: This field takes a Boolean value and indicates whether a request is a cross domain call.
- **type**: This field represents the request method to use, such as GET or POST. By default if the type is not specified, the call is assumed to be a GET method request.

To make an AJAX request via jQuery for all titles of type book, we can pass the type as a GET request named as the query string's parameter. The following code shows a function that takes the type parameter as an argument and makes the AJAX request to the servlet accordingly:

```
/*Returning jQuery Promise For a AJAX call with Product type*/
getProductDetails : function(type){
  var ajaxRequest=$.ajax("ProductServlet?type="+type);
  return ajaxRequest.promise();
}
```

The jQuery version that we have used for this application is 2.1.0. The method used in the preceding code returns a promise object on debugging. We will see what this promise object does in the next section.

Let's focus on the AJAX call for this method now. As the signature of the getProductDetails() method suggests, it takes a string as a parameter value and appends it to the URL with the type as a key.

The following screenshot shows the Firebug console of the jQuery AJAX call for the type book:

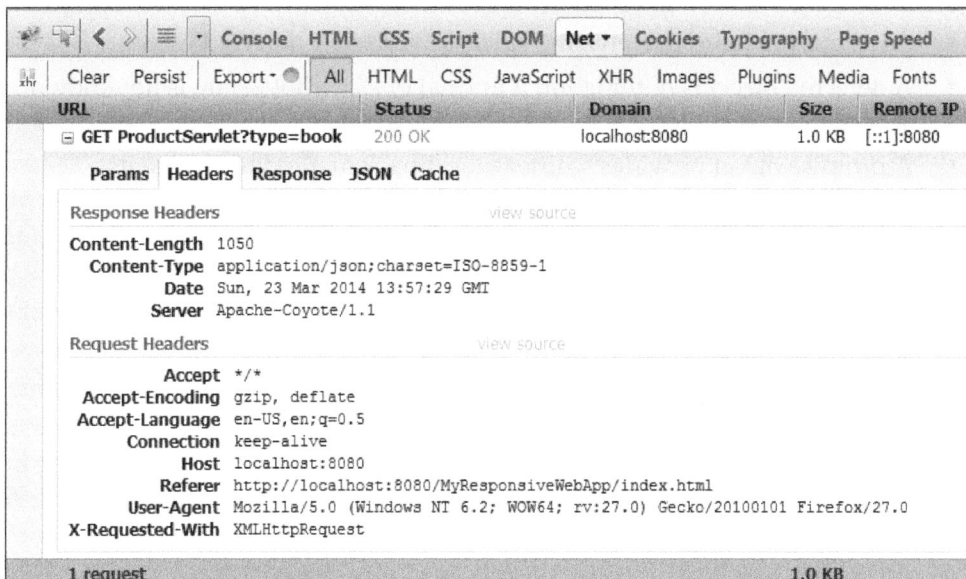

The following screenshot shows the Firebug console of the jQuery AJAX call for the type `video`:

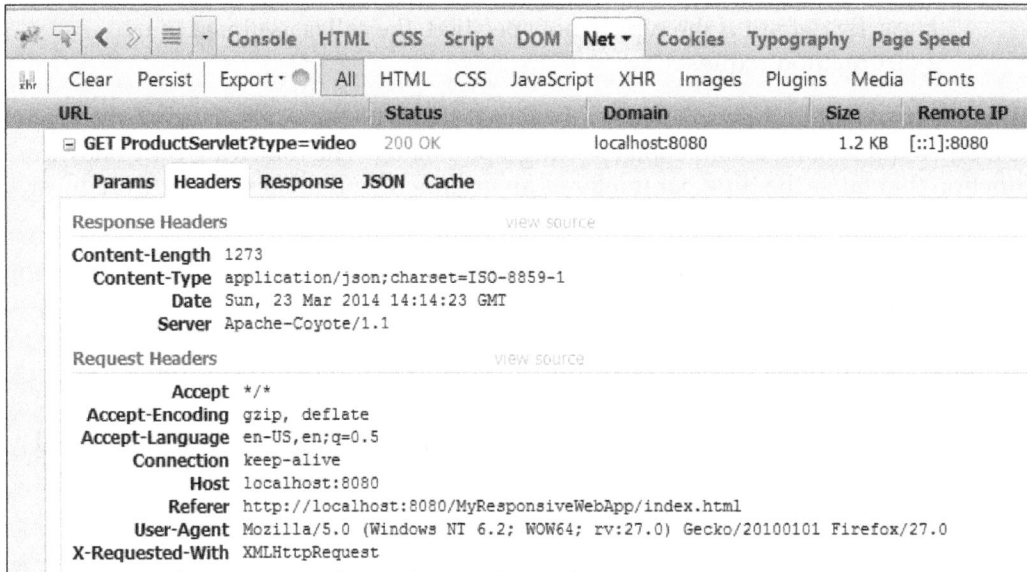

Console HTML CSS Script DOM **Net ▾** Cookies Typography Page Speed		

Clear Persist | Export ▾ ● | **All** HTML CSS JavaScript XHR Images Plugins Media Fonts

URL	Status	Domain	Size	Remote IP
⊟ **GET ProductServlet?type=video**	200 OK	localhost:8080	1.2 KB	[::1]:8080

Params **Headers** Response JSON Cache

Response Headers   view source

```
Content-Length  1273
  Content-Type  application/json;charset=ISO-8859-1
          Date  Sun, 23 Mar 2014 14:14:23 GMT
        Server  Apache-Coyote/1.1
```

Request Headers   view source

```
          Accept  */*
 Accept-Encoding  gzip, deflate
 Accept-Language  en-US,en;q=0.5
      Connection  keep-alive
            Host  localhost:8080
          Referer  http://localhost:8080/MyResponsiveWebApp/index.html
       User-Agent  Mozilla/5.0 (Windows NT 6.2; WOW64; rv:27.0) Gecko/20100101 Firefox/27.0
 X-Requested-With  XMLHttpRequest
```

jQuery promises

jQuery promises are a great mechanism to handle the asynchronous callback issue. Some of the key points about jQuery promises are listed as follows:

- A promise object represents the subset of a jQuery deferred object
- A deferred object is nothing but a normal object whose state is not known at present or is yet to be known in the future
- A promise object provides a different callback method to handle its future state

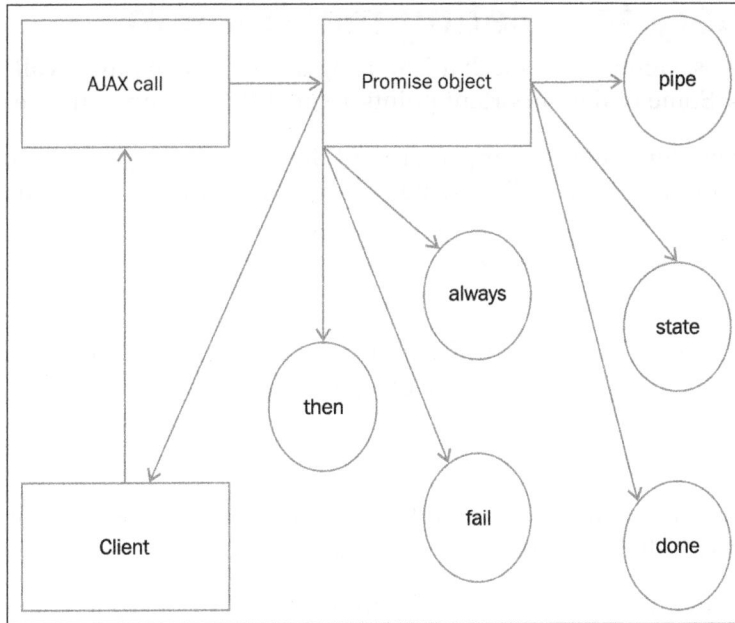

The preceding figure is a graphical representation of how a jQuery promise object works for an AJAX call.

The promise() method returns the promise object for handling. In our script code, we have used the done() callback method to handle the AJAX call's success state, as shown in the following code:

```
/*Handler For AJAX response*/
handleCallback : function(type){
    var promise = PACKT_PRODUCT_APP.getProductDetails(type);
    promise.done(function(data){
        PACKT_PRODUCT_APP.doProductRendering(data);
    });
}
```

The jQuery templating mechanism

jQuery provides a templating mechanism using an additional plugin called `jquery.tmpl.min.js`. Some of the important points about jQuery templating are as follows:

- A jQuery template is wrapped around the `<script>` tag with type as `text/x-jquery-tmpl`. The syntax of a jQuery template is shown as follows:

```
<script id="<templateid>" type="text/x-jquery-tmpl">
    HTML code goes here
</script>
```

- An expression is represented within a dollar ($) sign with curly braces and is used for representing the value of a JavaScript object in the string. The syntax is shown as follows:

```
${<expression>}
```

- The `tmpl()` method is for template compilation and is used for linking the data to produce the markup for a product.

The following figure shows a graphical representation of how jQuery templates work. It has two phases, which are the internal compilation phase and the linking phase, explored as follows:

- **The compilation phase**: In this phase, the HTML template is compiled and converted into a jQuery function
- **The linking phase**: In this phase, the JSON data is passed to the compiled jQuery method to generate the real HTML markup for rendering

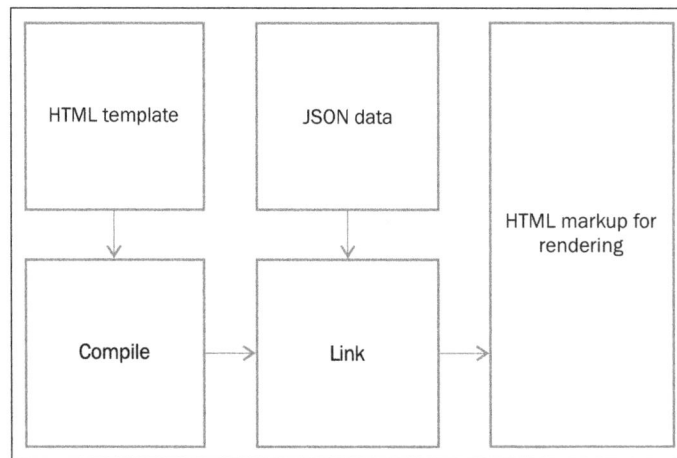

Let's create our product template to use it in the web application. To begin with templating, we need to decide which fields are to be displayed for a product while rendering, as shown in the following code:

```
<script id="aProductTemplate" type="text/x-Jquery-tmpl">
    <div class="ts-product panel panel-default">
        <div class="panel-body">
            <span class="glyphicon glyphicon-certificate ts-cost-
icon">
                <label>${cost}$</label>
            </span>
            <img class="img-responsive" src="${url}">
            <h5>${title}</h5>
        </div>
        <div class="panel-footer">
            <button type="button" class="btn btn-info btn-block">Buy</
button>
        </div>
    </div>
</script>
```

The HTML markup for a single product will render output as shown in the following screenshot:

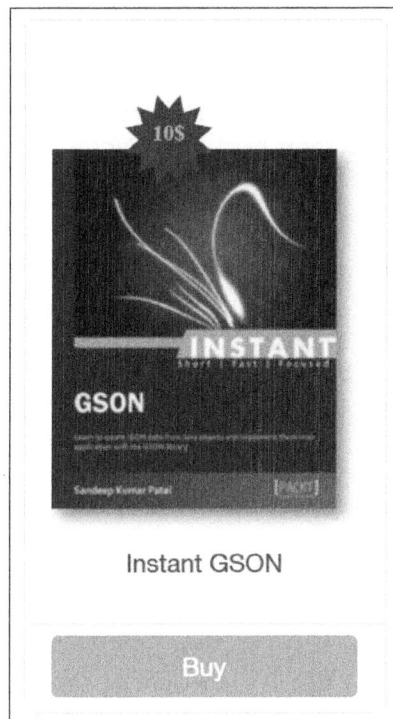

The combined jQuery code

The whole code for the web application is shown as follows, where PACKT_PRODUCT_
APP is the object that contains all methods for running the web application:

```
var PACKT_PRODUCT_APP={
    /*Returning jQuery Promise For a AJAX call with Product type*/
    getProductDetails : function(type){
        var ajaxRequest=$.ajax("ProductServlet?type="+type);
        return ajaxRequest.promise();
    },
    /*Handler For AJAX response*/
    handleCallback : function(type){
        var promise = PACKT_PRODUCT_APP.getProductDetails(type);
        promise.done(function(data){
            PACKT_PRODUCT_APP.doProductRendering(data);
        });
    },
    /*jQuery Template building with JSON data*/
    doProductRendering: function(data){
        var productContainer =$('.ts-product-container'),
            aProductTemplate = $('#aProductTemplate').tmpl( data ),
promiseOldPro = $(productContainer).find('.panel').fadeOut().
promise();

        $.when(promiseOldPro).then(function(){
            productContainer.html(aProductTemplate);
        });
    },
    /*Event Listener to Menu Item Click*/
    initCategoryClick:function(){
        $(".ts-bar").on('click','li',function(e){
            e.preventDefault();
            var li = e.currentTarget,
                type= $(li).attr('data-category');
            $(li).siblings('li').removeClass('active');
            $(li).addClass('active');
            PACKT_PRODUCT_APP.handleCallback(type);
        });
    }
};

$(document).ready(function(){
```

```
    /*Initial Load Call Books */
    PACKT_PRODUCT_APP.handleCallback('book');
    /*Initialize Click Of Menu Item*/
    PACKT_PRODUCT_APP.initCategoryClick();
});
```

The document ready function is calling the two methods: `handleCallback()` and `initCategoryClick()`. Some key points about these methods are as follows:

- `handleCallback()`: This method takes the `book` type as an input string to load the page for the product type `book`.

- `initCategoryClick()`: This method attaches a listener for menu click. When a book or video menu item is clicked, it attaches the active class to the target menu item and calls the AJAX for rendering the appropriate product type.

The combined HTML markup

The combined code of the markup present in the `index.html` file is shown as follows:

```html
<!DOCTYPE html>

<html>
<head>
  <link href="asset/css/bootstrap.min.css" rel="stylesheet">
  <link href="asset/css/ts-responsive-web-style.css" rel="stylesheet">
  <title>Responsive product Store</title>
</head>

<body>
  <div class="container packt-app">
    <div class="row">
      <nav class="navbar navbar-inverse navbar-static-top">
        <div class="container-fluid">
          <div class="navbar-header">
            <button class="navbar-toggle collapsed" data-target="#ts-top-menu"
            data-toggle="collapse" type="button"><span class="sr-only">Navigation buttons</span></button> <a class="navbar-brand" href="#">PRODUCTS</a>
          </div>
          <!-- Collect the nav links, forms, and other content for toggling -->
```

```
            <div class="navbar-collapse collapse" id="ts-top-menu">
              <ul class="nav navbar-nav ts-bar">
                <li class="active" data-category="book"><a
href="#">Books</a></li>

                <li data-category="video"><a href="#">Video</a></li>
              </ul>
            </div>
          </div>
        </nav>
      </div>

      <div class="row">
        <div class="jumbotron">
          <div class="row">
            <div class="col-sm-6"><img class="img-responsive"
src="asset/image/hero/1.jpg"></div>

            <div class="col-sm-6"><img class="img-responsive"
src="asset/image/hero/2.png"></div>
          </div>
        </div>
      </div>
      <div class="row">
        <div class="panel-body ts-product-container"></div>
      </div>
    </div>
    <script id="aProductTemplate" type="text/x-jquery-tmpl">
      <div class="ts-product panel panel-default">
          <div class="panel-body">
              <span class="glyphicon glyphicon-certificate ts-cost-
icon">
                  <label>${cost}$</label>
              </span>
              <img class="img-responsive" src="${url}">
              <h5>${title}</h5>
          </div>
          <div class="panel-footer">
              <button type="button" class="btn btn-info btn-block">Buy</
button>
          </div>
      </div>
    </script>
    <script src="asset/js/jquery-2.1.0.min.js"></script>
```

```
<script src="asset/js/jquery.tmpl.min.js"></script>
<script src="asset/js/bootstrap.min.js"></script>
<script src="asset/js/app.js"></script>
</body>
</html>
```

Modifying the style of the product

In this section, we will modify the style of our product. This change is desirable. There are two reasons to note, mentioned as follows:

- Even in a static (nonresponsive) layout, titles may be long enough to wrap to new lines, forcing the product title require multiple lines of height to display. It is possible to get around with this issue by forcing the height of all titles, but this will result in having unnecessary white spaces in the title area.

- In a fluid (responsive) layout, any content that varies in size, complicates the process of aligning the content across breakpoints, properly.

We have used the ellipsis symbol (...) when the title is too long to fill. This can be achieved using the overflow, white-space, text-overflow, and width properties, as shown in the following code:

```
.packt-app .ts-product-container .ts-product h5{
    overflow: hidden;
    white-space: nowrap;
    text-overflow:ellipsis;
    width:100%;
}
```

The combined style code is shown as follows:

```
.packt-app .ts-product-container{
    text-align:center;
    position:relative;
}
.packt-app .ts-product-container .ts-product{
    display: inline-block;
    float: left;
    margin: 10px 40px;
    width: 200px;
    background: #eee;
    font-weight: bold;
}
.packt-app .ts-product-container .ts-product .panel-body{
    background: #fff;
```

```
}
.packt-app .ts-product-container .ts-product .panel-footer{
    height:48px;
    padding: 6px 15px;
    background: #fff;
}
.packt-app .ts-product-container .ts-product img{
    position: relative;
    top: 0px;
}
.packt-app .ts-product-container .ts-product h5{
    overflow: hidden;
    white-space: nowrap;
    text-overflow:ellipsis;
    width:100%;
}
.packt-app .jumbotron{
    background:transparent;
    padding-left:0px;
}
.packt-app .glyphicon.glyphicon-certificate.ts-cost-icon{
    font-size:50px;
    z-index:2;
     position: relative;
    right: 20px;
    top: 25px;
}
.packt-app .glyphicon.glyphicon-certificate.ts-cost-icon label{
    color: #FFA500;
    font-size: 12px;
    left: 16px;
    position: absolute;
    top: 13px;
}
```

The web application can be called using the following URL:
`http://localhost:8080/MyResponsiveWebApp/index.html`

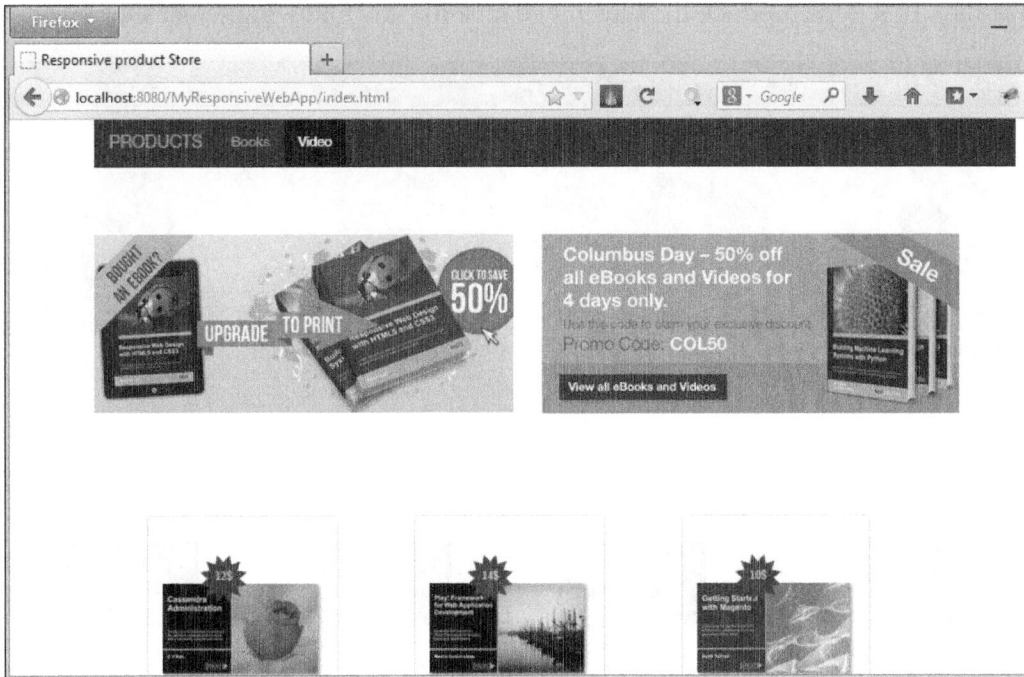

The output on our screen will look like the following screenshot:

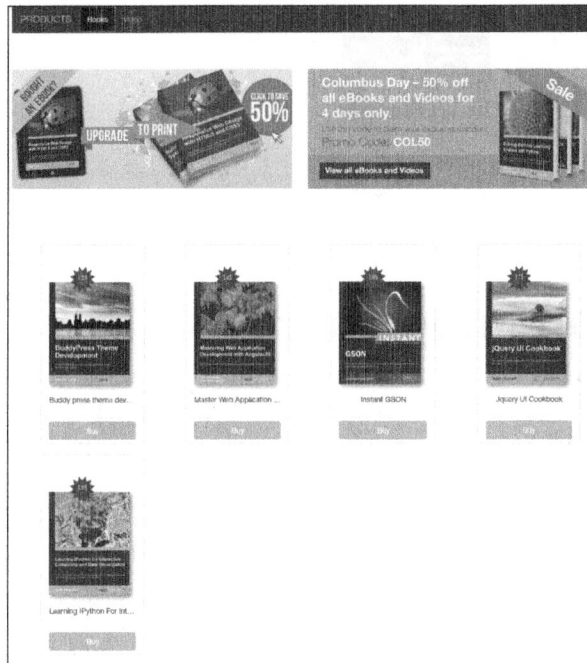

For the `video` type product, the screen will look like the following screenshot:

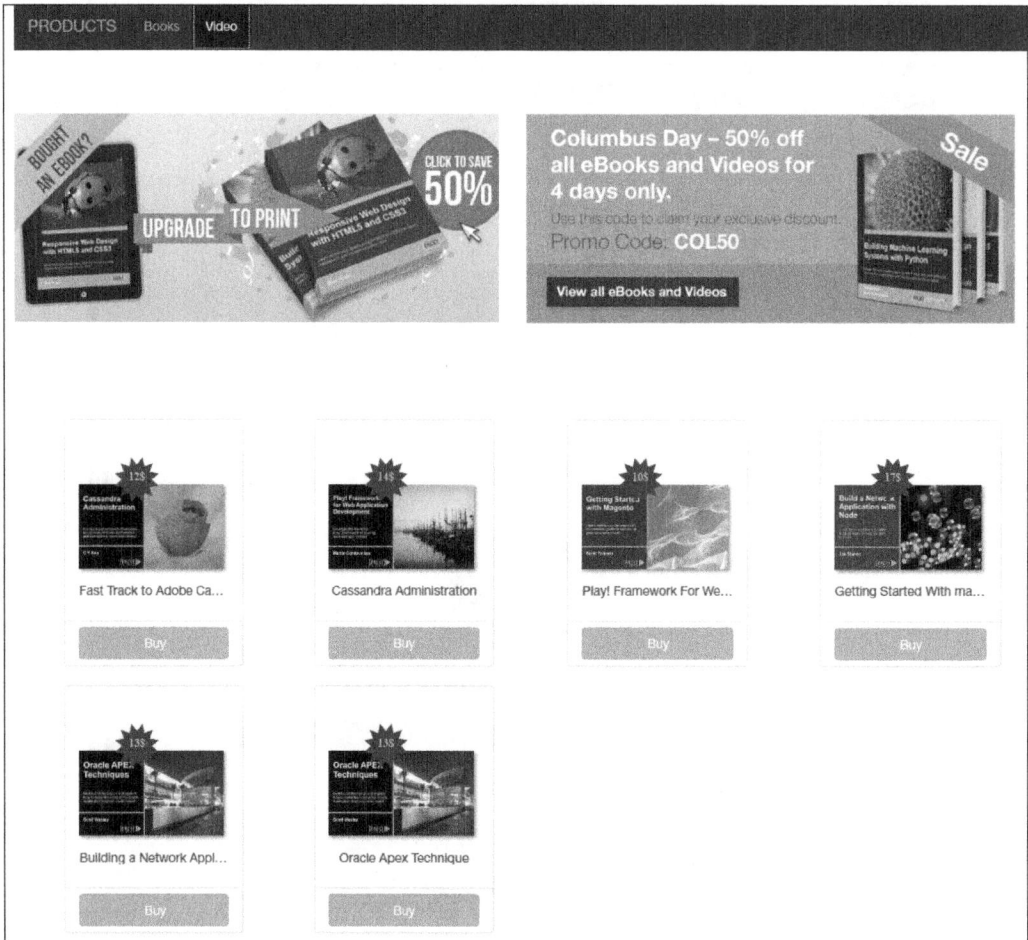

Building an image carousel

In this section, we will build an alternate version of our application's `index.html` file that displays the hero section as a carousel. Bootstrap 3 provides the carousel component based on jQuery.

Some of the key attributes about building a carousel are:

- `data-ride`: This attribute is used for the carousel animation on page load
- `data-slide-to`: This attribute is used for the carousel page indicator to navigate to that page

- data-slide: This attribute represents the navigation of the next and the previous item in the carousel

Some of the key classes of building carousel are:

- carousel: This represents the class of the whole carousel container
- carousel-inner: This class is the wrapper class for the inner carousel items
- item: This represents each carousel element
- carousel-control: This is the wrapper class for controls such as the previous and next actions
- carousel-indicators: This is the page indicator that is shown as a rounded circle for pagination

The code for the carousel component is shown as follows:

```html
<div id="carousel-packt-app" class="carousel slide" data-ride="carousel">
<ol class="carousel-indicators">
        <li data-target="#carousel-packt-app" data-slide-to="0"
class=""></li>
        <li data-target="#carousel-packt-app" data-slide-to="1"
class="active"></li>
</ol>
    <div class="carousel-inner">

        <div class="item">
          <img src="asset/image/hero/1.jpg">
          </div>
          <div class="item active">
          <img src="asset/image/hero/2.png">
          </div>
      </div>
    <a class="left carousel-control" href="#carousel-packt-app" data-slide="prev">
        <span class="glyphicon glyphicon-chevron-left"></span>
  </a>
    <a class="right carousel-control" href="#carousel-packt-app" data-slide="next">
        <span class="glyphicon glyphicon-chevron-right"></span>
    </a>
</div>
```

To position the carousel in the center of the page, we have included the `margin-left` property of the carousel item. The CSS code of the change is as follows:

```
#carousel-packt-app .item{
    margin-left:25%;
}
```

The carousel will look like the following screenshot:

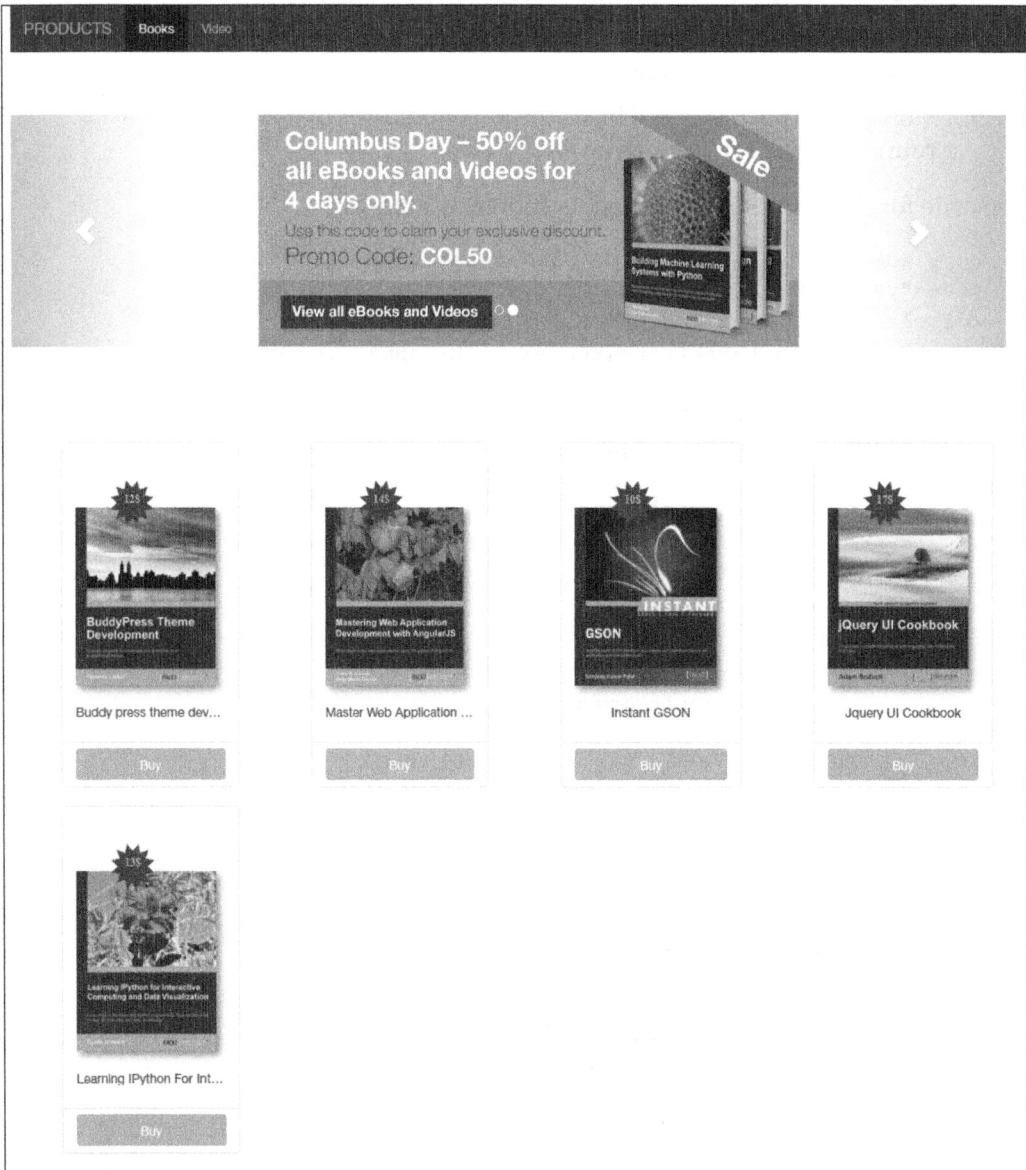

The combined HTML code for the `index-carousel.html` file is as follows:

```html
<!DOCTYPE html>

<html>
<head>
  <link href="asset/css/bootstrap.min.css" rel="stylesheet">
  <link href="asset/css/ts-responsive-web-style.css" rel="stylesheet">
  <title>Responsive product Store</title>
</head>

<body>
  <div class="container packt-app">
    <div class="row">
      <nav class="navbar navbar-inverse navbar-static-top">
        <div class="container-fluid">
          <div class="navbar-header">
            <button class="navbar-toggle collapsed" data-target="#ts-
top-menu"
              data-toggle="collapse" type="button"><span class=
              "sr-only">Navigation buttons</span></button> <a class=
              "navbar-brand" href="#">PRODUCTS</a>
          </div>
          <!-- Collect the nav links, forms, and other content for
toggling -->

          <div class="navbar-collapse collapse" id="ts-top-menu">
            <ul class="nav navbar-nav ts-bar">
              <li class="active" data-category="book"><a href=
              "#">Books</a></li>

              <li data-category="video"><a href="#">Video</a></li>
            </ul>
          </div>
        </div>
      </nav>
    </div>

    <div class="row">
      <div class="jumbotron">
        <div id="carousel-packt-app" class="carousel slide" data-
ride="carousel">
          <ol class="carousel-indicators">
            <li data-target="#carousel-packt-app" data-slide-to="0"
class=""></li>
            <li data-target="#carousel-packt-app" data-slide-to="1"
class="active"></li>
```

```
        </ol>
        <div class="carousel-inner">
          <div class="item">
            <img src="asset/image/hero/1.jpg">
          </div>
          <div class="item active">
            <img src="asset/image/hero/2.png">
          </div>
        </div>
        <a class="left carousel-control" href="#carousel-packt-app"
data-slide="prev">
          <span class="glyphicon glyphicon-chevron-left"></span>
        </a>
        <a class="right carousel-control" href="#carousel-packt-app"
data-slide="next">
          <span class="glyphicon glyphicon-chevron-right"></span>
        </a>
      </div>
    </div>
  </div>

  <div class="row">
    <div class="panel-body ts-product-container"></div>
  </div>
</div>
<script id="aProductTemplate" type="text/x-jquery-tmpl">
  <div class="ts-product panel panel-default">
      <div class="panel-body">
          <span class="glyphicon glyphicon-certificate ts-cost-
icon">
              <label>${cost}$</label>
          </span>
          <img class="img-responsive" src="${url}">
          <h5>${title}</h5>
      </div>
      <div class="panel-footer">
          <button type="button" class="btn btn-info btn-block">Buy</
button>
      </div>
  </div>
</script>
<script src="asset/js/jquery-2.1.0.min.js"></script>
<script src="asset/js/jquery.tmpl.min.js"></script>
<script src="asset/js/bootstrap.min.js"></script>
<script src="asset/js/app.js"></script>
</body>
</html>
```

Summary

In this chapter, we learned to create a Java servlet followed by converting a POJO object to a JSON string, and learned how jQuery AJAX calls are made to the remote servlet. We have also seen the use of jQuery promises to handle the callback issues for the asynchronous method, the use of jQuery templates for compiling a HTML template and building the rendering markup by linking the compiled template with JSON data, and building a Carousel for the hero section.

In the next chapter, we will learn to integrate Twitter's social features into our web application.

4
Twitter Integration

Social networking sites such as Twitter are the most powerful tool for online marketing and lead generation for an e-commerce web application site. In this chapter, we will learn how to integrate the Twitter4J API into our web application. We will also explore the different features provided by Twitter4J.

Introduction to Twitter4J

Twitter4J is a Java library for developing Twitter-based Java applications. It is an unofficial Twitter API. This can be downloaded from `http://twitter4j.org/en/index.html`. The library is zipped in a `twitter4j-4.0.1.zip` file. When unzipped, it contains a `lib` folder containing all the required `.jar` files. The included `.jar` files are listed as follows:

- `twitter4j-core-4.0.1.jar`: This contains the core class for the Twitter API.

- `twitter4j-stream-4.0.1.jar`: This contains the API classes for streaming. Threads can be created to consume the stream generated by listener classes that implement Twitter.

- `twitter4j-async-4.0.1.jar`: This contains API classes and the method for asynchronous access to Twitter.

- `twitter4j-media-support-4.0.1`: This contains API classes and the methods to work with different media types.

We also need to download a dependent JAR file, `commons-codec-1.9-bin`, from `http://commons.apache.org/proper/commons-codec/`.

Configuring Twitter4J in a web application

All of the previous JAR files need to be copied to the `lib` folder present inside the `WEB-INF` directory. The following screenshot shows the `WEB-INF` directory containing all the required JAR files for this application:

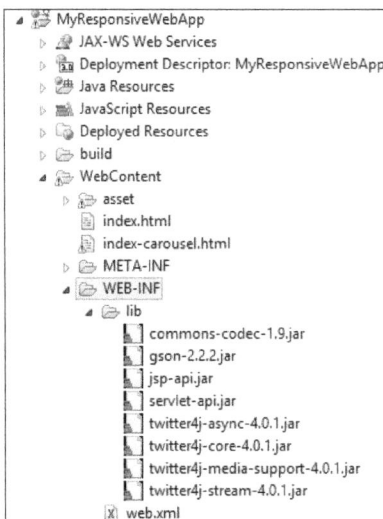

All these JAR files need to be added to the classpath. We can verify that these JAR files are added to the application by looking in the **Java Build Path** option present in the project properties. The following screenshot shows the build path with all the Twitter4J JAR files added properly to our application:

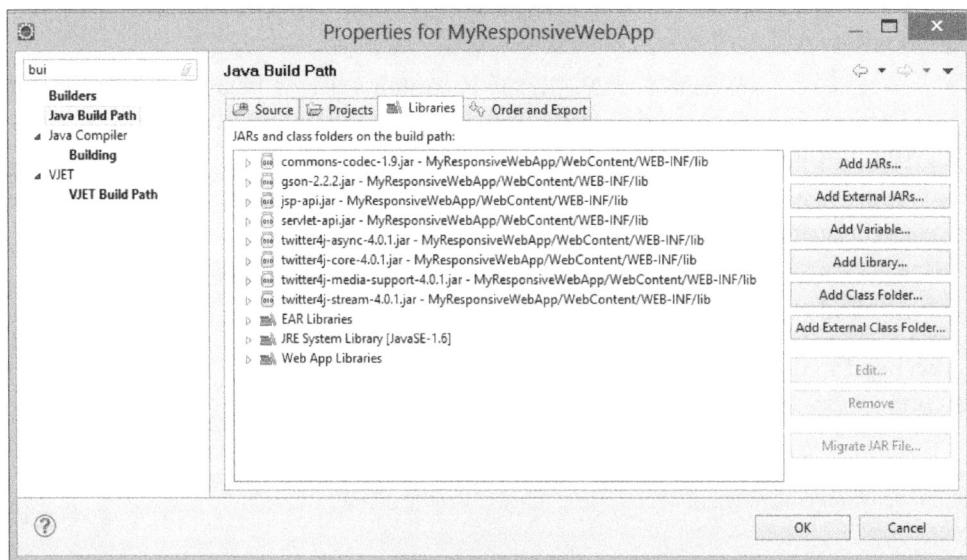

Posting a tweet

In this section, we will learn how to tweet about a product using the Twitter4J API. The approach to achieve this is as follows:

- Create a Twitter button
- Set up a new Twitter application
- Develop a Twitter servlet
- Develop a Twitter callback servlet

The following diagram shows the important entities involved in a Twitter-based client application. The arrow marks represent the communication between each component while posting a tweet to a user timeline:

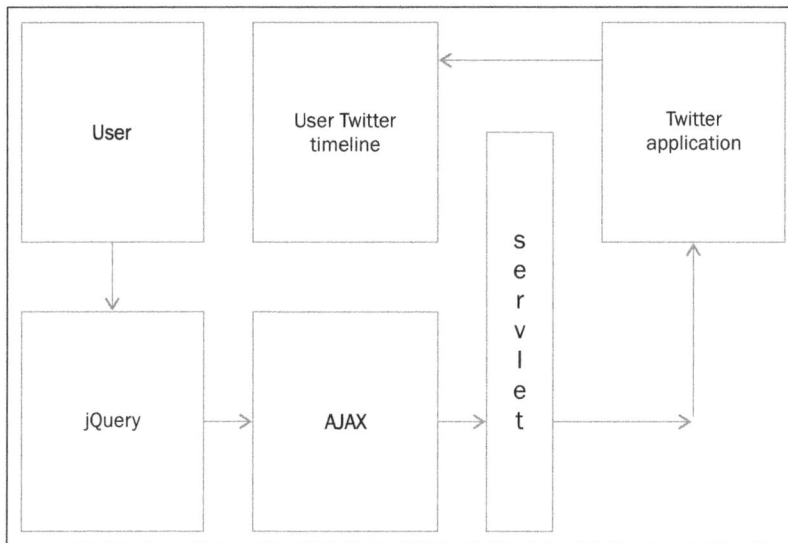

Creating a Twitter button

In this section, we will create a Tweet button for each product. When this button is clicked, a message is posted to the user's timeline about the product. The following steps are executed to develop a Tweet button:

1. Additional HTML markup is added to the jQuery product template as follows:

```
<script id="aProductTemplate" type="text/x-jquery-tmpl">
<div class="ts-product panel panel-default">
  <div class="panel-body">
```

```
            <span class="glyphicon glyphicon-certificate ts-cost-icon">
                <label>${cost}$</label>
            </span>
            <img class="img-responsive" src="${url}">
                <h5>${title}</h5>
        </div>
        <div class="panel-footer">
            <button type="button" class="btn btn-info btn-block">Buy</
button>
            <button type="button" class="btn btn-info btn-block tweet-me"
data-bookTitle="${title}">Tweet</button>
        </div>
        </div>
</script>
```

2. Additional CSS styles are added to make the appearance of the Tweet button similar to the Twitter theme. The change in style is as follows:

```
.packt-app .btn.tweet-me{
background: #55acee;
}
```

3. An additional `click` event handler is added to the script, which will be called when the Tweet button is clicked:

```
/*Event Listener to Tweet Button Click*/
initTwitterApp: function () {
   $(".ts-product-container").on('click', '.tweet-me', function (e)
{
      e.preventDefault();
      var target = e.target, bookTitle = $(target).attr("data-
bookTitle"), message = "I like this book ''" + bookTitle + "''
.What's your opinion?'", aReqTwitPromise = PACKT_PRODUCT_APP.
postTwitAboutProduct(message);
      aReqTwitPromise.done(function (data) {
        window.open(data.url, "_self");
      });
   });
},
/*Calls the Servlet with message in parameter*/
postTwitAboutProduct: function (message) {
```

```
var aReqTwitPromise = $.ajax({
  url: "TwitterServlet",
  type: "POST",
  data: {
    msg: message
  }
}).promise();
return aReqTwitPromise;
}
```

The following screenshot shows the updated product with a Tweet button on it. The Tweet button is present in the footer section of the product, and the background color matches with the Twitter theme too:

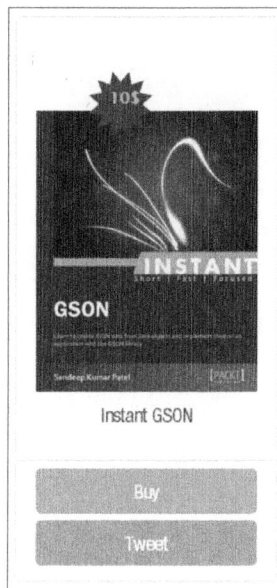

Setting up a new Twitter application

A new Twitter application needs to be created using the `https://dev.twitter.com/apps/new` link. The following screenshot shows a blank form to register a new application:

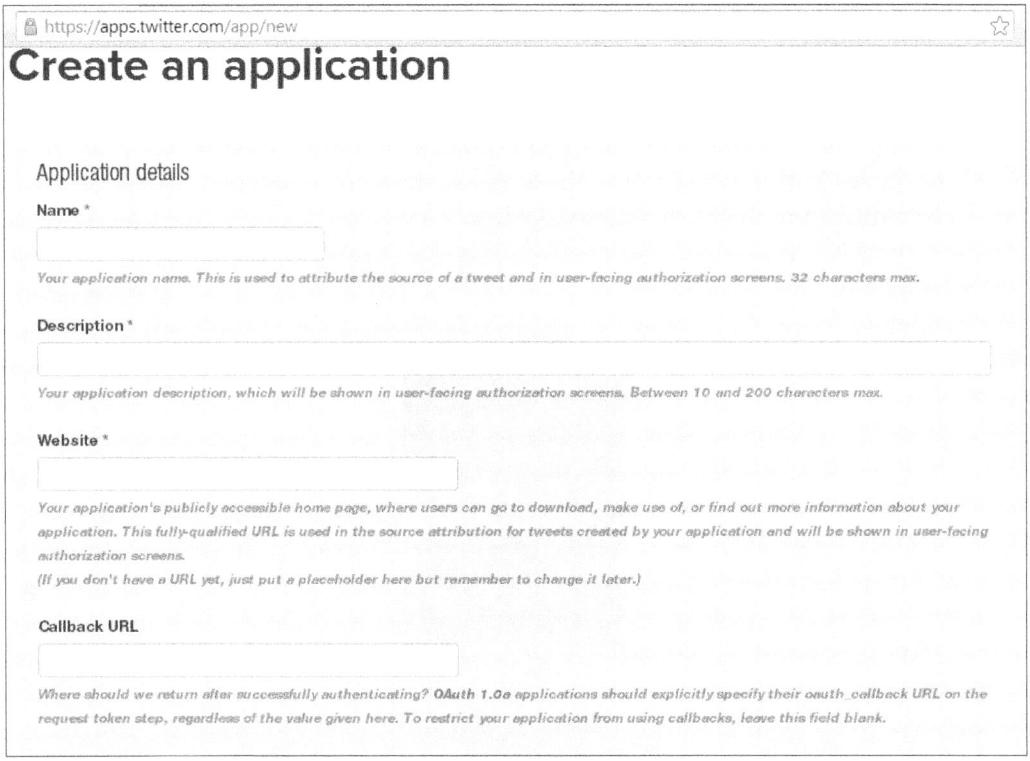

The form has various fields asking about the application details. For our application, we have entered the name as `MyResponsiveWebAppTwitClient`, and the callback URL is `http://127.0.0.1:8080/MyResponsiveWebApp/TwitterCallbackServlet`. The following screenshot shows the filled form for our application:

Application details

Name *

MyResponsiveWebAppTwitClient

Your application name. This is used to attribute the source of a tweet and in user-facing authorization screens. 32 characters max.

Description *

This application is for MyResponsiveWebAppTwitClient. It is used for exploring Twitter4J API.

Your application description, which will be shown in user-facing authorization screens. Between 10 and 200 characters max.

Website *

http://127.0.0.1:8080

Your application's publicly accessible home page, where users can go to download, make use of, or find out more information about your application. This fully-qualified URL is used in the source attribution for tweets created by your application and will be shown in user-facing authorization screens.
(if you don't have a URL yet, just put a placeholder here but remember to change it later.)

Callback URL

http://127.0.0.1:8080/MyResponsiveWebApp/TwitterCallbackServlet

Where should we return after successfully authenticating? OAuth 1.0a applications should explicitly specify their oauth_callback URL on the request token step, regardless of the value given here. To restrict your application from using callbacks, leave this field blank.

☐ Allow this application to be used to Sign in with Twitter

Finally, in the bottom section of the page, there is an application agreement. The following screenshot shows the agreement for our new application. By checking the checkbox, we are agreeing to the terms and conditions:

Developer Rules of the Road

Last Update: July 2, 2013.

Twitter maintains an open platform that supports the millions of people around the world who are sharing and discovering what's happening now. We want to empower our ecosystem partners to build valuable businesses around the information flowing through Twitter. At the same time, we aim to strike a balance between encouraging interesting development and protecting both Twitter's and users' rights.

So, we've come up with a set of Developer Rules of the Road ("**Rules**") that describes the policies and philosophy around what type of innovation is permitted with the content and information shared on Twitter.

The Rules will evolve along with our ecosystem as developers continue to innovate and find new, creative ways to use the Twitter API, so please check back periodically to see the current version. Don't do anything prohibited by the Rules and talk to us if you think we should make a change or give you an exception.

If your application will eventually need more than 1 million user tokens, or you expect your embedded Tweets and embedded timelines to exceed 10 million daily impressions, you will need to talk to us directly about your access to the Twitter API as you may be subject to additional terms. Furthermore, applications that attempt to replicate Twitter's core user experience (as described in Section I.5 below) will need our permission to have more than 100,000 user tokens and are subject to additional terms.

☑ Yes, I agree

Create your Twitter application

Once you have agreed to the agreement and clicked on the **Create Your Twitter application** button, it will create and register the application. We can verify that the application is listed in the / link. The following screenshot shows that the new application is listed in the app list:

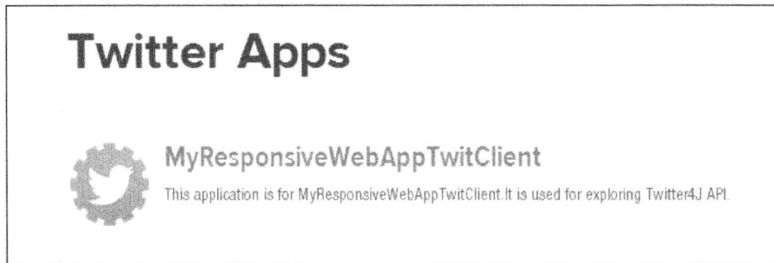

It generates the application ID, 5956893, for our application. If you click on the application, it will navigate to the details page, https://apps.twitter.com/ app/5956893/show. This page has four different tabs: **Details**, **Settings**, **API Keys**, and **Permissions**.

The Twitter Permissions tab

The **Permissions** tab has all the settings related to the specific application. Every Twitter application has the **Read, Write and Access direct messages** permission. By default, each Twitter application has **Read only** access. Check out the following screenshot showing the default permissions for the application:

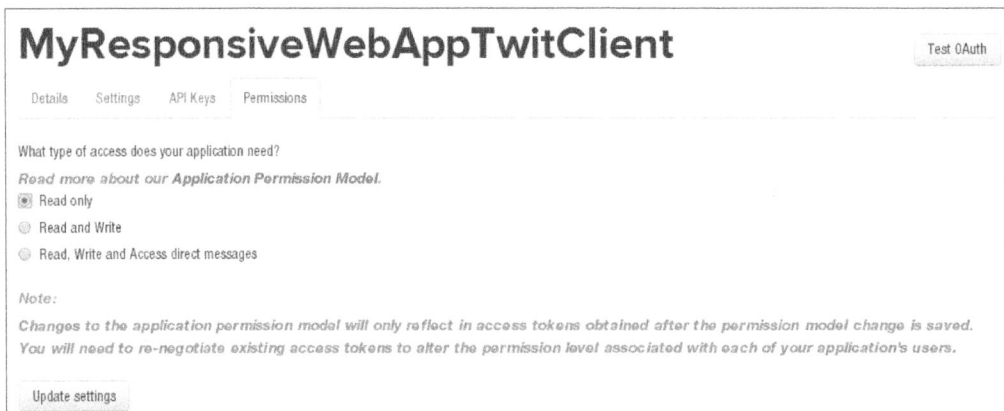

For our application requirement, we need write access too. Select the third radio button **Read, Write and Access direct messages** from the screen, and save the settings using the **Update settings** button present at the bottom of the page:

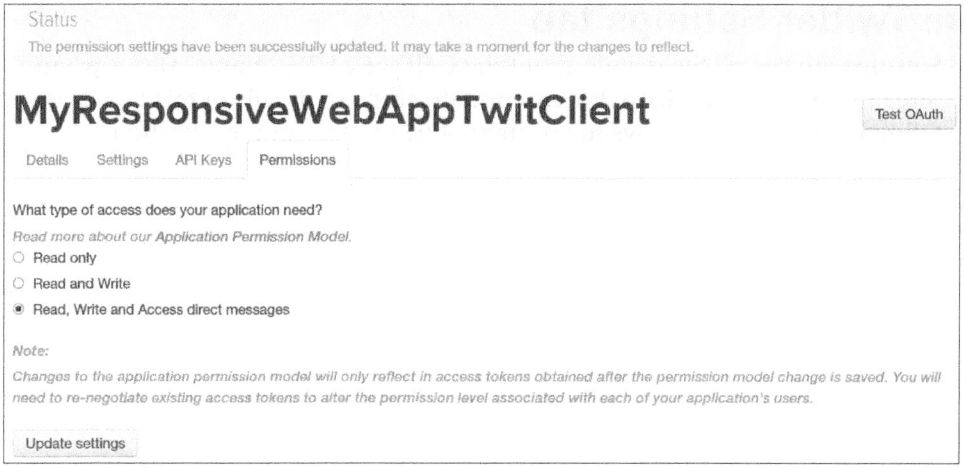

Status
The permission settings have been successfully updated. It may take a moment for the changes to reflect.

MyResponsiveWebAppTwitClient

Test OAuth

Details   Settings   API Keys   **Permissions**

What type of access does your application need?

Read more about our Application Permission Model.

○ Read only

○ Read and Write

⦿ Read, Write and Access direct messages

Note:

Changes to the application permission model will only reflect in access tokens obtained after the permission model change is saved. You will need to re-negotiate existing access tokens to alter the permission level associated with each of your application's users.

Update settings

The Twitter Details tab

The **Details** tab has all the details about the application, such as **Access level**, **API key**, **Callback URL**, **App-only authentication**, **Request token URL**, **Authorize URL**, and **Access token URL**, as shown in the following screenshot:

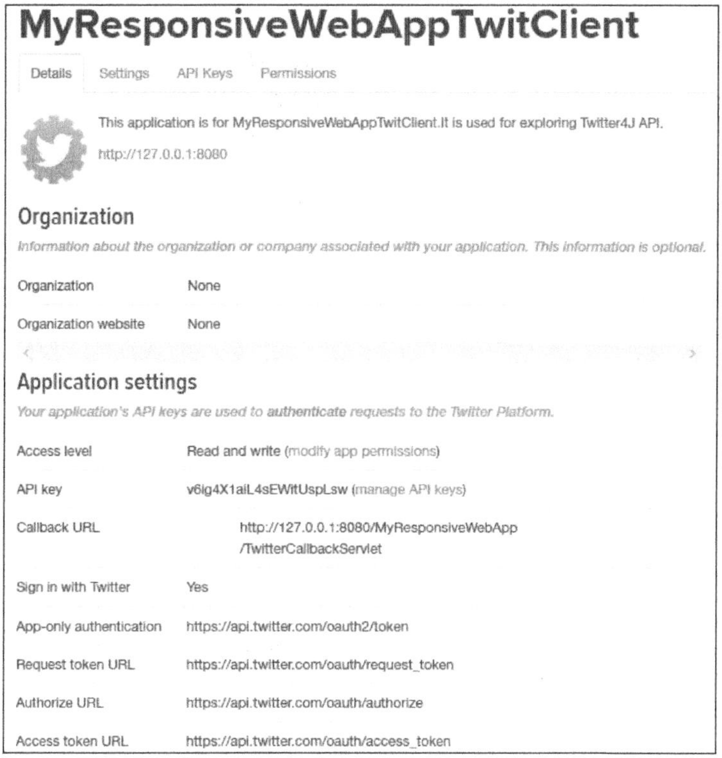

MyResponsiveWebAppTwitClient

Details   Settings   API Keys   Permissions

This application is for MyResponsiveWebAppTwitClient.It is used for exploring Twitter4J API.

http://127.0.0.1:8080

Organization

Information about the organization or company associated with your application. This information is optional.

Organization   None

Organization website   None

Application settings

Your application's API keys are used to authenticate requests to the Twitter Platform.

Access level	Read and write (modify app permissions)
API key	v6ig4X1aiL4sEWftUspLsw (manage API keys)
Callback URL	http://127.0.0.1:8080/MyResponsiveWebApp /TwitterCallbackServlet
Sign in with Twitter	Yes
App-only authentication	https://api.twitter.com/oauth2/token
Request token URL	https://api.twitter.com/oauth/request_token
Authorize URL	https://api.twitter.com/oauth/authorize
Access token URL	https://api.twitter.com/oauth/access_token

The Twitter Settings tab

The **Settings** tab has all the details about the **Callback URL**, **Name**, **Description**, **Website**, and **Application icon**. We can update all these details in this tab. The following screenshot shows the content of this tab for our application:

Application details

Name *

MyResponsiveWebAppTwitClient

Your application name. This is used to attribute the source of a tweet and in user-facing authorization screens. 32 characters max.

Description *

This application is for MyResponsiveWebAppTwitClient. It is used for exploring Twitter4J API.

Your application description, which will be shown in user-facing authorization screens. Between 10 and 200 characters max.

Website *

http://127.0.0.1:8080

Your application's publicly accessible home page, where users can go to download, make use of, or find out more information about your application. This fully-qualified URL is used in the source attribution for tweets created by your application and will be shown in user-facing authorization screens.
(If you don't have a URL yet, just put a placeholder here but remember to change it later.)

Callback URL

http://127.0.0.1:8080/MyResponsiveWebApp/TwitterCallbackServlet

Where should we return after successfully authenticating? OAuth 1.0a applications should explicitly specify their oauth_callback URL on the request token step, regardless of the value given here. To restrict your application from using callbacks, leave this field blank.

☐ Allow this application to be used to Sign in with Twitter

Application icon

Change icon

Browse... No file selected.

Maximum size of 700k. JPG, GIF, PNG.

The Twitter API Keys tab

The **API Keys** tab has all the information about the keys that are being used by the application to access Twitter user data. The following screenshot shows all the content of this tab:

MyResponsiveWebAppTwitClient

Details   Settings   API Keys   Permissions

Application settings

Keep the "API secret" a secret. This key should never be human-readable in your application.

API key	v6ig4X1aiL4sEWitUspLsw
API secret	sRUJ3YyVPvUkM78Fv5cJONzf0ZwvGY7VXR96yFI94
Access level	Read, write, and direct messages (modify app permissions)
Owner	MySmallTutorial
Owner ID	984628201

Application actions

Regenerate API keys   Change App Permissions

Your access token

This access token can be used to make API requests on your own account's behalf. Do not share your access token secret with anyone.

Access token	984628201-O71E5B7b2qGxCVFcwVjRUVEeQYeU2sPPpjPGoR2T
Access token secret	FrN3NG90R3kZc1AQO4kvOl94rZNAVgOXSWBt531knsV9c
Access level	Read, write, and direct messages
Owner	MySmallTutorial
Owner ID	984628201

Token actions

Regenerate my access token   Revoke token access

Developing a Twitter servlet

In the previous section, we registered our new Twitter application to post tweets about our product to the respective user's timeline. The Twitter timeline posting feature starts from the client side where the user needs to click on the Tweet button, which calls a servlet, `TwitterServlet.java`, in the background to receive the authorization URL of the application.

The following screenshot shows the new project structure. There are a few new Java classes added to the project to enable Twitter application integration:

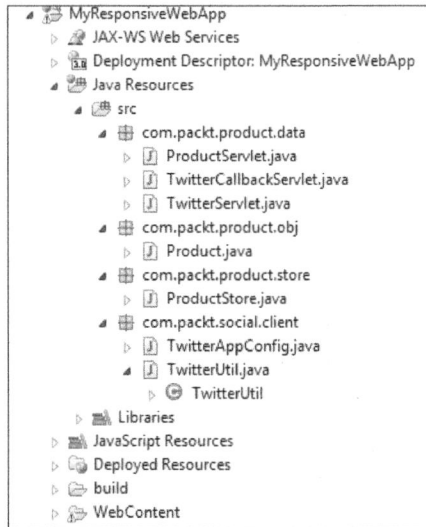

A Twitter application works by a set of token communications. The following diagram shows the main building blocks of a Twitter application lifecycle:

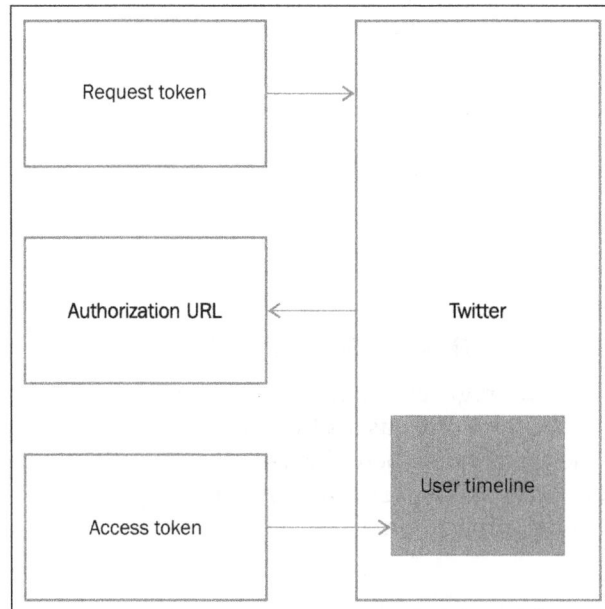

Request token

Each registered Twitter application has an **API key token** and an **API secret token**. These tokens when combined are known as a **request token** for the application. The following diagram shows the two different keys combined to form a request token:

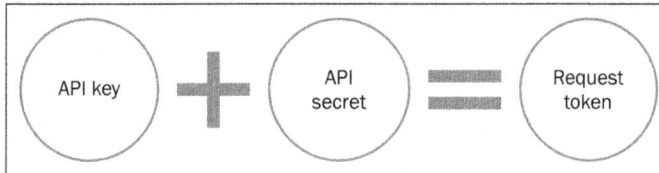

A request token is used to get the authorization URL for the application. In our application, we have saved these tokens in the `TwitterAppConfig.java` file. The code for `TwitterAppConfig` is listed as follows:

```
package com.packt.social.client;
public interface TwitterAppConfig{
    final static String TWIT_CONSUMER_KEY = "v6ig4X1aiL4sEWitUspLsw";
    final static String TWIT_CONSUMER_SECRET_KEY =
"sRUJ3YyVPvUkM78Fv5cJONzf0ZwvGY7VXR96yFI94";
}
```

`TwitterServlet` is the middleware code for our application which will make use of this request token to get the authorization URL. The steps involved to get the authorization URL are explained in the following list of points:

- A Twitter object needs to be created from `TwitterFactory`
- The API key and secret string need to be added to create an OAuth consumer
- This OAuth consumer is required to get an OAuth request token
- This OAuth request token will generate the authorization URL for our Twitter application

Additionally, we are saving the request token to reuse it on the callback servlet. You can save it in persistent storage or as a user session object. The following diagram shows a graphical representation of the preceding process:

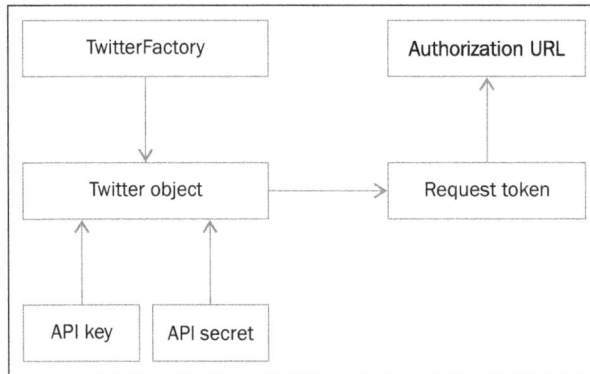

A `TwitterUtil` class is created so we have some reusable code for this application. The code for this utility class is listed in the next code snippet. This utility has methods for temporary storage of messages. In a real-time application, this can be optimized with a better persistence mechanism. Have a look at the following code:

```
package com.packt.social.client;
import java.io.InputStream;
import twitter4j.auth.RequestToken;
public class TwitterUtil {
    public  static RequestToken reqToken =null;
    public static String message;
    public static InputStream imgStrem;
    public static  void saveRequestToken(RequestToken req, String msg)
{
        reqToken =req;
        message = msg;
    }
    public static  void saveRequestToken(RequestToken req, String
msg,InputStream imageStrem) {
        reqToken =req;
        message = msg;
        imgStrem = imageStrem;
    }
}
```

The code for `TwitterServlet.java` is listed as follows:

```java
package com.packt.product.data;
import java.io.IOException;
import java.io.PrintWriter;
import javax.servlet.ServletException;
import javax.servlet.annotation.WebServlet;
import javax.servlet.http.HttpServlet;
import javax.servlet.http.HttpServletRequest;
import javax.servlet.http.HttpServletResponse;
import twitter4j.JSONException;
import twitter4j.JSONObject;
import twitter4j.Twitter;
import twitter4j.TwitterException;
import twitter4j.TwitterFactory;
import twitter4j.auth.RequestToken;
import com.packt.social.client.TwitterAppConfig;
import com.packt.social.client.TwitterUtil;
@WebServlet("/TwitterServlet")
public class TwitterServlet extends HttpServlet implements
TwitterAppConfig {
    private static final long serialVersionUID = 1L;
    public TwitterServlet() {
        super();
    }
    protected void doPost(HttpServletRequest request,
HttpServletResponse response) throws ServletException, IOException {
        Twitter twitter = new TwitterFactory().getInstance();
        twitter.setOAuthConsumer(TWIT_CONSUMER_KEY, TWIT_CONSUMER_
SECRET_KEY);
        RequestToken requestToken = null;
        String url = null;
        String twitMsgPost = request.getParameter("msg");
        try {
        requestToken = twitter.getOAuthRequestToken();
      /* Saving the Request Token:
      * Can be implemented in Database.
    * In this example, we have saved the token
      * in static field for the purposes of demonstration.
      * For real implementation, please use other mechanisms.
      */
        TwitterUtil.saveRequestToken(requestToken, twitMsgPost);
          url = requestToken.getAuthorizationURL();
        } catch (TwitterException e){
```

```
          e.printStackTrace();
    }
    response.setContentType("application/json");
    PrintWriter out = response.getWriter();
    JSONObject reqToken = new JSONObject();
     try {
       reqToken.put("url", url);
       reqToken.put("token", requestToken.getToken());
       reqToken.put("tokenSecret",requestToken.getTokenSecret());
     } catch (JSONException e) {
         e.printStackTrace();
    }
      out.write(reqToken.toString());
   }
 }
```

Developing a Twitter callback servlet

A callback URL is required for a Twitter application. After successful authorization, this is the location that the application returns to for further processing. While creating the application, this callback option is present for configuration. For our application, we have used `http://127.0.0.1:8080/MyResponsiveWebApp/ TwitterCallbackServlet`.

Access token

An access token is used to post a tweet in the user timeline. An access token is made up of a combination of `oauth_verifier` and an API secret.

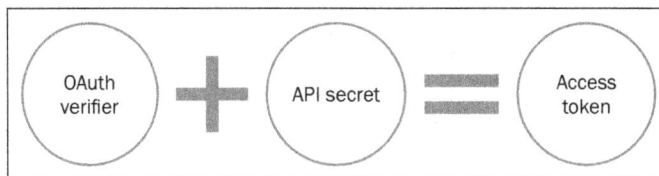

After authorization, the control returns to the callback servlet .The callback servlet retrieves the request token saved in the storage. Using the request token and the `oauth_verifier` key, it generates the access token. This OAuth token is then set to a Twitter object to post the tweet or status in the user timeline.

The code for `TwitterCallbackServlet.java` is listed as follows:

```java
package com.packt.product.data;
import java.io.IOException;
import javax.servlet.ServletException;
import javax.servlet.annotation.WebServlet;
import javax.servlet.http.HttpServlet;
import javax.servlet.http.HttpServletRequest;
import javax.servlet.http.HttpServletResponse;
import twitter4j.Twitter;
import twitter4j.TwitterException;
import twitter4j.TwitterFactory;
import twitter4j.auth.AccessToken;
import twitter4j.auth.RequestToken;
import com.packt.social.client.TwitterAppConfig;
import com.packt.social.client.TwitterUtil;
@WebServlet("/TwitterCallbackServlet")
public class TwitterCallbackServlet extends HttpServlet implements
TwitterAppConfig{
    private static final long serialVersionUID = 1L;
     public TwitterCallbackServlet() {
         super();
     }
    protected void doGet(HttpServletRequest request,
HttpServletResponse response) throws ServletException, IOException {
         Twitter twitter = new TwitterFactory().getInstance();
         twitter.setOAuthConsumer(TWIT_CONSUMER_KEY, TWIT_CONSUMER_
SECRET_KEY);
         AccessToken aToken = null;
         RequestToken reqToken = TwitterUtil.reqToken;
         try{
          aToken = twitter.getOAuthAccessToken(reqToken,request.
getParameter("oauth_verifier"));
         twitter.setOAuthAccessToken(aToken);
         twitter.updateStatus(TwitterUtil.message);
         } catch (TwitterException e) {
             e.printStackTrace();
         }
     request.getRequestDispatcher("/index.html").forward(request,
response);
     }
}
```

The next screenshot shows the pop-up window asking for the user's authorization to post the tweet in the user's timeline; the user can authorize the application by providing the correct username and password:

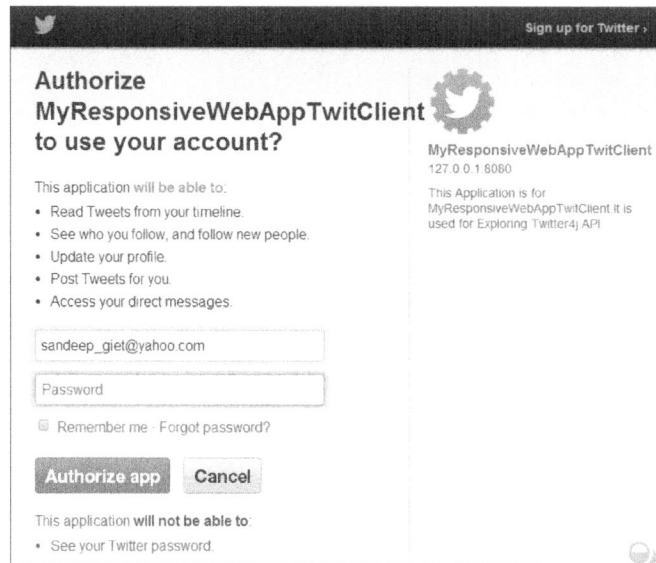

You can check the list of tweets on the timeline. The following screenshot shows the tweet list of the user:

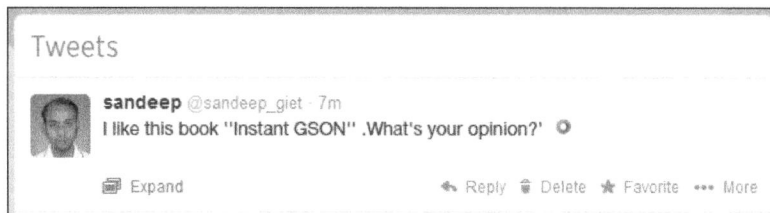

Combining all the pieces

In this section, we will see the combined code for the whole application and the look and feel of the entire page.

The updated code for the `index.html` file is listed as follows:

```
<!DOCTYPE html>
<html>
<head>
  <link href="asset/css/bootstrap.min.css" rel="stylesheet">
```

```
    <link href="asset/css/ts-responsive-web-style.css" rel="stylesheet">
    <title>Responsive product Store</title>
  </head>
  <body>
    <div class="container packt-app">
      <div class="row">
        <nav class="navbar navbar-inverse navbar-static-top">
          <div class="container-fluid">
            <div class="navbar-header">
              <button class="navbar-toggle collapsed" data-target="#ts-
top-menu"
                data-toggle="collapse" type="button"><span class=
                "sr-only">Navigation buttons</span></button> <a class=
                "navbar-brand" href="#">PRODUCTS</a>
            </div>
            <!-- Collect the nav links, forms, and other content for
toggling -->
            <div class="navbar-collapse collapse" id="ts-top-menu">
              <ul class="nav navbar-nav ts-bar">
                <li class="active" data-category="book"><a href=
                "#">Books</a></li>
                <li data-category="video"><a href="#">Video</a></li>
              </ul>
            </div>
          </div>
        </nav>
      </div>
      <div class="row">
        <div class="jumbotron">
          <div class="row">
            <div class="col-sm-6"><img class="img-responsive" src=
            "asset/image/hero/1.jpg"></div>
            <div class="col-sm-6"><img class="img-responsive" src=
            "asset/image/hero/2.png"></div>
          </div>
        </div>
      </div>
      <div class="row">
        <div class="panel-body ts-product-container"></div>
      </div>
    </div>
    <script id="aProductTemplate" type="text/x-jquery-tmpl">
      <div class="ts-product panel panel-default">
        <div class="panel-body">
```

```
                <span class="glyphicon glyphicon-certificate ts-cost-
    icon">
                    <label>${cost}$</label>
                </span>
                <img class="img-responsive" src="${url}">
                <h5>${title}</h5>
            </div>
            <div class="panel-footer">
                <button type="button" class="btn btn-info btn-block">Buy</
    button>
                <button type="button" class="btn btn-info btn-block tweet-
    me" data-bookTitle="${title}">Tweet</button>
            </div>
        </div>
    </script>
    <script src="asset/js/jquery-2.1.0.min.js"></script>
    <script src="asset/js/jquery.tmpl.min.js"></script>
    <script src="asset/js/bootstrap.min.js"></script>
    <script src="asset/js/app.js"></script>
</body>
</html>
```

The updated code for app.js is listed as follows:

```
var PACKT_PRODUCT_APP={
    /*Returning jQuery Promise For a AJAX call with Product type*/
    getProductDetails : function(type){
        var ajaxRequest=$.ajax("ProductServlet?type="+type);
        return ajaxRequest.promise();
    }
    /*Handler For AJAX response*/
    handleCallback : function(type){
        var promise = PACKT_PRODUCT_APP.getProductDetails(type);
        promise.done(function(data){
            PACKT_PRODUCT_APP.doProductRendering(data);
        });
    },
    /*jquery Template building with  JSON data*/
    doProductRendering: function(data){
        var productContainer =$('.ts-product-container'),
        aProductTemplate = $('#aProductTemplate').tmpl(data),
promiseOldPro = $(productContainer).find('.panel').fadeOut().
promise();
            $.when(promiseOldPro).then(function(){
                productContainer.html(aProductTemplate);
```

```
            });
        }
        /*Event Listener to Menu Item Click*/
        initCategoryClick:function(){
            $(".ts-bar").on('click','li',function(e){
                e.preventDefault();
                 var li = e.currentTarget, type= $(li).attr('data-
category');
                $(li).siblings('li').removeClass('active');
                $(li).addClass('active');
                PACKT_PRODUCT_APP.handleCallback(type);
            });
        }
        /*Event Listener to Twitter Button Click*/
        initTwitterApp : function(){
        $(".ts-product-container").on('click','.tweet-me',function(e){
        e.preventDefault();
        var target = e.target,
        bookTitle = $(target).attr("data-bookTitle"),
        message= "I like this book ''"+bookTitle+"'' .What's your
opinion?'",
 aReqTwitPromise = PACKT_PRODUCT_APP.postTwitAboutProduct(message);
        aReqTwitPromise.done(function(data){
          window.open(data.url,"_self");
          });
        });
}
        /*Calls the Servlet with message in parameter*/
        postTwitAboutProduct:function(message){
        var aReqTwitPromise=$.ajax({url:"TwitterServlet",type:"POST",data:
{msg:message}}).promise();
        return aReqTwitPromise;
        }
};
$(document).ready(function(){
    /*Initial Load Call Books */
    PACKT_PRODUCT_APP.handleCallback('book');
    /*Initialize Click Of Menu Item*/
    PACKT_PRODUCT_APP.initCategoryClick();
    /*Initialize Click Of Twitter Button*/
    PACKT_PRODUCT_APP.initTwitterApp();
});
```

The screen will look like the following screenshot:

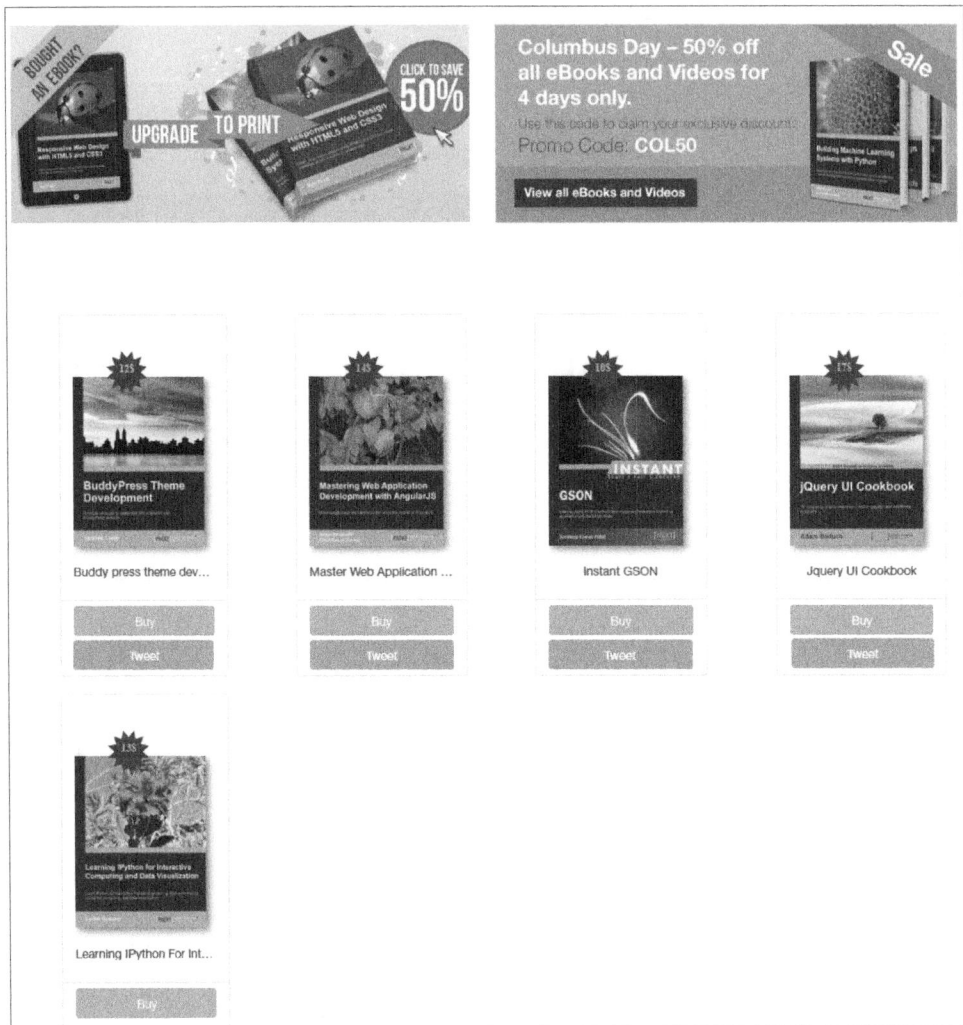

Posting a tweet with an image

In this section, we will learn how to post a tweet with an image included in the message. In the previous section, we developed the Twitter client for text message status updates. This section is all about posting a media item.

To demonstrate this, we have made some changes to the code.

Product store with an image

The product store, where all our products have been stored, now points to a URL to display the corresponding images. Have a look at the following code:

```
package com.packt.product.store;
import java.util.ArrayList;
import java.util.List;
import com.google.gson.Gson;
import com.google.gson.GsonBuilder;
import com.packt.product.obj.Product;
public class ProductStore{
    public static List<Product> getAllListedBook(){
        List<Product> listProduct = new ArrayList<Product>();
        Product product2 = new Product();
        product2.setTitle("Buddy press theme development");
        product2.setCost(12);
        product2.setDescription("Lorem ipsum dollar.Lorem ipsum
dollar.Lorem ipsum dollar.");
product2.setUrl("http://127.0.0.1:8080/MyResponsiveWebApp/asset/image/
books/2.png");
        product2.setType("book");
        Product product3 = new Product();
        product3.setTitle("Master Web Application Development with
AngularJS");
        product3.setCost(14);
        product3.setDescription("Lorem ipsum dollar.Lorem ipsum
dollar.Lorem ipsum dollar.");
product3.setUrl("http://127.0.0.1:8080/MyResponsiveWebApp/asset/image/
books/3.png");
        product3.setType("book");
        Product product4 = new Product();
        product4.setTitle("Instant GSON");
        product4.setCost(10);
        product4.setDescription("Lorem ipsum dollar.Lorem ipsum
dollar.Lorem ipsum dollar.");
    product4.setUrl("http://127.0.0.1:8080/MyResponsiveWebApp/asse
t/image/books/4.png");
        product4.setType("book");
        Product product5 = new Product();
        product5.setTitle("Jquery UI Cookbook");
        product5.setCost(17);
        product5.setDescription("Lorem ipsum dollar.Lorem ipsum
dollar.Lorem ipsum dollar.");
```

```
product5.setUrl("http://127.0.0.1:8080/MyResponsiveWebApp/asset/image/
books/5.png");
        product5.setType("book");
        Product product6 = new Product();
    product6.setTitle("Learning IPython For Interactive Computing And
Data Visualization");
        product6.setCost(13);
        product6.setDescription("Lorem ipsum dollar.Lorem ipsum
dollar.Lorem ipsum dollar.");
product6.setUrl("http://127.0.0.1:8080/MyResponsiveWebApp/asset/image/
books/6.png");
        listProduct.add(product2);
        listProduct.add(product3);
        listProduct.add(product4);
        listProduct.add(product5);
        listProduct.add(product6);
        return listProduct;
    }
    public static List<Product> getAllListedVideo() {
        List<Product> listProduct = new ArrayList<Product>();
        Product product1 = new Product();
        product1.setTitle("Fast Track to Adobe Captivate 6");
        product1.setCost(12);
        product1.setDescription("Lorem ipsum dollar.Lorem ipsum
dollar.Lorem ipsum dollar.");
product1.setUrl("http://127.0.0.1:8080/MyResponsiveWebApp/asset/
image/video/2.png");
        product1.setType("video");
        Product product2 = new Product();
        product2.setTitle("Cassandra Administration");
        product2.setCost(14);
        product2.setDescription("Lorem ipsum dollar.Lorem ipsum
dollar.Lorem ipsum dollar.");
product2.setUrl("http://127.0.0.1:8080/MyResponsiveWebApp/asset/image/
video/3.png");
        product2.setType("video");
        Product product3 = new Product();
        product3.setTitle("Play! Framework For Web Application
Development");
        product3.setCost(10);
        product3.setDescription("Lorem ipsum dollar.Lorem ipsum dollar.
Lorem ipsum dollar.");
```

```
product3.setUrl("http://127.0.0.1:8080/MyResponsiveWebApp/asset/image/
video/4.png");
        product3.setType("video");
        Product product4 = new Product();
        product4.setTitle("Getting Started With Magento");
        product4.setCost(17);
        product4.setDescription("Lorem ipsum dollar.Lorem ipsum
dollar.Lorem ipsum dollar.");
product4.setUrl("http://127.0.0.1:8080/MyResponsiveWebApp/asset/image/
video/5.png");
        product4.setType("video");
        Product product5 = new Product();
        product5.setTitle("Building a Network Application With Node");
        product5.setCost(13);
        product5.setDescription("Lorem ipsum dollar.Lorem ipsum
dollar.Lorem ipsum dollar.");
product5.setUrl("http://127.0.0.1:8080/MyResponsiveWebApp/asset/image/
video/6.png");
        product5.setType("video");
        Product product6 = new Product();
        product6.setTitle("Oracle Apex Technique");
        product6.setCost(13);
        product6.setDescription("Lorem ipsum dollar.Lorem ipsum
dollar.Lorem ipsum dollar.");
product6.setUrl("http://127.0.0.1:8080/MyResponsiveWebApp/asset/image/
video/6.png");
        product6.setType("video");
        listProduct.add(product1);
        listProduct.add(product2);
        listProduct.add(product3);
        listProduct.add(product4);
        listProduct.add(product5);
        listProduct.add(product6);
        return listProduct;
    }
    public static String createStaticJSON(List<Product>
listOfProduct){
    Gson gson = new GsonBuilder().setPrettyPrinting().create();
        String json = gson.toJson(listOfProduct);
        return json;
    }
}
```

Markup changes

The product template now has the new attribute `data-imgURI`. This attribute has the URL to the book image. The modified jQuery template is listed in the following code:

```
<script id="aProductTemplate" type="text/x-jquery-tmpl">
    <div class="ts-product panel panel-default">
        <div class="panel-body">
            <span class="glyphicon glyphicon-certificate ts-cost-
icon">
                <label>${cost}$</label>
            </span>
            <img class="img-responsive" src="${url}">
            <h5>${title}</h5>
        </div>
        <div class="panel-footer">
         <button type="button" class="btn btn-info btn-block">Buy</
button>
        <button type="button" class="btn btn-info btn-block tweet-me"
data-bookTitle="${title}" data-imgURI="${url}">Tweet</button>
        </div>
    </div>
</script>
```

The following screenshot from the Firebug console shows the HTML markup for the product; you can notice the attribute containing the URL to the image:

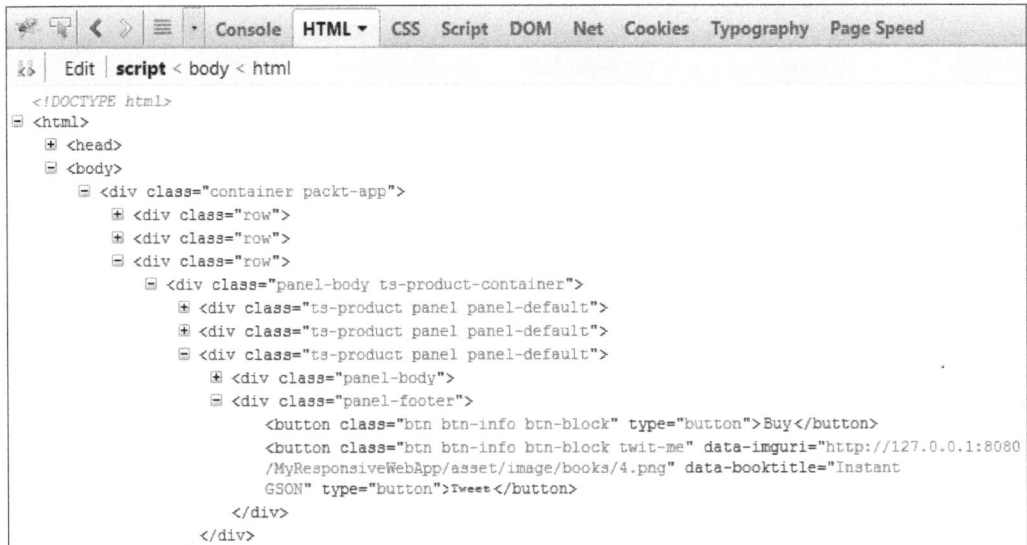

Changes in app.js

When the Tweet button is clicked now, the `data-imgURI` value will be posted to the servlet. The changes in the jQuery code are listed as follows:

```
var PACKT_PRODUCT_APP={
    /*Returning jQuery Promise For an AJAX call with Product type*/
    getProductDetails : function(type){
        var ajaxRequest=$.ajax("ProductServlet?type="+type);
        return ajaxRequest.promise();
    }
    /*Handler For AJAX response*/
    handleCallback : function(type){
        var promise = PACKT_PRODUCT_APP.getProductDetails(type);
        promise.done(function(data){
        PACKT_PRODUCT_APP.doProductRendering(data);
        });
    }
    /*jQuery Template building with  JSON data*/
    doProductRendering: function(data){
        var productContainer =$('.ts-product-container'),
aProductTemplate = $('#aProductTemplate').tmpl( data ), promiseOldPro
= $(productContainer).find('.panel').fadeOut().promise();
    $.when(promiseOldPro).then(function(){
        productContainer.html(aProductTemplate);
    });
    }
    /*Event Listener to Menu Item Click*/
    initCategoryClick:function(){
        $(".ts-bar").on('click','li',function(e){
            e.preventDefault();
            var li = e.currentTarget,
                type= $(li).attr('data-category');
            $(li).siblings('li').removeClass('active');
            $(li).addClass('active');
            PACKT_PRODUCT_APP.handleCallback(type);
        });
    }
    /*Event Listener to Twitter Button Click*/
    initTwitterApp : function(){
        $(".ts-product-container").on('click','.tweet-me',function(e){
            e.preventDefault();
            var target = e.target,
                bookTitle = $(target).attr("data-bookTitle"),
                imgURI = $(target).attr("data-imgURI"),
```

```
                         message= "I like this book ''"+bookTitle+"''
    .What's your opinion?'", aReqTwitPromise = PACKT_PRODUCT_APP.
postTwitAboutProduct(message, imgURI);
        aReqTwitPromise.done(function(data){
            window.open(data.url,"_self");
        });
            });
        }
        /*Calls the Servlet with message in parameter*/
        postTwitAboutProduct:function(message,imgURI){
            var aReqTwitPromise=$.ajax({url:"TwitterServlet",type:"POST",d
ata:{msg:message, imgUri:encodeURI(imgURI)}}).promise();
            return aReqTwitPromise;
        }
};
$(document).ready(function(){
    /*Initial Load Call Books */
    PACKT_PRODUCT_APP.handleCallback('book');
    /*Initialize Click Of Menu Item*/
    PACKT_PRODUCT_APP.initCategoryClick();
    /*Initialize Click Of Twitter Button*/
    PACKT_PRODUCT_APP.initTwitterApp();
});
```

Twitter servlet changes

In the Twitter servlet, we have added some code to catch the image URI parameter and saved it to the input stream. The code changes are listed as follows:

```
package com.packt.product.data;
import java.io.IOException;
import java.io.InputStream;
import java.io.PrintWriter;
import java.net.URL;
import java.net.URLConnection;
import javax.servlet.ServletException;
import javax.servlet.annotation.WebServlet;
import javax.servlet.http.HttpServlet;
import javax.servlet.http.HttpServletRequest;
import javax.servlet.http.HttpServletResponse;
import twitter4j.JSONException;
import twitter4j.JSONObject;
import twitter4j.Twitter;
import twitter4j.TwitterException;
import twitter4j.TwitterFactory;
```

```
import twitter4j.auth.RequestToken;
import com.packt.social.client.TwitterAppConfig;
import com.packt.social.client.TwitterUtil;
@WebServlet("/TwitterServlet")
public class TwitterServlet extends HttpServlet implements
TwitterAppConfig {
    private static final long serialVersionUID = 1L;
    public TwitterServlet() {
        super();
    }
    protected void doPost(HttpServletRequest request,
            HttpServletResponse response) throws ServletException,
IOException {
        Twitter twitter = new TwitterFactory().getInstance();
        twitter.setOAuthConsumer(TWIT_CONSUMER_KEY, TWIT_CONSUMER_
SECRET_KEY);
        RequestToken requestToken = null;
        String url = null;
        String twitMsgPost = request.getParameter("msg");
        String twitImgUri = request.getParameter("imgUri");
        URL imgUri = null;
        InputStream imageStrem = null;
        try {
            imgUri = new URL(twitImgUri);
            URLConnection conn = imgUri.openConnection();
            requestToken = twitter.getOAuthRequestToken();
            imageStrem = conn.getInputStream();
            TwitterUtil.saveRequestToken(requestToken, twitMsgPost,
imageStrem);
            url = requestToken.getAuthorizationURL();
        } catch (TwitterException e) {
            e.printStackTrace();
        }
        response.setContentType("application/json");
        PrintWriter out = response.getWriter();
        JSONObject reqToken = new JSONObject();
        try{
            reqToken.put("url", url);
            reqToken.put("token", requestToken.getToken());
            reqToken.put("tokenSecret", requestToken.
getTokenSecret());
        } catch (JSONException e) {
            e.printStackTrace();
        }
        out.write(reqToken.toString());
    }
}
```

Changes in the Twitter callback servlet

In the callback servlet, we have created a status object and we have added the text content and the image media input stream to be posted on the user client. The following code has the change in the callback servlet:

```java
package com.packt.product.data;
import java.io.IOException;
import javax.servlet.ServletException;
import javax.servlet.annotation.WebServlet;
import javax.servlet.http.HttpServlet;
import javax.servlet.http.HttpServletRequest;
import javax.servlet.http.HttpServletResponse;
import twitter4j.StatusUpdate;
import twitter4j.Twitter;
import twitter4j.TwitterException;
import twitter4j.TwitterFactory;
import twitter4j.auth.AccessToken;
import twitter4j.auth.RequestToken;
import com.packt.social.client.TwitterAppConfig;
import com.packt.social.client.TwitterUtil;
@WebServlet("/TwitterCallbackServlet")
public class TwitterCallbackServlet extends HttpServlet implements
TwitterAppConfig{
    private static final long serialVersionUID = 1L;
    public TwitterCallbackServlet() {
        super();
    }
    protected void doGet(HttpServletRequest request,
HttpServletResponse response) throws ServletException, IOException {
        Twitter twitter = new TwitterFactory().getInstance();
        twitter.setOAuthConsumer(TWIT_CONSUMER_KEY, TWIT_CONSUMER_
SECRET_KEY);
        AccessToken aToken = null;
        RequestToken reqToken = TwitterUtil.reqToken;
        try{
            aToken = twitter.getOAuthAccessToken(reqToken,request.
getParameter("oauth_verifier"));
            twitter.setOAuthAccessToken(aToken);
            StatusUpdate status = new StatusUpdate(TwitterUtil.
message);
            status.setMedia("Book", TwitterUtil.imgStrem);
            twitter.updateStatus(status);
        } catch (TwitterException e) {
```

```
            e.printStackTrace();
        }
    request.getRequestDispatcher("/index.html").forward(request,
response);
        }
}
```

User Twitter timeline

Now, when a user tweets about a product, the tweet has both text and image in the content. This can be verified in the timeline. The following screenshot shows my timeline, which contains the tweet about my book *Instant GSON*.

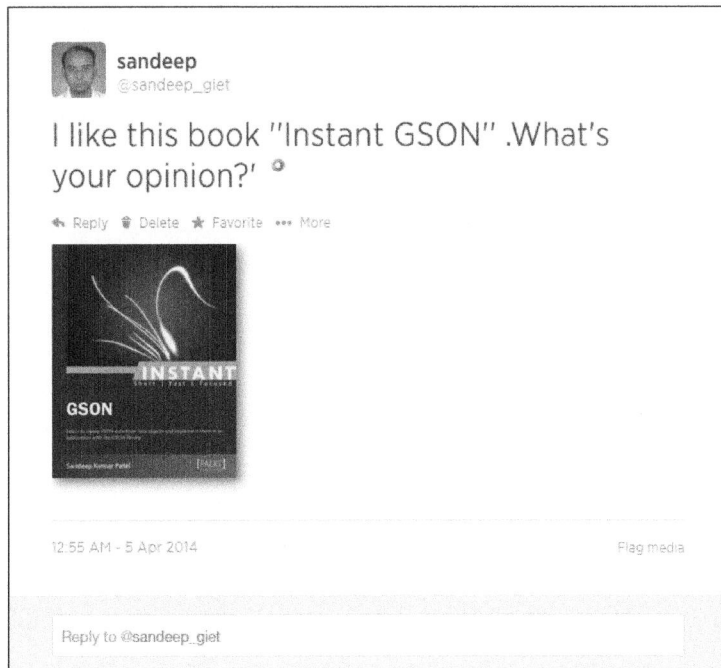

Summary

In this chapter, we learned how to configure the Twitter4J API for a web application, create a new Twitter client application to work with our web application, and integrate the Twitter application to the web application using Twitter4J, jQuery, and AJAX.

In the next chapter, we will learn how to integrate Facebook features to our web application.

5
Facebook Integration

In this chapter, we will learn how to integrate Facebook into our responsive web application. We will learn how to integrate different features, such as logging in using a Facebook account and integrating a Like button into each product as well as integrating comments. The presence of Facebook features enables users to share information about the product on their timeline, which includes visibility of the web application.

Introduction to the Facebook SDK for JavaScript

In this section, we will learn how to configure the Facebook JavaScript SDK for our application. There are no specific files to be downloaded to configure the SDK. Facebook provides a JavaScript all.js file to call the Facebook API.

```
<script src="http://connect.facebook.net/en_US/all.js">
</script>
```

Facebook supports different locales for configuration. For our application, we have called the US English locale. In the preceding script, en_US represents the locale parameter.

This JavaScript file can be called in the bottom section of the body to be loaded. It can also be called asynchronously by script injection. The following code shows the code to load the JavaScript library asynchronously:

```
<script>
(function(d, s, id){
   var js,
       fjs = d.getElementsByTagName(s)[0];
   if (d.getElementById(id)) {return;}
   js = d.createElement(s);
   js.id = id;
```

```
        js.src = "//connect.facebook.net/en_US/all.js";
        fjs.parentNode.insertBefore(js, fjs);
    }(document, 'script', 'facebook-jssdk'));
    </script>
```

There are some standard methods provided by the Facebook SDK that will be used by the client application to use different features. The following diagram shows all the methods supported by the Facebook SDK:

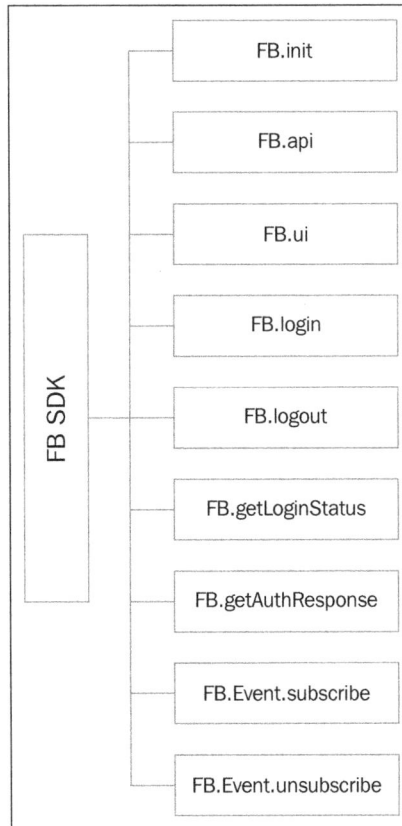

SDK method	Description
FB.init	This initializes the SDK with your Application ID generated during configuration
FB.api	This is useful to make API calls to the Graph API
FB.ui	This is used to trigger Facebook dialogs to the end user, asking for various permissions
FB.login	This is used to log in to Facebook using the OAuth dialog box
FB.logout	This is used to log the user out from Facebook
FB.getLoginStatus	This is used to check whether the user is logged in and authenticated for the application
FB.getAuthResponse	This method is similar to FB.getLoginStatus, but it is synchronous and returns the authResponse object
FB.Event.subscribe	This method is used to subscribe to Facebook events auth.login, auth.authResponseChange, and auth.statusChange, and get callbacks to your function when an event is fired
FB.Event.unsubscribe	This method is used to unsubscribe the specified Facebook events

To initialize the Facebook SDK, the HTML markup must be present inside the page. This HTML element is the base for the Facebook application's integration.

Creating a Facebook application

In this section, we will learn how to create and register a Facebook application. Facebook provides a portal to register a new application. You can access this application using the https://developers.facebook.com/apps link. The following screenshot shows the page for the application:

You can see a button for creating a new application. You will then see the following screenshot come up when you click on the **Create New App** button:

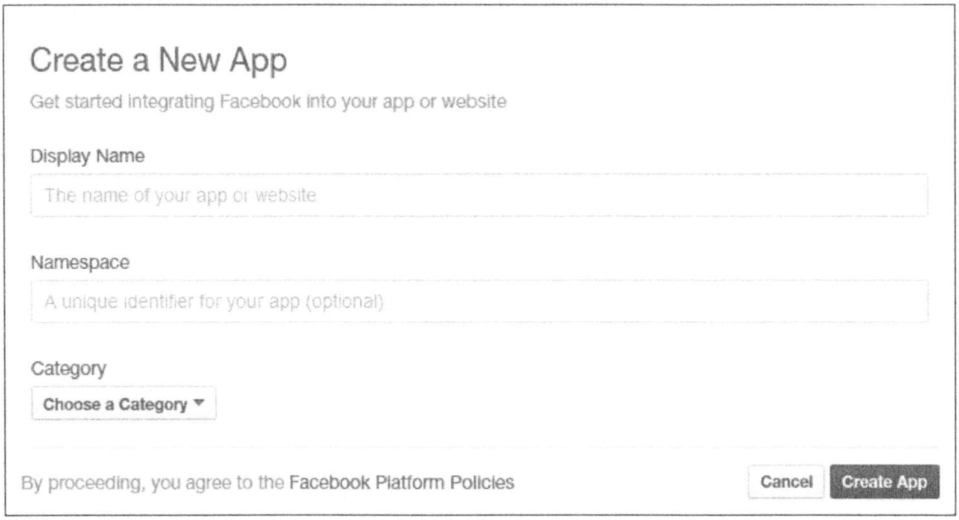

Create a New App

Get started integrating Facebook into your app or website

Display Name

The name of your app or website

Namespace

A unique identifier for your app (optional)

Category

Choose a Category ▼

By proceeding, you agree to the Facebook Platform Policies   Cancel   Create App

The preceding form is for creating a new application. It will ask for the **Display Name**, **Namespace**, and **Category** of the application. We have filled in the form and given the application name as `MyResponsivePacktApp`. The following screenshot shows the completed form:

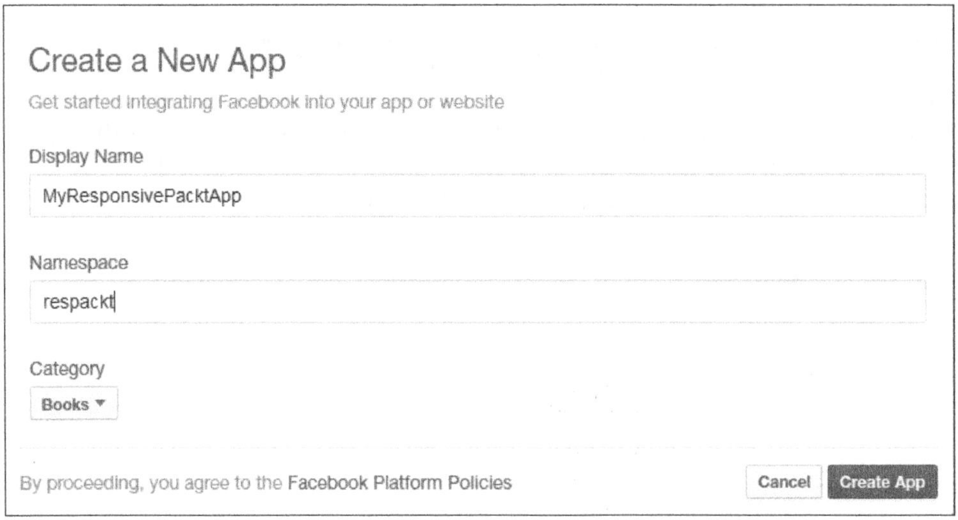

Create a New App

Get started integrating Facebook into your app or website

Display Name

MyResponsivePacktApp

Namespace

respackt

Category

Books ▼

By proceeding, you agree to the Facebook Platform Policies   Cancel   Create App

After filling in these input elements and clicking on the **Create App** button, it will navigate you to the application dashboard. This dashboard has the application ID and other details. The following screenshot shows the application ID for our application:

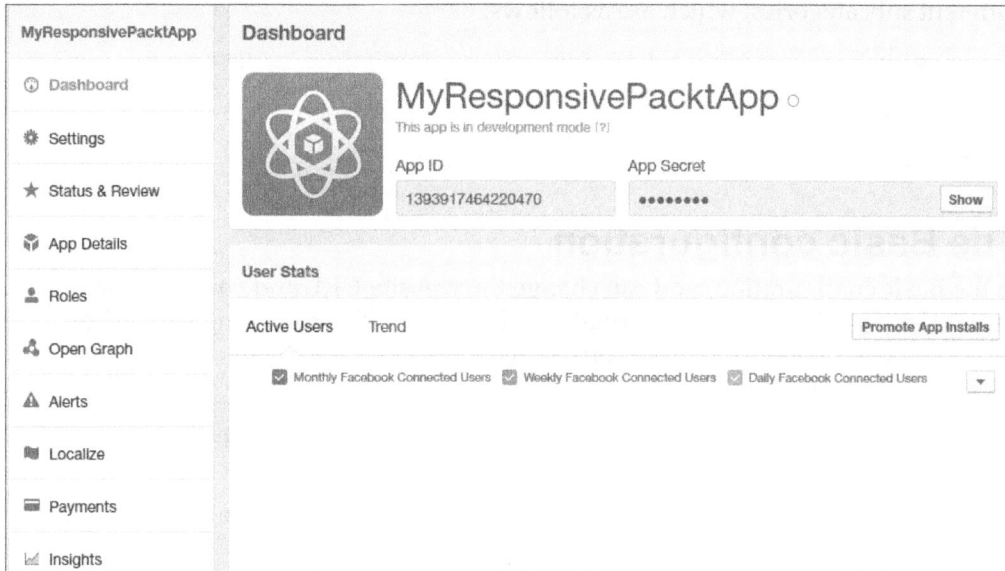

Now, the application is listed, and you can see it present in the table. The following screenshot shows the application as a card:

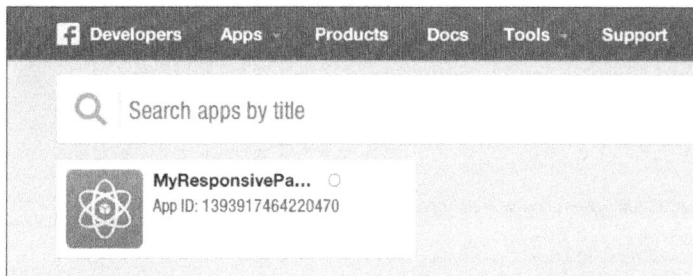

Configuring the Facebook SDK

In this section, we will learn how to initialize the Facebook JavaScript SDK for our application. The **Settings** tab of the Facebook application has all the fields to configure our application based on our requirements.

The Settings tab

The **Settings** tab has the configuration parameters such as domain name, site URL, mobile site URL, and contact mail. Generally, the settings are divided into three different subcategories, which are as follows:

- **Basic**
- **Advanced**
- **Migrations**

The Basic configuration

In the **Basic** configuration, you can change the website URL and contact person name. Generally, it has all the normal standard fields. The following screenshot shows the **Basic** configuration for our application:

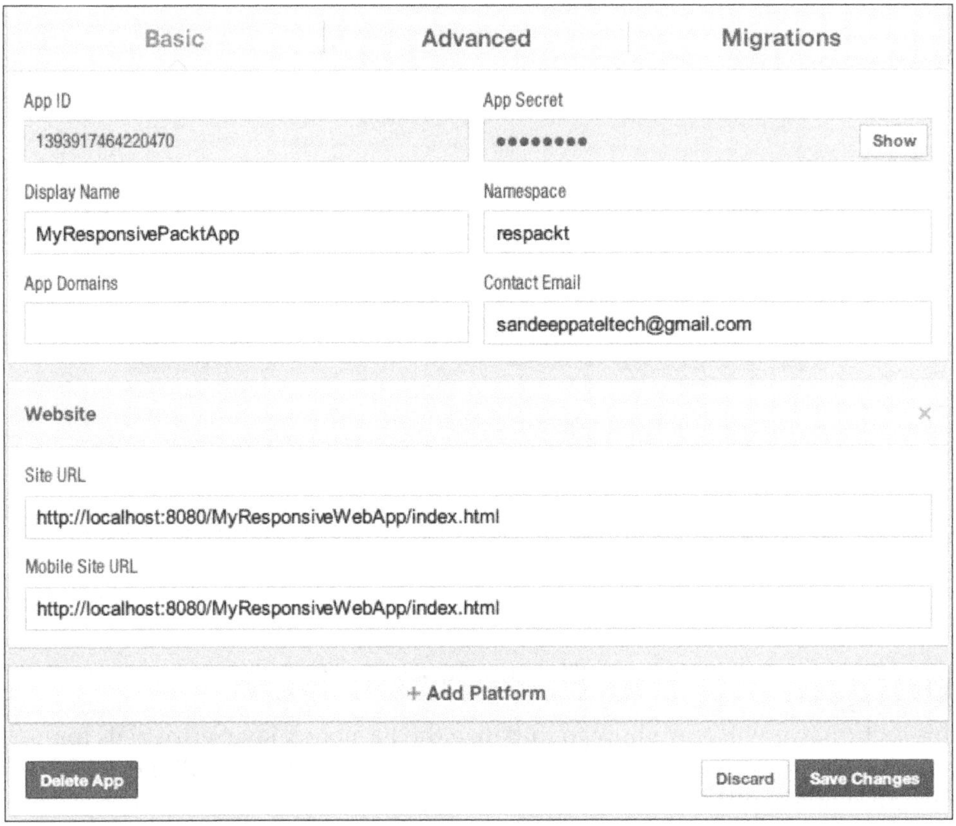

The Advanced configuration

The **Advanced** configuration tab has all the configuration parameters for application restrictions and security parameters. The following screenshot shows the **Advanced** configuration for our application:

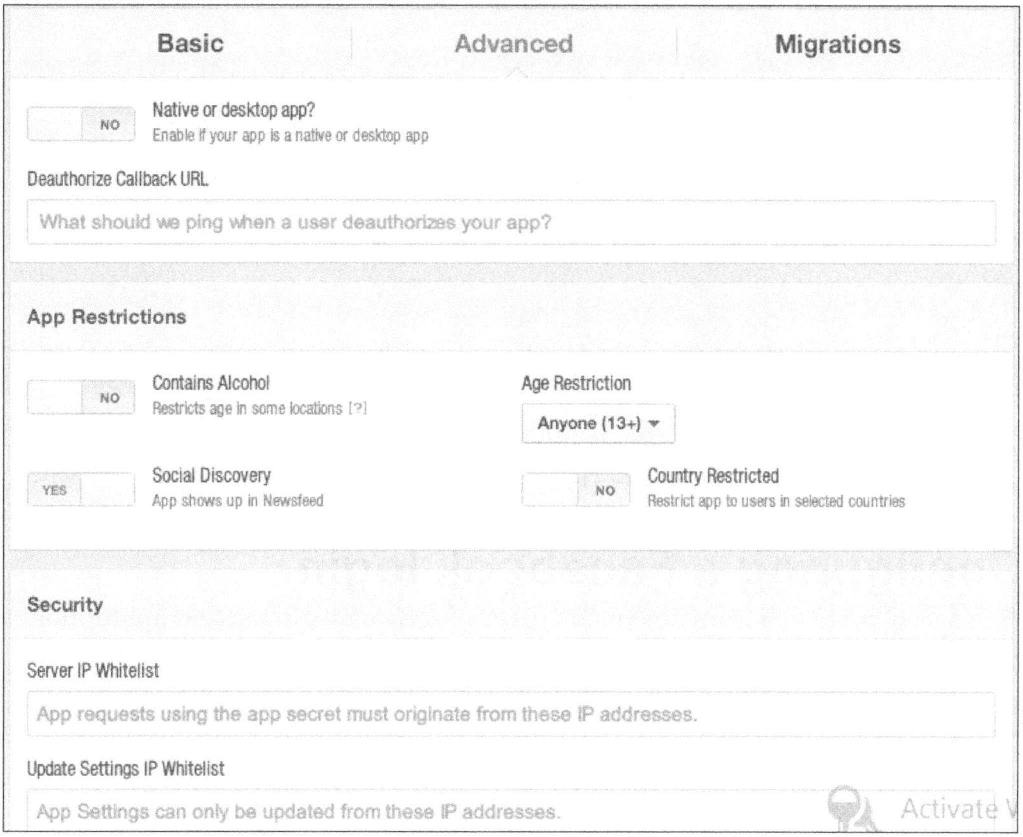

Basic	Advanced	Migrations

NO   Native or desktop app?
Enable if your app is a native or desktop app

Deauthorize Callback URL

What should we ping when a user deauthorizes your app?

App Restrictions

NO   Contains Alcohol
Restricts age in some locations [?]

Age Restriction
Anyone (13+) ▼

YES   Social Discovery
App shows up in Newsfeed

NO   Country Restricted
Restrict app to users in selected countries

Security

Server IP Whitelist

App requests using the app secret must originate from these IP addresses.

Update Settings IP Whitelist

App Settings can only be updated from these IP addresses.

The Migrations configuration

The **Migrations** tab has all the configuration parameters for streaming security, publishing scopes, and offers. The following screenshot shows the **Migrations** configuration for our application:

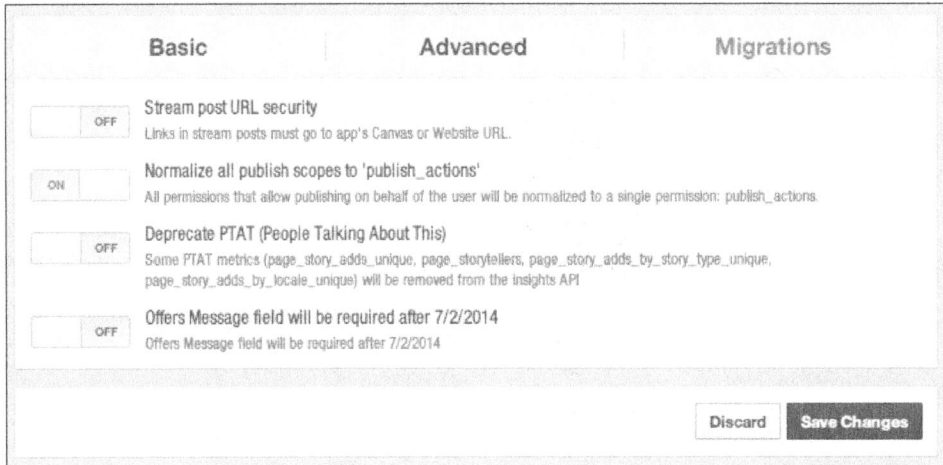

Configuring a Facebook login

In this section, we will learn how to integrate a Facebook login into our application. The markup that generates the Facebook login button is listed in the following code:

```
<div class="fb-login-button pull-left"
perms='read_stream'
data-width="200"
data-colorscheme="dark"
show-faces="true"
autologoutlink="true">
</div>
```

The attributes used in the markup are explained as follows:

- `perms`: This attribute represents the permissions asked by the application from the user account

- `data-width`: This attribute represents the width of the container for the login button

- `data-colorscheme`: This attribute represents the color scheme for the login widget

- `show-faces`: This attribute has the Boolean value and represents whether to show the user image or not
- `Autologoutlink`: This attribute has the Boolean value and represents whether to show the log out button on successful login

The following screenshot shows the Facebook **Log In** component rendered in our application:

Once you click on this **Log In** button, a dialog box opens up in a new window asking for the username and password of the user for Facebook authentication. The following screenshot shows the dialog box for our application:

After successful login, the **Log Out** box will appear, as shown in the
following screenshot:

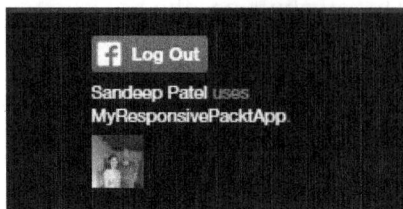

Configuring the Facebook Like and Share buttons

In this section, we will learn how to integrate the Facebook Like button into our
product pages. Facebook provides the markup and attributes to create a Like
and Share button. The following HTML syntax shows the required markup for
these buttons:

```
<div class="fb-like"
    data-href="${url}"
    data-layout="button_count"
    data-action="like"
    data-show-faces="true"
    data-share="true">
</div>
```

The attributes used in the markup are explained as follows:

- `data-href`: This attribute has the value for the targeted link for the
  Like button.

- `data-layout`: This attribute has the value for the style of the button.

- `data-action`: This attribute has the value for the action to be done when a
  user clicks on the **Like** button.

- `data-show-faces`: This attribute has a Boolean value. It represents whether
  the users' faces have to be shown or not.

- `data-share`: This attribute has a Boolean value and represents whether the
  Share button should be displayed or not.

The init() method must be called to initialize the Facebook object. The following code shows the init() method with parameters:

```
FB.init({
    appId: '1393917464220470',
    status: true,
    cookie: true,
    xfbml: true,
    oauth: true
});
```

The init() method takes a number of parameters in its configuration. The parameters are explained as follows:

- appId: This contains the ID for the Facebook application.
- status: This field takes a Boolean value and ensures that the current login status of the user is freshly retrieved on every page load.
- cookie: This determines whether a cookie is created for the session or not. If enabled, it can be accessed by the server-side code.
- xfbml: This determines whether XFBML tags used by social plugins are parsed, and therefore, whether the plugins are rendered or not.
- oauth: This takes the Boolean value to determine whether it supports the OAuth mechanism.

The modified jQuery template is listed in the following code:

```
<script id="aProductTemplate" type="text/x-jquery-tmpl">
    <div class="ts-product panel panel-default">
        <div class="panel-head">
            <div class="fb-like" data-href="${url}" data-
layout="button_count" data-action="like" data-show-faces="true"
data-share="true">
            </div>
        </div>
        <div class="panel-body">
            <span class="glyphicon glyphicon-certificate ts-cost-
icon">
                <label>${cost}$</label>
            </span>
            <img class="img-responsive" src="${url}">
            <h5>${title}</h5>
        </div>
        <div class="panel-footer">
```

```
                <button type="button" class="btn btn-info btn-block">Buy</
button>
                <button type="button" class="btn btn-info btn-block tweet-
me" data-bookTitle="${title}" data-imgURI="${url}">Tweet</button>
        </div>
    </div>
  </script>
```

The following screenshot shows the Facebook **Like** and **Share** buttons added to one of the books:

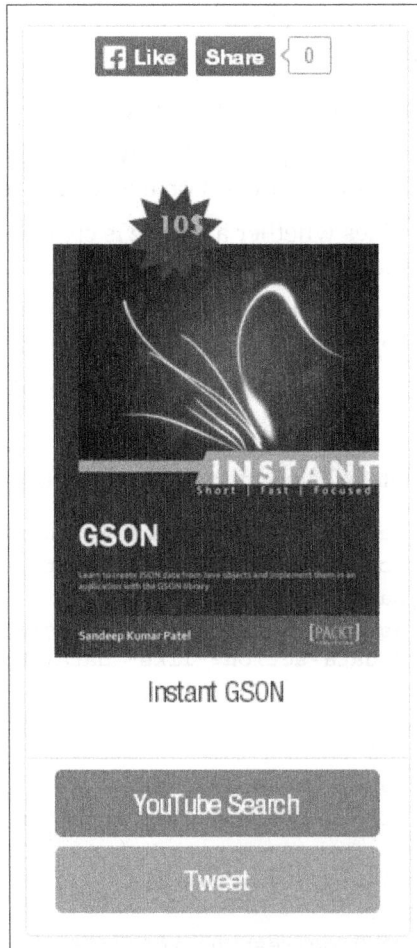

On clicking on the **Share** button, it will ask for authentication, and after successful authentication, a new dialog box comes up with a text area element asking for the message to be shared on the user timeline. This dialog box looks like the following screenshot:

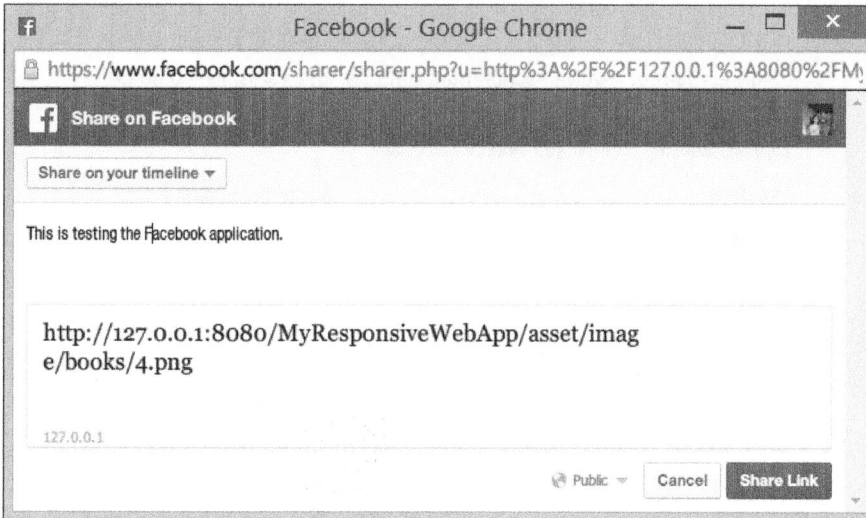

After writing the message and clicking on the **Share Link** button, it will be shared on the user's timeline. The following screenshot shows the message shared on my timeline:

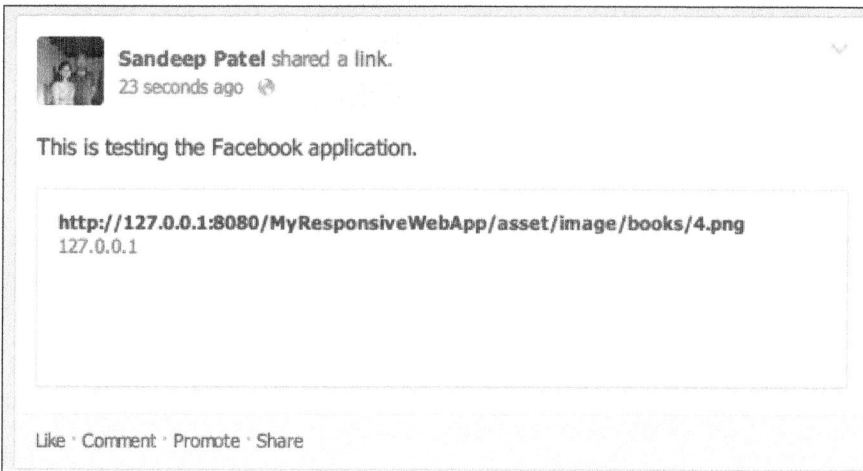

To embed this post, we can get the code by clicking on the **Embed this Post** option in the dropdown. The following screenshot shows the dialog box with the code required to embed the post:

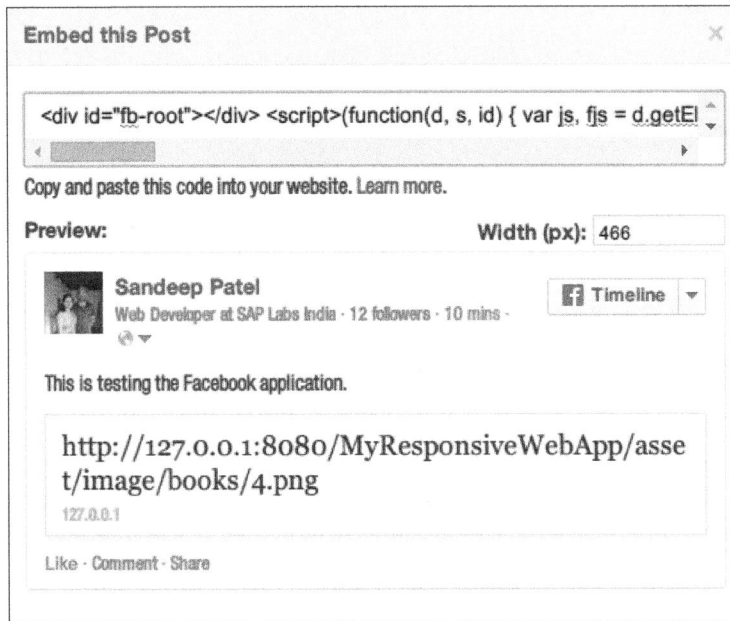

The code is listed as follows:

```
<div id="fb-root"></div>
<script>
    (function(d, s, id) {
        var js, fjs = d.getElementsByTagName(s)[0];
        if (d.getElementById(id))
            return;
        js = d.createElement(s);
        js.id = id;
        js.src = "//connect.facebook.net/en_US/all.js#xfbml=1";
        fjs.parentNode.insertBefore(js, fjs);
    }(document, 'script', 'facebook-jssdk'));
</script>
<div class="fb-post" data-href="https://www.facebook.com/permalink.
php?story_fbid=684830454911033&amp;id=100001522557151" data-
width="466">
```

```
<div class="fb-xfbml-parse-ignore">
      <a href="https://www.facebook.com/permalink.php?story_fbid=684
830454911033&amp;id=100001522557151">Post</a>
      by <a href="https://www.facebook.com/profile.
php?id=100001522557151">Sandeep Patel</a>.
   </div>
</div>
```

Configuring Facebook comments

In this section, we will learn how to integrate a Facebook comment section into the application so that each client can comment on their experience with the product and application.

The following HTML markup is used to generate the comment box for our application:

```
<div class="fb-comments"
data-href="http://localhost:8080/MyResponsiveWebApp/index.html" data-
numposts="5"
data-colorscheme="light">
</div>
```

The attributes used in the markup are explained as follows:

- `data-href`: This attribute has the link for the targeted application
- `data-numposts`: This attribute has the value for the number of posts to be displayed in the comment box
- `data-colorscheme`: This attribute has the theme name for the look and feel of the comment box

The following screenshot shows the comment box generated by the HTML markup:

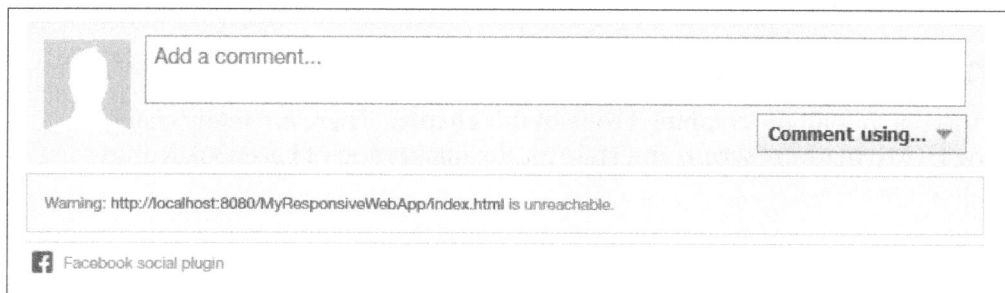

Users can comment on this application using Facebook, Microsoft Outlook, AOL, and Hotmail. The following screenshot shows all the options that can be used to comment:

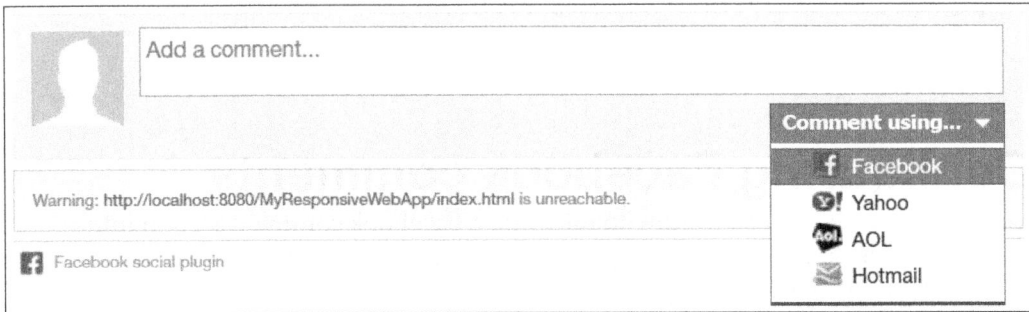

After posting a comment, it will appear at the bottom section of the comment box. The following screenshot shows the comment that we have posted to test the application:

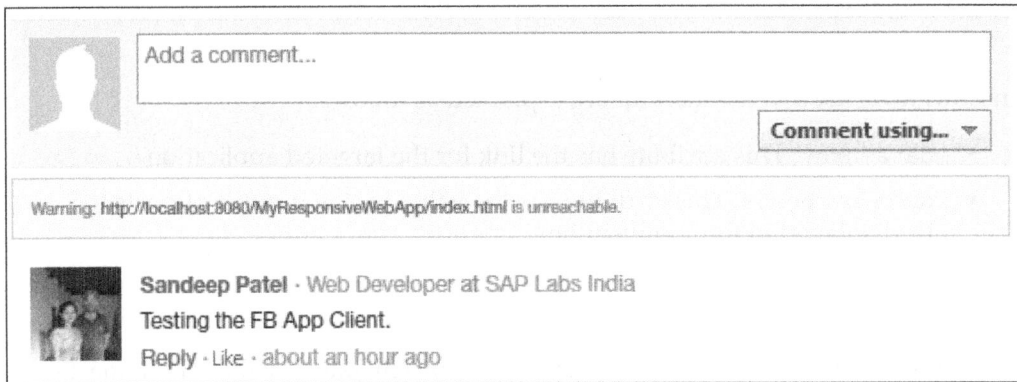

The combined code

This section has all the combined code of this chapter. There are many changes in the HTML markup, script, and style for the integration of Facebook features in our application.

All the markup and template code is present in the index.html file listed as follows:

```html
<!DOCTYPE html>
<html>
<head>
  <link href="asset/css/bootstrap.min.css" rel="stylesheet">
  <link href="asset/css/ts-responsive-web-style.css" rel="stylesheet">
  <title>Responsive product Store</title>
</head>
<body>
  <div class="container packt-app">
    <div class="row">
      <nav class="navbar navbar-inverse navbar-static-top">
        <div class="container-fluid">
          <div class="navbar-header">
            <button class="navbar-toggle collapsed" data-target="#ts-top-menu"
            data-toggle="collapse" type="button"><span class=
            "sr-only">Navigation buttons</span></button> <a class=
            "navbar-brand" href="#">PRODUCTS</a>
          </div>
          <!-- Collect the nav links, forms, and other content for
toggling -->
          <div class="navbar-collapse collapse" id="ts-top-menu">
            <ul class="nav navbar-nav ts-bar">
              <li class="active" data-category="book"><a href=
              "#">Books</a></li>
              <li data-category="video"><a href="#">Video</a></li>
            </ul>
          </div>
        </div>
      </nav>
    </div>
    <div class="row">
    <div class="fb-login-button pull-left" perms='read_stream,friends_
birthday'data-width="200"  data-colorscheme="dark" show-faces="true"
autologoutlink="true" ></div>
      <div class="jumbotron">
        <div class="row">
          <div class="col-sm-6"><img class="img-responsive" src=
          "asset/image/hero/1.jpg"></div>
```

```
            <div class="col-sm-6"><img class="img-responsive" src=
            "asset/image/hero/2.png"></div>
          </div>
        </div>
      </div>
      <div class="row">
        <div class="panel-body ts-product-container"></div>
      </div>
      <div class="fb-comments" data-href="http://localhost:8080/
MyResponsiveWebApp/index.html" data-numposts="5" data-
colorscheme="light"></div>
    </div>
    <script id="aProductTemplate" type="text/x-jquery-tmpl">
      <div class="ts-product panel panel-default">
        <div class="panel-head">
          <div class="fb-like" data-href="${url}" data-
layout="button_count"
              data-action="like" data-show-faces="true" data-
share="true">
          </div>
        </div>
        <div class="panel-body">
          <span class="glyphicon glyphicon-certificate ts-cost-
icon">
              <label>${cost}$</label>
          </span>
          <img class="img-responsive" src="${url}">
          <h5>${title}</h5>
        </div>
        <div class="panel-footer">
          <button type="button" class="btn btn-info btn-block">Buy</
button>
          <button type="button" class="btn btn-info btn-block tweet-
me" data-bookTitle="${title}" data-imgURI="${url}">Tweet</button>
        </div>
      </div>
    </script>
    <script src="asset/js/jquery-2.1.0.min.js"></script>
    <script src="//connect.facebook.net/en_US/all.js"></script>
    <script src="asset/js/jquery.tmpl.min.js"></script>
    <script src="asset/js/bootstrap.min.js"></script>
    <script src="asset/js/app.js"></script>
</body>
</html>
```

All the script changes are present in the app.js file listed as follows:

```
var PACKT_PRODUCT_APP={
    /*Returning jQuery Promise For an AJAX call with Product type*/
    getProductDetails : function(type){
        var ajaxRequest=$.ajax("ProductServlet?type="+type);
        return ajaxRequest.promise();
    }
    /*Handler For AJAX response*/
    handleCallback : function(type){
        var promise = PACKT_PRODUCT_APP.getProductDetails(type);
        promise.done(function(data){
            PACKT_PRODUCT_APP.doProductRendering(data);
        });
    },
    /*jQuery Template building with JSON data*/
    doProductRendering: function(data){
        var productContainer =$('.ts-product-container'),
            aProductTemplate = $('#aProductTemplate').tmpl( data
), promiseOldPro = $(productContainer).find('.panel').fadeOut().
promise();
        $.when(promiseOldPro).then(function(){
            productContainer.html(aProductTemplate);
        });
    },
    /*Event Listener to Menu Item Click*/
    initCategoryClick:function(){
        $(".ts-bar").on('click','li',function(e){
            e.preventDefault();
            var li = e.currentTarget,
                type= $(li).attr('data-category');
            $(li).siblings('li').removeClass('active');
            $(li).addClass('active');
            PACKT_PRODUCT_APP.handleCallback(type);
        });
    },
    /*Event Listener to Twitter Button Click*/
    initTwitterApp : function(){
        $(".ts-product-container").on('click','.tweet-me',function(e){
            e.preventDefault();
            var target = e.target,
```

```
                    bookTitle = $(target).attr("data-bookTitle"),
                    imgURI = $(target).attr("data-imgURI"),
                    message= "I like this book ''"+bookTitle+"'' .What's
        your opinion?'",
                    aReqTwitPromise = PACKT_PRODUCT_APP.
        postTwitAboutProduct(message, imgURI);
                    aReqTwitPromise.done(function(data){
                        window.open(data.url,"_self");
                    });
            });
        },
        /*Calls the Servlet with message in parameter*/
        postTwitAboutProduct:function(message,imgURI){
            var aReqTwitPromise=$.ajax({url:"TwitterServlet",type:"POST",d
        ata:{msg:message, imgUri:encodeURI(imgURI)}}).promise();
            return aReqTwitPromise;
        },
        /*Initialize Facebook Login*/
        initFBLogin: function () {
            FB.init({
                appId: '1393917464220470',
                status: true,
                cookie: true,
                xfbml: true,
                oauth: true
            });
            FB.Event.subscribe('auth.login',
                function (response) {
                    var accessToken = response.authResponse.accessToken;
                    if (response.status === 'connected') {
                        console.log("Successfully Logged in.")
                    }
                });
            FB.Event.subscribe('auth.logout',
                function (response) {
                    location.reload();
                });
        }
    };
    $(document).ready(function(){
        /*Initial Load Call Books */
```

```
        PACKT_PRODUCT_APP.handleCallback('book');
        /*Initialize Click Of Menu Item*/
        PACKT_PRODUCT_APP.initCategoryClick();
        /*Initialize Click Of Tweet Button*/
        PACKT_PRODUCT_APP.initTwitterApp();
        /*Initialize Click Of Facebook Login Button*/
        PACKT_PRODUCT_APP.initFBLogin();
});
```

All the CSS style changes are present in the `ts-responsive-web-style.css` file listed as follows:

```
.packt-app .ts-product-container{
    text-align:center;
    position:relative;
}
.packt-app .ts-product-container .ts-product{
    display: inline-block;
    float: left;
    margin: 10px 40px;
    width: 200px;
    background: #eee;
    font-weight: bold;
}
.packt-app .ts-product-container .ts-product .panel-body{
    background: #fff;
}
.packt-app .ts-product-container .ts-product .panel-footer{
    height: 100%;
    padding: 6px 15px;
    background: #fff;
}
.packt-app .ts-product-container .ts-product img{
    position: relative;
    top: 0px;
}
.packt-app .ts-product-container .ts-product h5{
    overflow: hidden;
    white-space: nowrap;
    text-overflow:ellipsis;
    width:100%;
}
```

```css
.packt-app .jumbotron{
    background:transparent;
    padding-left:0px;
}
.packt-app .glyphicon.glyphicon-certificate.ts-cost-icon{
    font-size:50px;
    z-index:2;
    position: relative;
    right: 20px;
    top: 25px;
}
.packt-app .glyphicon.glyphicon-certificate.ts-cost-icon label{
    color: #FFA500;
    font-size: 12px;
    left: 16px;
    position: absolute;
    top: 13px;
}
#carousel-packt-app .item{
    margin-left:25%;
}
.packt-app .btn.tweet-me{
    background: #55acee;
}
.fb-login-button {
    background: none repeat scroll 0 0 #000000;
    padding: 14px 0 17px 55px;
    position: absolute !important;
    top: 45px;
    z-index: 1001;
}
.packt-app .panel-head{
    background: #fff;
    height: 40px;
    padding:5px;
}
.fb-comments {
    margin-left:20%;
}
```

The following screenshot shows the home page for our application after integrating the Facebook features:

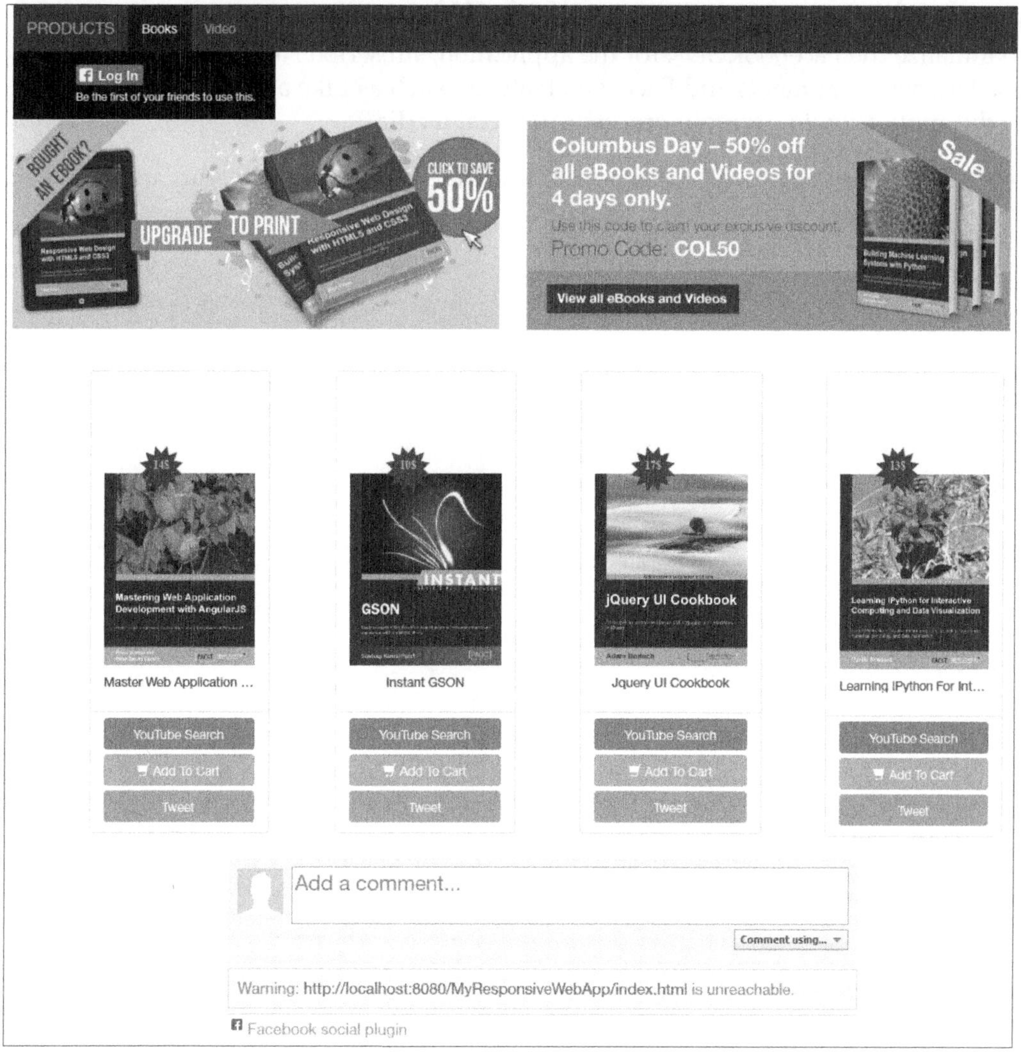

Summary

In this chapter, we have learned about integrating Facebook features into our web application. The key things that we have learned from this chapter are how to initialize the Facebook SDK for the application, subscribe Facebook Events, and use Facebook comments and Facebook features, such as Like and Share buttons, in the application to promote products in social media.

In the next chapter, we will learn how to integrate the Google+1 feature into our web application.

6
Google+ Integration

In this chapter, we will learn about the Google+ integration to our responsive web application. We will understand how to integrate different features such as login using a Google+ account and integrating a +1 button to each product. Integrating the Google feature helps to promote the web application, which increases the probability of a lead generation.

Introduction to the Google+ API

Google+ is another famous social network by Google Inc. The Google+ API provides access to its features through the programming interface to integrate in the web application. To access the API, we need to register a client application in **Google Developers Console**. This developer console can be accessed by visiting `https://console.developers.google.com`. The following screenshot shows the default view of the developer console:

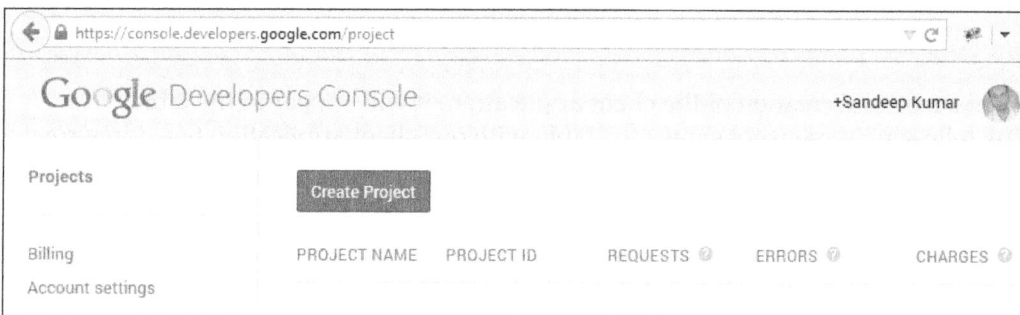

We can see a **Create Project** button to register a new client application to access the Google+ API. After clicking on this button, a new pop up is displayed on the screen to register a new application. The following screenshot shows the window that appears when you need to register a new application:

New Project

PROJECT NAME

Packt Responsive Application

PROJECT ID

packt-responsive-app

Create   Cancel

For our application, we have used `Packt Responsive Application` in the **Project name** field and `packt-responsive-app` in the **Project ID** field. During the creation of the application, there is one inner window showing the activities. The following screenshot shows the activity window:

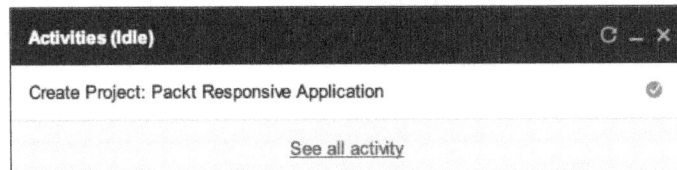

Activities (Idle)

Create Project: Packt Responsive Application

See all activity

After successful creation of the client application, it will appear in the table. The following screenshot shows the table with our client application listed in a row:

Projects	Create Project				
Billing	PROJECT NAME	PROJECT ID	REQUESTS	ERRORS	CHARGES
Account settings	Packt Responsive Application	packt-responsive-app	0	0	—

Configuring Google+

Google+ supports OAuth 2.0 access for its API. OAuth 2.0 allows users to share specific data while keeping their usernames, passwords, and other information private. Configuring the Google+ API on a web application needs the following steps to be executed:

- Creating a client ID
- Including Google script

Creating a client ID

In this section, we will learn how to create a client ID for our application. To create a new client ID, we need to go to the **APIS & AUTH** tab. The following screenshot shows the details inside the **APIS & AUTH** section:

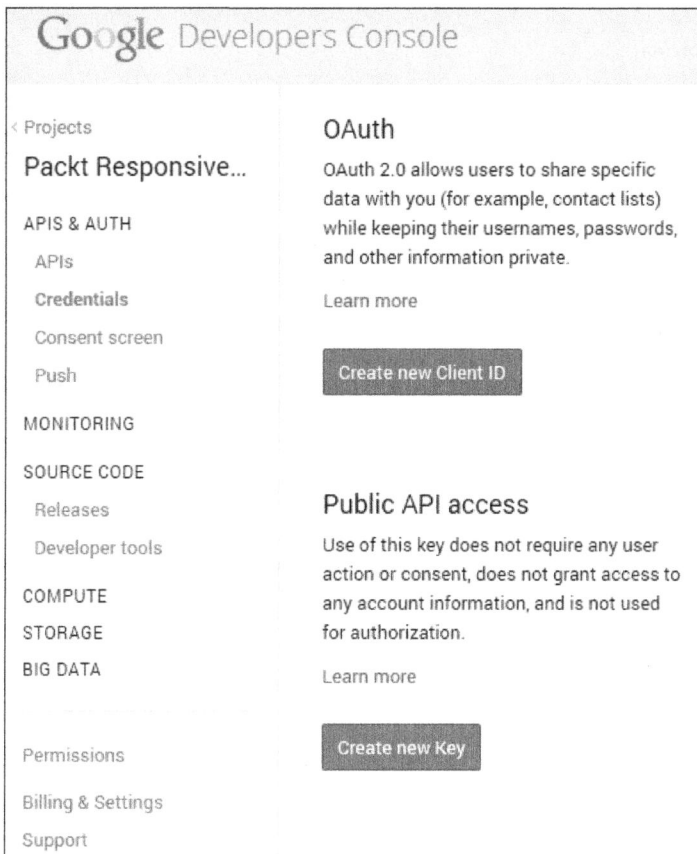

You can see a button to create a new application ID for our application. After clicking on this button, a new window opens up to create the new application ID. In this window, we have the following two important fields:

- **Authorized JavaScript origins**: For development purposes, we have given `http://localhost:8080` as the URL. This should be changed before going live to a real domain name.

- **Authorized redirect URI**: For development purposes, we have given `http://localhost:8080/MyResponsiveWebApp` as the URL. This URL needs to be changed to a real domain path before going live.

The following screenshot shows the window that appears when you create the new client ID:

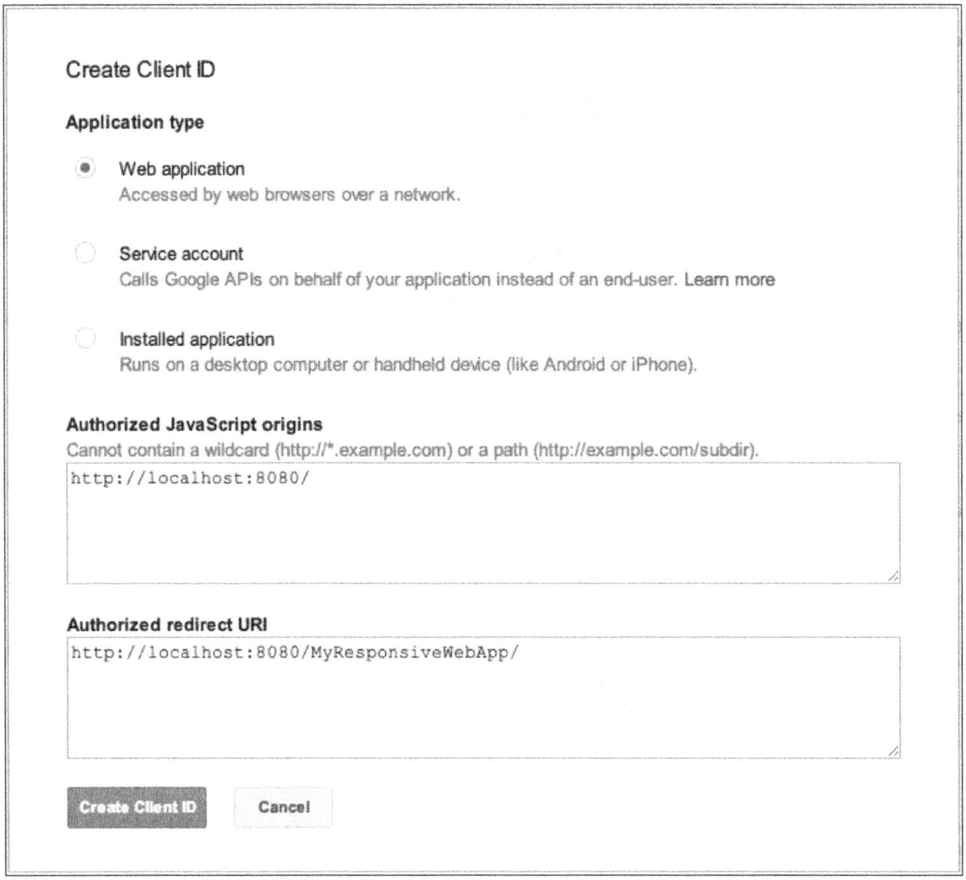

Create Client ID

Application type

- ● Web application
  Accessed by web browsers over a network.

- ○ Service account
  Calls Google APIs on behalf of your application instead of an end-user. Learn more

- ○ Installed application
  Runs on a desktop computer or handheld device (like Android or iPhone).

Authorized JavaScript origins
Cannot contain a wildcard (http://*.example.com) or a path (http://example.com/subdir).

```
http://localhost:8080/
```

Authorized redirect URI

```
http://localhost:8080/MyResponsiveWebApp/
```

Create Client ID   Cancel

After the successful creation of the client ID, it is listed on the page. The following screenshot shows **Client ID**, **Client secret**, and other details about the application:

Client ID for web application	
Client ID	781737073387-254c6ldrq9pcep1gs76tj92fr4dfdmri.apps.googleusercontent.com
Email address	781737073387-254c6ldrq9pcep1gs76tj92fr4dfdmri@developer.gserviceaccount.com
Client secret	DT7F8k4awF-798aPzUpdowBV
Redirect URIs	http://localhost:8080/MyResponsiveWebApp
Javascript Origins	http://localhost:8080
Edit settings Download JSON Delete	

Including the Google script

We need to include a JavaScript library provided by the Google API in our application. The JavaScript file client:plusone.js has all the required methods in order to use Google+ features. We can include this file just before the </body> tag to load the file synchronously. The following code shows the <script> tag in order to load this file:

```
<script src="https://apis.google.com/js/client:plusone.js"></
script>
```

Also, we can load this file asynchronously by using the script injection technique. The following code loads the library asynchronously in our page:

```
<script type="text/javascript">
        (function() {
         var po = document.createElement('script');
 po.type = 'text/javascript';
 po.async = true;
         po.src = 'https://apis.google.com/js/client:plusone.js';
         var s = document.getElementsByTagName('script')[0];
s.parentNode.insertBefore(po, s);
     })();
</script>
```

Log in using Google+

The Google+ **Sign in** button can be added using HTML markup or through JavaScript. We will follow the markup approach for development. The following HTML code shows the syntax to add the Google+ sign in the button:

```
<span id="signinButton" class="pull-right">
    <span
      class="g-signin"
      data-callback="signinCallback"
      data-clientid="YOUR_CLIENT_ID"
      data-cookiepolicy="single_host_origin"
      data-scope="https://www.googleapis.com/auth/plus.login">
    </span>
</span>
```

The details of these attributes are listed as follows:

- `data-callback`: This function is called when the **Sign in** button is rendered and also after the sign in flow is complete.

- `data-clientid`: This client ID is obtained from the **Google Developers Console**.

- `data-cookiepolicy`: This parameter determines the policy for storing users' session information.

- `data-scope`: This parameter takes the single or multiscope values. For authentication purpose, login is the scope.

You can find an attribute in the previous code asking for the client ID. In the *Creating a client ID* section, we created the client ID. We can use this client ID in the previous markup.

> More about this attribute can be found on `https://developers.google.com/+/web/signin/reference#sign-in_button_attributes`.

The following code shows the markup for our application to add a **Sign in** button:

```
<span id="signinButton" class="pull-right">
    <span
      class="g-signin"
      data-callback="signinCallback"
      data-clientid="781737073387-254c61drq9pcep1gs76tj92fr4dfdmri.
apps.googleusercontent.com"
```

```
      data-cookiepolicy="single_host_origin"
      data-scope="https://www.googleapis.com/auth/plus.login">
   </span>
</span>
```

The preceding markup will create a Google+ sign in the button similar to the following button:

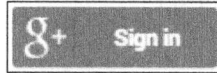

After clicking on this **Sign in** button, a pop-up window comes up asking for permission from the user to authenticate the application. The following screenshot shows the permission window for the Google+ authentication:

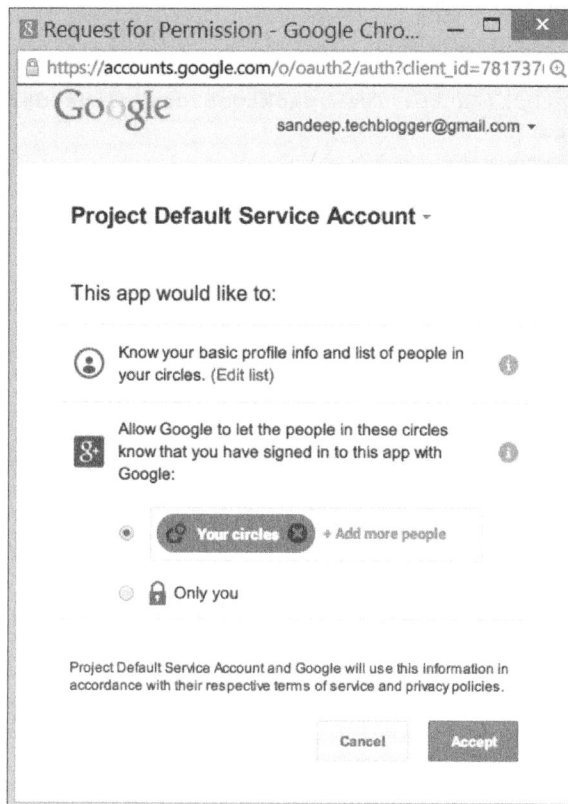

Integrating +1 recommendations

In this section, we will learn how to add a Google +1 button to our products. Before integrating the Google +1 button, we have to change the product image URL for the books to point to real live links. It is required for the demonstration of Google+ recommendations. The following code shows the `getAllListedBook()` method. You can see that we have changed the image URL links to the images hosted on the `http://www.packtpub.com` website:

```
public class ProductStore {
 public static List<Product> getAllListedBook() {
    List<Product> listProduct = new ArrayList<Product>();
    Product product3 = new Product();
    product3.setTitle("Master Web Application Development with
AngularJS");
    product3.setCost(14);
    product3.setDescription("Lorem ipsum dollar.Lorem ipsum dollar.
Lorem ipsum dollar.");
    product3.setUrl("http://www.packtpub.com/sites/default/
files/1820OS.jpg");
    product3.setType("book");
    Product product4 = new Product();
    product4.setTitle("Instant GSON");
    product4.setCost(10);
    product4.setDescription("Lorem ipsum dollar.Lorem ipsum dollar.
Lorem ipsum dollar.");
    product4.setUrl("http://www.packtpub.com/sites/default/
files/2036OS_GSON_Froncover.jpg");
    product4.setType("book");
    Product product5 = new Product();
    product5.setTitle("Jquery UI Cookbook");
    product5.setCost(17);
    product5.setDescription("Lorem ipsum dollar.Lorem ipsum dollar.
Lorem ipsum dollar.");
    product5.setUrl("http://www.packtpub.com/sites/default/
files/2186OS.jpg");
    product5.setType("book");
    Product product6 = new Product();
    product6.setTitle("Learning IPython For Interactive Computing And
Data Visualization");
    product6.setCost(13);
    product6.setDescription("Lorem ipsum dollar.Lorem ipsum dollar.
Lorem ipsum dollar.");
```

```
        product6.setUrl("http://www.packtpub.com/sites/default/
files/99320S.jpg");
        listProduct.add(product3);
        listProduct.add(product4);
        listProduct.add(product5);
        listProduct.add(product6);
        return listProduct;
        }
    }
```

Google provides the HTML markup to be used in order to create the Google +1 recommendation button. The required markup is listed as follows:

```
<div class="g-plus-button">
    <div class="g-plusone"
data-width="180"
data-href="${url}">
    </div>
</div>
```

The attributes in the preceding markup are explained as follows:

- `data-width`: This specifies the width of the Google+ button
- `data-href`: This specifies the link to be shared and recommended

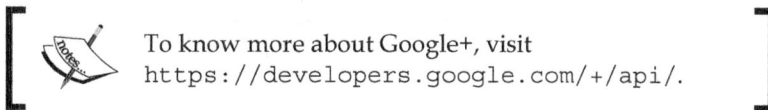

> To know more about Google+, visit
> `https://developers.google.com/+/api/`.

Google also provides JavaScript code in the `platform.js` file to be included in the application. The following code shows the `platform.js` file loaded asynchronously:

```
<script type="text/javascript">
  (function() {
    var po = document.createElement('script');
 po.type = 'text/javascript';
 po.async = true;
    po.src = 'https://apis.google.com/js/platform.js';
    var s = document.getElementsByTagName('script')[0];
s.parentNode.insertBefore(po, s);
  })();
</script>
```

We have modified our jQuery template to include the +1 button. The following code shows the modified jQuery template:

```
<script id="aProductTemplate" type="text/x-jquery-tmpl">
  <div class="ts-product panel panel-default">
      <div class="panel-head">
          <div class="fb-like" data-href="${url}" data-
layout="button_count"  data-action="like" data-show-faces="true"
data-share="true">
          </div>
      </div>
      <div class="panel-body">
          <span class="glyphicon glyphicon-certificate ts-cost-
icon">
              <label>${cost}$</label>
          </span>
          <img class="img-responsive" src="${url}">
          <h5>${title}</h5>
      </div>
      <div class="panel-footer">
          <button type="button" class="btn btn-info btn-block">Buy</
button>
          <button type="button" class="btn btn-info btn-block twit-
me" data-bookTitle="${title}" data-imgURI="${url}">Twit</button>
          <div class="g-plus-button">
              <div class="g-plusone" data-width="180" data-
href="${url}"></div>
          </div>
      </div>
  </div>
</script>
```

The following screenshot shows the product with the Google +1 button integrated in the footer section of the code:

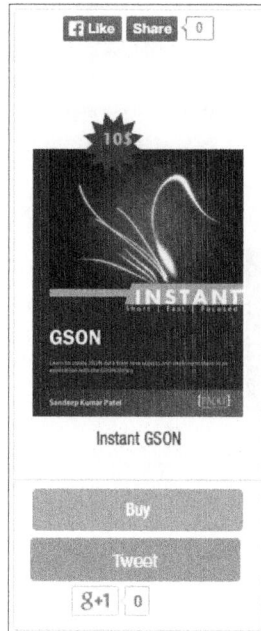

The following screenshot shows the Firebug console view of the Google +1 button markup. An IFrame is created automatically around the +1 button markup. The main reason to use an IFrame is that the other CSS will not hamper the style of the button. The following screenshot shows the IFrame created for wrapping the +1 button:

After clicking on the +1 button, a pop-up window appears asking for the comment to be written in the post. The following screenshot shows the pop-up window:

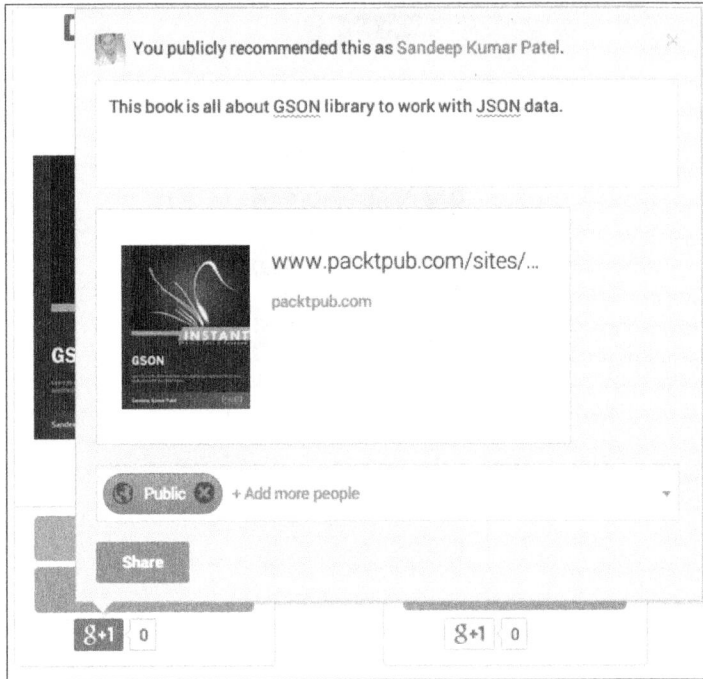

After filling in the comment text area in the pop-up window and clicking on the **Share** button, the post will be shared in the user timeline as a card. The following screenshot shows the user timeline with the post:

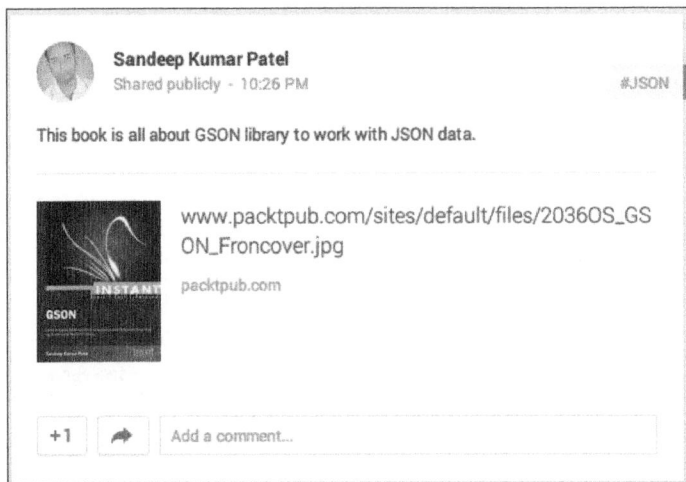

Summary

In this chapter, we learned about the Google+ API configuration for our application along with configuring **Google Developers Console**, integrating Google+ login, and integrating Google +1 recommendations to the product. In the next chapter, we will explore the YouTube API that will be integrated into our web application.

7
Linking Dynamic Content from External Websites

In this chapter, you will learn how to integrate the YouTube API into our web application. We will explore and learn to use the video-search feature for our web application. Users of the web application can get an instant review and key features of the product. This will help users in making a quick buying decision and increase the number of leads.

Introduction to the YouTube API

YouTube provides three different APIs for a client application to access. The following figure shows the three different APIs provided by YouTube:

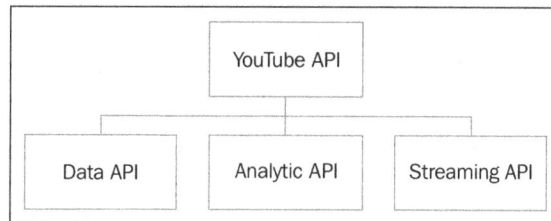

Configuring a YouTube API

In the Google Developers Console, we need to create a client project. We will be creating a new project, called PacktYoutubeapi. The URL for the Google Developers Console is https://console.developers.google.com.

The following screenshot shows the pop-up window that appears when you want to create a new client project in the Developers Console:

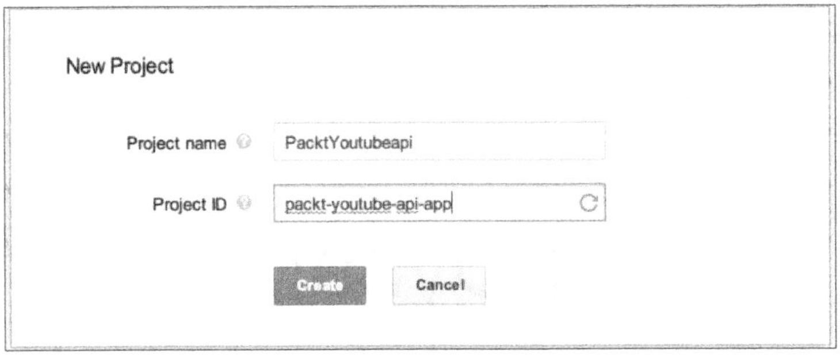

After the successful creation of the new client project, it will be available in the Console's project list. The following screenshot shows our new client project listed in the Developers Console:

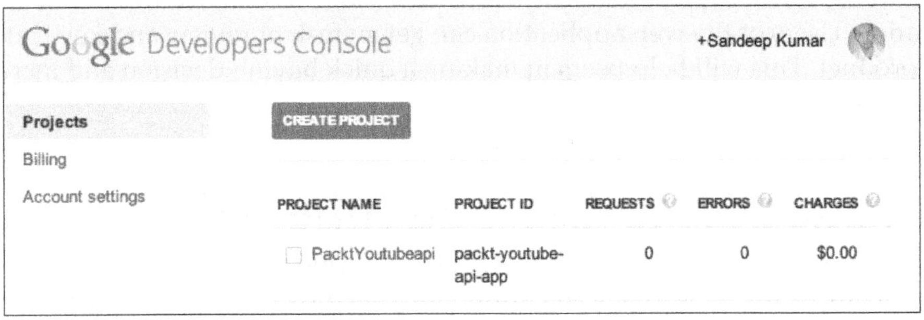

There is an option available to enable access to the YouTube API for our application. The following screenshot shows the YouTube API listed in the Developers Console. By default, the status of this API is **OFF** for the application.

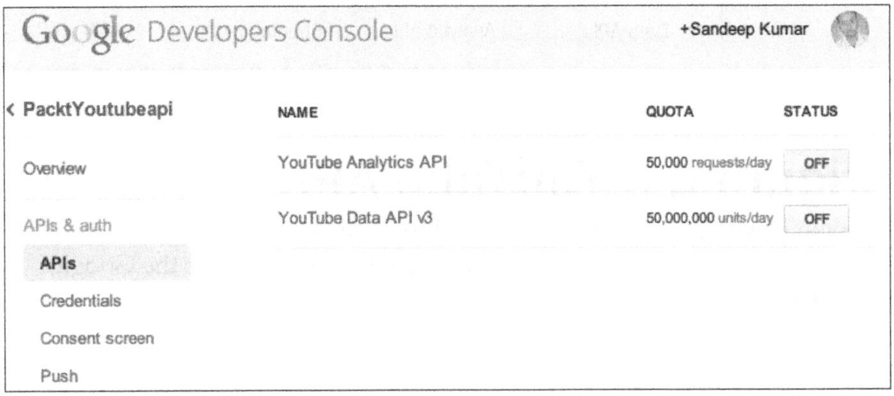

To enable this API for our application, we need to toggle the **STATUS** button to **ON**. The following screenshot shows the status of the YouTube API, which is **ON** for our application:

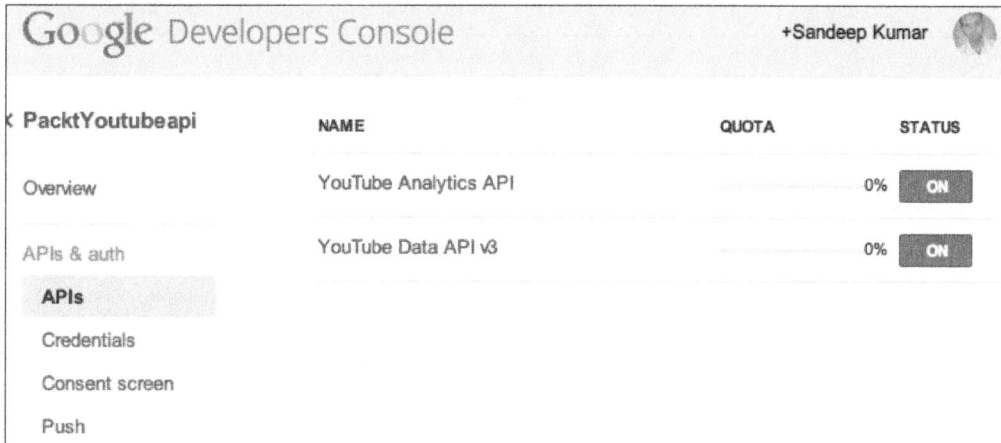

To access YouTube API methods, we need to create an API key for our client application. You can find the option to create a public API key in the **APIs & auth** section. The following screenshot shows the **Credentials** subsection where you can create an API key:

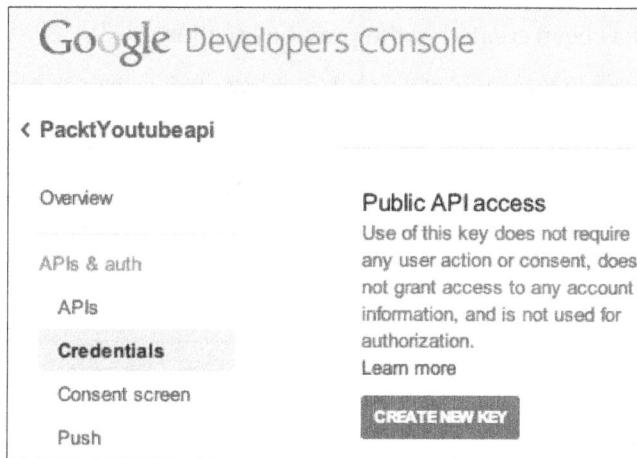

In the preceding screenshot, you can see a button to create a new API key. After clicking on this button, it provides some choices to create an API key, and after the successful creation of an API key, the key will be listed in the **Credentials** section. The following screenshot shows the API key generated for our application:

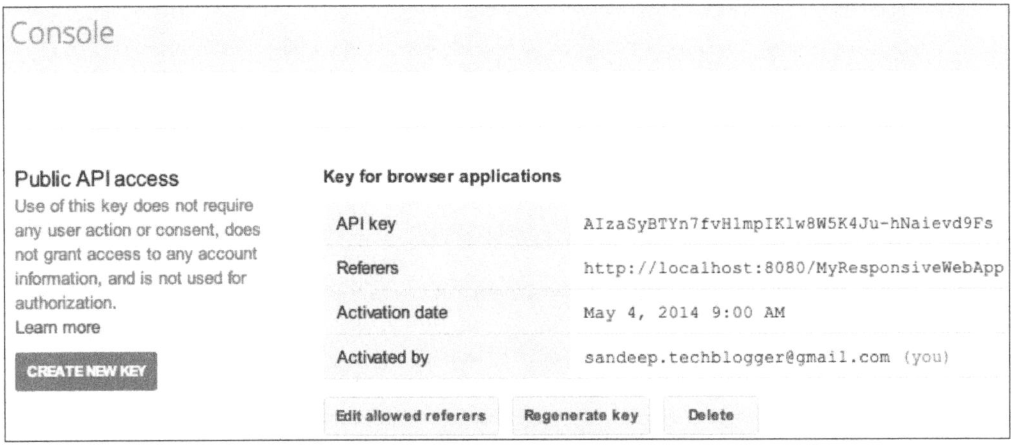

Searching for a YouTube video

In this section, we will learn about integrating a YouTube-related search video. YouTube Data API Version 3.0 is the new API to access YouTube data. It requires the API key that has been created in the previous section.

The main steps that we have to follow to do a YouTube search are:

1. After adding the `YouTube Search` button, click on it to trigger the search process.

2. The script reads the `data-booktitle` attribute to get the title. This will serve as a keyword for the search. Check the following screenshot for the HTML markup showing the `data-booktitle` attribute:

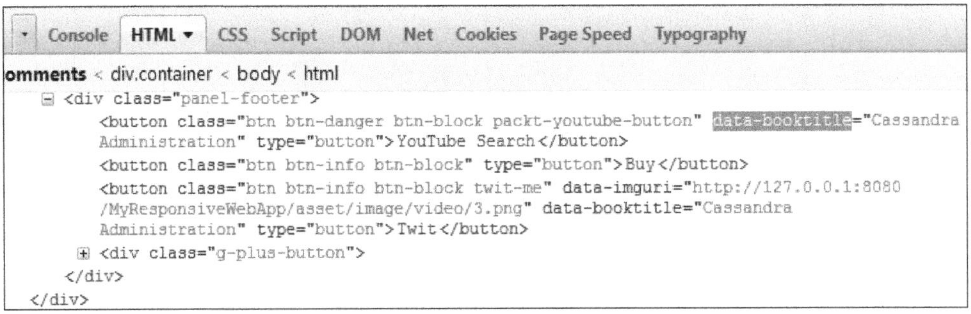

3. Then, it creates an AJAX request to make an asynchronous call to the YouTube API, and returns a promise object.

4. After the successful completion of the AJAX call, the promise object is resolved successfully.

5. Once the data is available, we fetch the jQuery template for the search results and compile it with a `script` function. We then link it to the search data returned by the AJAX call and generate the HTML markup for rendering.

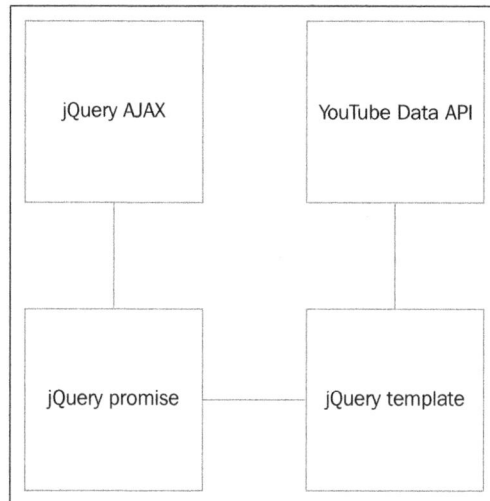

The base URL for the YouTube search is through a secure HTTP protocol, `https://www.googleapis.com/youtube/v3/search`. It takes different parameters as input for the search and filter criteria. Some of the important parameters are `field` and `part`.

The part parameter

The `part` parameter is about accessing a resource from a YouTube API. It really helps the application to choose resource components that your application actually uses. The following figure shows some of the resource components:

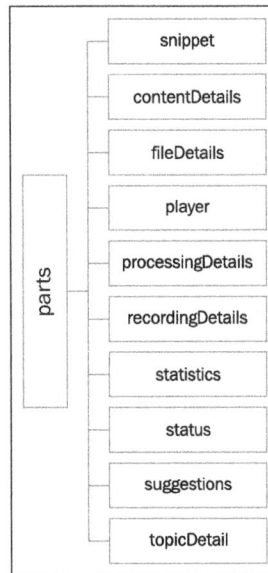

The fields parameter

The `fields` parameter is used to filter out the exact fields that are needed by the client application. This is really helpful to reduce the size of the response.

For example, `fields = items(id, snippet(title))` will result in a small footprint of a response containing an ID and a title.

The YouTube button markup

We have added a button in our jQuery product template to display the search option in the product. The following code shows the updated template:

```
<script id="aProductTemplate" type="text/x-jquery-tmpl">
    <div class="ts-product panel panel-default">
        <div class="panel-head">
            <div class="fb-like" data-href="${url}" data-
layout="button_count"
                data-action="like" data-show-faces="true" data-
share="true">
```

```
                </div>
            </div>
            <div class="panel-body">
                <span class="glyphicon glyphicon-certificate ts-cost-
icon">
                    <label>${cost}$</label>
                </span>
                <img class="img-responsive" src="${url}">
                <h5>${title}</h5>
            </div>
            <div class="panel-footer">
                <button type="button" class="btn btn-danger btn-block
packt-youtube-button" data-bookTitle="${title}">YouTube Search</
button>
                <button type="button" class="btn btn-info btn-block">Buy</
button>
                <button type="button" class="btn btn-info btn-block twit-
me" data-bookTitle="${title}" data-imgURI="${url}">Tweet</button>
                <div class="g-plus-button">
                    <div class="g-plusone" data-width="180" data-
href="${url}"></div>
                </div>
            </div>
        </div>
    </div>
</script>
```

The following screenshot shows the updated product markup with a YouTube
button added to the product template:

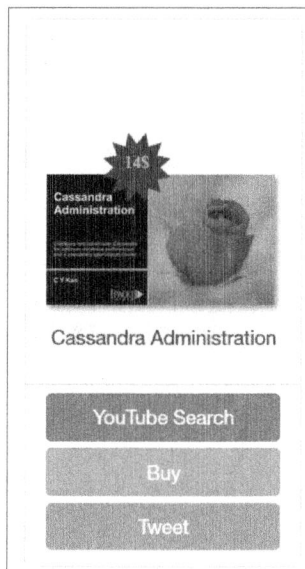

Asynchronous search in YouTube

When any user clicks on the **YouTube Search** button, a list of related videos will appear at the top of the page. In this chapter, we are mainly focusing on the search feature of YouTube using the keyword option. The `query` parameter that does this work is `q`.

The following URL shows an example of how to search the Cassandra Administration:

```
https://www.googleapis.com/youtube/v3/search?q=Cassandra+Administrati
on&part=snippet&key=AIzaSyBTYn7fvH1mpIKlw8W5K4Ju-hNaievd9Fs
```

JSON's data object response for the preceding URL has five item objects as a response but due to the space constraint, only one item detail is listed as follows:

```
{
    "kind": "youtube#searchListResponse",
    "etag": "\"ePFRUfYBkeQ2ncpP9OLHKB0fDw4/7OUuUA4io00-
QTaWxOM2dzJxZ14\"",
    "nextPageToken": "CAUQAA",
    "pageInfo": {
        "totalResults": 14063,
        "resultsPerPage": 5
    },
    "items": [
        {
        "kind": "youtube#searchResult",
        "etag": "\"ePFRUfYBkeQ2ncpP9OLHKB0fDw4/
BUpjVqlJL1lhr3TGWJnPVlmTM0g\"",
            "id": {
                "kind": "youtube#video",
                "videoId": "UTE6kQXVa-M"
            },
            "snippet": {
                "publishedAt": "2013-11-22T12:27:36.000Z",
                "channelId": "UC3VydBGBl132baPCLeDspMQ",
                "title": "Cassandra Administration Tutorial: Building a
Cluster of Multiple Nodes | packtpub.com",
                "description": "Learn how to scale out a Cassandra cluster
from a single node.  Prepare the seed node Configure the cluster
Conduct verification tests Part of Cassandra...",
                "thumbnails": {
                    "default": {
                        "url": "https://i.ytimg.com/vi/UTE6kQXVa-M/
default.jpg"
                    },
```

```
            "medium": {
                "url": "https://i.ytimg.com/vi/UTE6kQXVa-M/
mqdefault.jpg"
            },
            "high": {
                "url": "https://i.ytimg.com/vi/UTE6kQXVa-M/
hqdefault.jpg"
            }
        },
        "channelTitle": "packt1000",
        "liveBroadcastContent": "none"
    }
  },
  ]
}
```

The response JSON format from YouTube is shown in the following screenshot:

```
https://www.googleapis.com/you...    +

https://www.googleapis.com/youtube/v3/search?&q=Cassandra+Administration&part=snippet&key=AIzaSyBTYn7fvH1mplKlw8W5K4Ju-hNaievd9Fs    C

{
   kind: "youtube#searchListResponse",
   etag: "\"ePFRUfYBkeQ2ncpP9OLHKB0fDw4/7enAfkhaBPOGq-namWuIQ98s2hg\"",
   nextPageToken: "CAUQAA",
 - pageInfo: {
       totalResults: 14242,
       resultsPerPage: 5
   },
 + items: [ ... ]
}
```

The details of the fields are explained as follows:

- kind: This represents a type of JSON object. As this JSON object is a list of search results, the type is searchListResponse.

- etag: This represents the unique tag of this resource.

- nextPageToken: This represents a unique token value that needs to be passed on the subsequent request in order to access the next set of results through pagination.

- pageInfo: This consists of the pagination information:

  ○ totalResults: This returns the total number of results for a query.

  ○ resultsPerPage: This returns the maximum number of records per page.

- items: This contains the actual result of the search.

> To know more about etag, refer to
> http://en.wikipedia.org/wiki/HTTP_ETag.

The following screenshot shows the details of the items property:

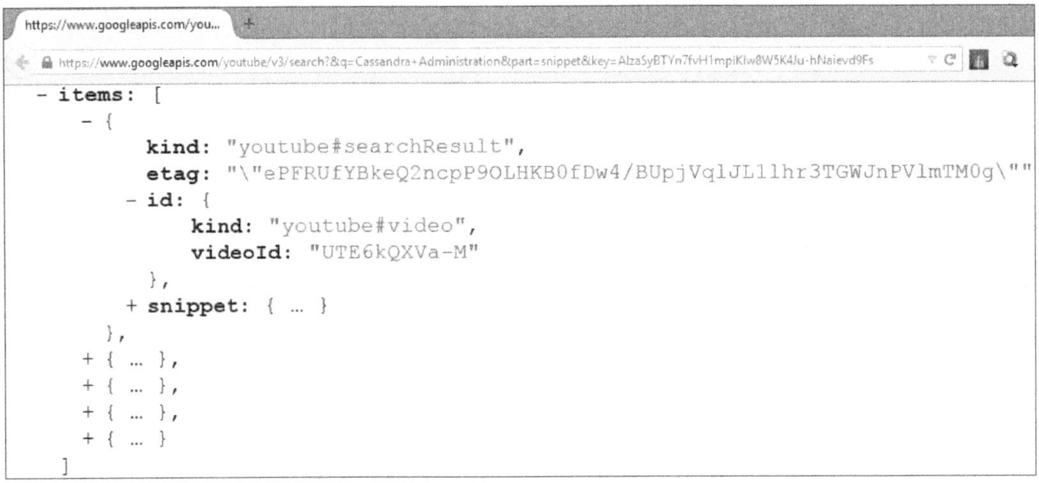

```
https://www.googleapis.com/you...   +

     https://www.googleapis.com/youtube/v3/search?&q=Cassandra+Administration&part=snippet&key=AIzaSyBTYn7fvH1mpiKIw8W5K4Ju-hNaievd9Fs          C

   - items: [
     - {
         kind: "youtube#searchResult",
         etag: "\"ePFRUfYBkeQ2ncpP9OLHKB0fDw4/BUpjVqlJLl1hr3TGWJnPVlmTM0g\""
         - id: {
             kind: "youtube#video",
             videoId: "UTE6kQXVa-M"
           },
         + snippet: { ... }
       },
     + { ... },
     + { ... },
     + { ... },
     + { ... }
   ]
```

The details of the fields are explained as follows:

- kind: This represents a type of object. As this represents an individual record of every search, the type is seacrhResult.

- etag: This represents a unique string for the resource object.

- id: This represents a unique identifier and has two subfields kind and videoId:

  - kind: This represents the type as video.

  - videoId: This represents a unique video ID of the resultant video. This ID can further be used to embed videos to a page.

- snippet: This represents the actual value of the video.

The following screenshot shows the inside details of the `items` property:

```
https://www.googleapis.com/you...                                       — □  ✕
  ←  🔒 https://www.googleapis.com/youtube/v3/search?&q=Cassandra+Administration&part=snippet&key:  ▽ C'   📔  ▼   ≡
            - snippet: {
                publishedAt: "2013-11-22T12:27:36.000Z",
                channelId: "UC3VydBGBl132baPCLeDspMQ",
                title: "Cassandra Administration Tutorial:
                Building a Cluster of Multiple Nodes |
                packtpub.com",
                description: "Learn how to scale out a
                Cassandra cluster from a single node. • Prepare
                the seed node • Configure the cluster • Conduct
                verification tests Part of Cassandra...",
                - thumbnails: {
                    - default: {
                        url: https://i.ytimg.com/vi/UTE6kQXVa-
                        M/default.jpg
                    },
                    - medium: {
                        url: https://i.ytimg.com/vi/UTE6kQXVa-
                        M/mqdefault.jpg
                    },
                    - high: {
                        url: https://i.ytimg.com/vi/UTE6kQXVa-
                        M/hqdefault.jpg
                    }
                },
                channelTitle: "packt1000",
                liveBroadcastContent: "none"
            }
        },
```

The details of the fields are explained as follows:

- `publishedAt`: This represents the date and time of when the API is published.
- `channelId`: This represents a unique channel identifier and designates the channel to which the video belongs.
- `title`: This represents title of the video.
- `description`: This represents the description of the video.
- `thumbnails`: This contains the image URL for the video and has three different subfields:
    - `default`: This contains the URL for the thumbnail image with default quality.
    - `medium`: This contains the URL for the thumbnail image with medium quality.
    - `high`: This contains the URL for the thumbnail image with high quality.

- `channelTitle`: This represents the name of the channel to which the video belongs.

- `liveBroadcastContent`: This represents the live broadcast information, if any, which exists for a video.

Rendering the YouTube search results

We have created a separate jQuery template to represent individual search results. Once the markup is ready to be rendered, we place the markup in a video container. For this, we have added an additional row in our page layout. The following code shows the additional row markup to render YouTube-related results in the page:

```
<div class="row youtube-video-container hide">
   <div class="page-header text-default">
     <h2>YouTube Related Search Video</h2>
   </div>
   <div class="col-sm-6">
     <ul class="media-list ts-video-container"></ul>
   </div>
   <div class="col-sm-6">
     <!--Space for Embedding video-->
   </div>
</div>
```

The following code has the jQuery template to represent each video result in the list:

```
<script id="aVideoTemplate" type="text/x-jquery-tmpl">
     <li class="media btn-link youtube-video" data-videoId="${id.
videoId}">
       <a class="pull-left" href="#">
       <img class="media-object" src="${snippet.thumbnails.default.
url}" alt="${snippet.title}">
       </a>
       <div class="media-body">
         <h4 class="media-heading">${snippet.title}</h4>
              ${snippet.description}
       </div>
   </li>
  </script>
```

The following screenshot shows YouTube's response rendered at the top of the page. The search keyword is Cassandra Administration for a q parameter value. It returns five results per page. We have only rendered the first page as an unordered elements list.

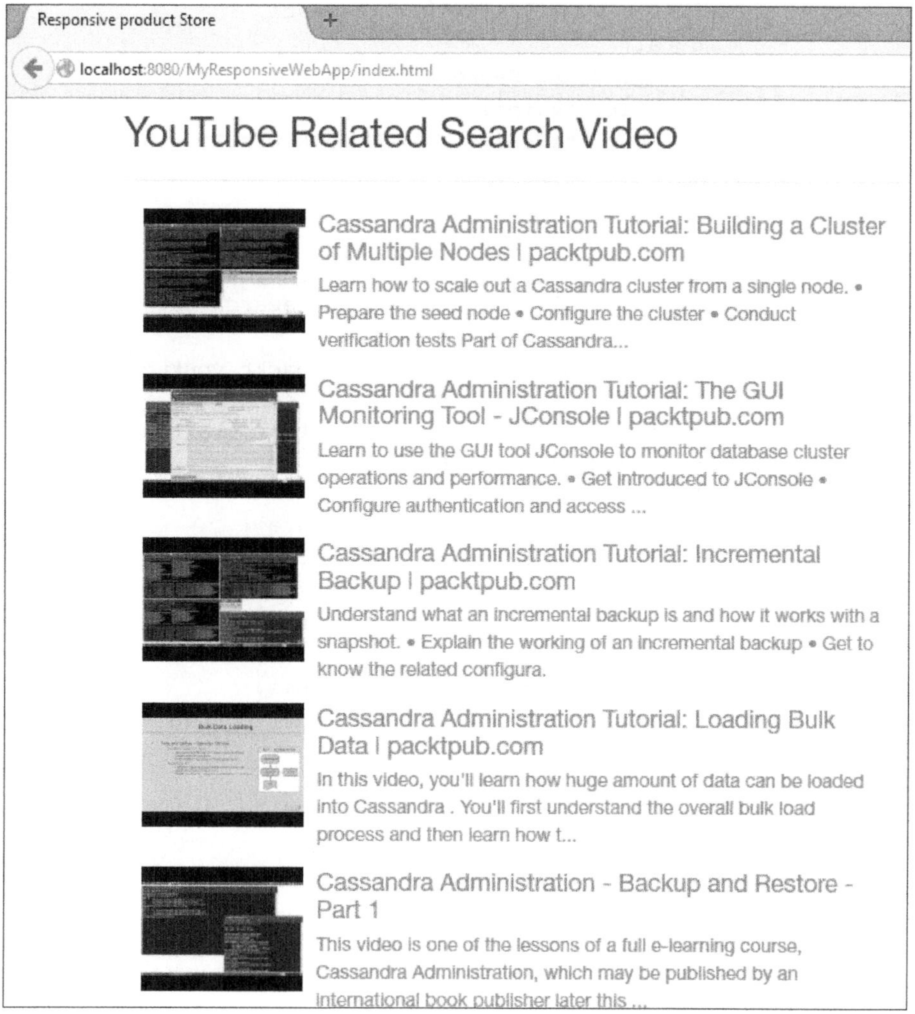

The jQuery code that implemented this search is listed in the following code:

```
/*Returns a jQuery Promise Object For YouTube Search*/
doYouTubeSearch : function(searchKeyWord){
    var baseUrl ="https://www.googleapis.com/youtube/v3/search",
        searchRequest = $.ajax({url:baseUrl,
            data:{
                q: searchKeyWord,
                part:"snippet",
                key :"AIzaSyBTYn7fvH1mpIKlw8W5K4Ju-hNaievd9Fs"
            }
        });
    return searchRequest.promise();
},
/*Event Listener for click event YouTube search button*/
initYouTubeButton : function(){
    $('.packt-app').on('click',' button.packt-youtube-
button',function(e){
        var title = $(e.target).attr('data-bookTitle'),
            promisedData = PACKT_PRODUCT_APP.
doYouTubeSearch(title);
            promisedData.done(function(data){
            /*By Default, Initial result returns only 5 video,
             *other related video can be called using
             *Pagination info returned in the response
             */
            var videoItemArray = data.items;
            PACKT_PRODUCT_APP.doVideoRendering(videoItemArray);
        });
    });
},
/*jQuery Template building with JSON data*/
doVideoRendering: function(data){
    var videoItemContainer =$('.ts-video-container'),
        aVideoTemplate = $('#aVideoTemplate').tmpl( data ),
promiseOldPro = $(videoItemContainer).find('.panel').fadeOut().
promise();
        $.when(promiseOldPro).then(function(){
            $('.youtube-video-container').removeClass('hide');
            videoItemContainer.html(aVideoTemplate);
        });
    }
```

The Firebug inspection shows the following markup generated in the container:

```
Console   HTML ▼   CSS   Script   DOM   Net   Cookies   Page Speed   Typography

div.col-sm-6 < div.row < div.container < body < html

<div class="row youtube-video-container">
  <div class="page-header text-default">
    <h2>YouTube Related Search Video</h2>
  </div>
  <div class="col-sm-6">
    <ul class="media-list ts-video-container">
      <li class="media btn-link youtube-video" data-videoid="UTE6kQXVa-M">
        <a class="pull-left" href="#">
          <img class="media-object" alt="Cassandra Administration Tutorial:
          Building a Cluster of Multiple Nodes |
          packtpub.com" src="https://i.ytimg.com/vi/UTE6kQXVa-M/default.jpg">
        </a>
        <div class="media-body">
          <h4 class="media-heading">Cassandra Administration Tutorial: Building
          a Cluster of Multiple Nodes | packtpub.com</h4>
          Learn how to scale out a Cassandra cluster from a single node. •
          Prepare the seed node • Configure the cluster • Conduct verification
          tests Part of Cassandra...
        </div>
      </li>
      <li class="media btn-link youtube-video" data-videoid="RDd35Lszpq4">
      <li class="media btn-link youtube-video" data-videoid="60p53oXTCGs">
      <li class="media btn-link youtube-video" data-videoid="n4_KhB5Xn_o">
      <li class="media btn-link youtube-video" data-videoid="MilEGIc_90U">
    </ul>
  </div>
</div>
```

Embedding a YouTube video

There are different approaches to embed a YouTube video in an HTML page. YouTube provides two different APIs to embed a video to a page: the JavaScript API and IFrame API. In this section, we have used the IFrame API in order to embed the video in our page. To use this API, we need to include the iframe_api API provided by YouTube. The script code to include this API in our page is as follows:

```
<script src="https://www.youtube.com/iframe_api"></script>
```

We have added `iframe` in the container. When we click on one of the search results, it receives the video ID and renders it on IFrame as a video. The jQuery code performing this is listed as follows:

```
initVideoPlay: function(){
    $('.packt-app').on('click',' li.youtube-video',function(e){
      var videoId = $(e.currentTarget).attr('data-videoId'),
        embedURL= "https://www.youtube.com/embed/"+videoId;
      $('iframe#ytplayer').attr('src',embedURL);
    });
}
```

The embedded URL has the format `https://www.youtube.com/embed/<videoId>`. IFrame takes this URL to render the video player of YouTube. We have added an IFrame in the layout and kept it hidden initially. The following code shows the IFrame embedded in the markup:

```
<div class="row youtube-video-container hide">
    <div class="page-header text-default">
      <h2>YouTube Related Search Video</h2>
    </div>
     <div class="col-sm-6">
       <ul class="media-list ts-video-container"></ul>
     </div>
     <div class="col-sm-6">
        <iframe id="ytplayer" type="text/html" width="100%"
height="300" src="" frameborder="0" allowfullscreen></iframe>
     </div>
</div>
```

In the preceding code, the width of the IFrame is 100 percent. So, it will be a fluid layout on the available size of the container. The following screenshot shows the video player loaded with the target video on clicking the first item from the list of video links:

YouTube Related Search Video

Cassandra Administration Tutorial: Building a Cluster of Multiple Nodes | packtpub.com
Learn how to scale out a Cassandra cluster from a single node. • Prepare the seed node • Configure the cluster • Conduct verification tests Part of Cassandra...

Cassandra Administration Tutorial: The GUI Monitoring Tool - JConsole | packtpub.com
Learn to use the GUI tool JConsole to monitor database cluster operations and performance. • Get introduced to JConsole • Configure authentication and access ...

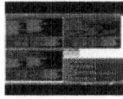
Cassandra Administration Tutorial: Incremental Backup | packtpub.com
Understand what an incremental backup is and how it works with a snapshot. • Explain the working of an incremental backup • Get to know the related configura.

Cassandra Administration Tutorial: Loading Bulk Data | packtpub.com
In this video, you'll learn how huge amount of data can be loaded into Cassandra . You'll first understand the overall bulk load process and then learn how t...

Cassandra Administration - Backup and Restore - Part 1
This video is one of the lessons of a full e-learning course, Cassandra Administration, which may be published by an international book publisher later this ...

The HTML markup for the IFrame video player in Firebug looks like the following screenshot:

```
Console  HTML ▼  CSS  Script  DOM  Net  Cookies  Page Speed  Typography

div.fb-comments < div.container < body < html

⊟ <div class="col-sm-6">
    ⊟ <iframe id="ytplayer" width="" height="300" frameborder="0" allowfullscreen="" s
      rc="https://www.youtube.com/embed/UTE6kQXVa-M" type="text/html">
        <!DOCTYPE html>
        ⊟ <html lang="en" data-cast-api-enabled="true" dir="ltr">
            ⊞ <head>
            ⊟ <body id="" class="date-20140508 en_US ltr site-center-aligned site-as-
              giant-card gecko gecko-29 exp-css-ellipsis" dir="ltr">
                ⊞ <div id="player" class="full-frame" style="width: 100%; height: 100%;
                  overflow: hidden;">
                ⊞ <div id="player-unavailable" class="ytp-error hid">
                    <div id="html5-player-messages" style="display:none"> </div>
                ⊞ <script name="www-embed-player" src="//s.ytimg.com/yts/jsbin
                  /www-embed-player-vflZJ0dax.js">
                ⊞ <script>
                ⊞ <script>
            </body>
        </html>
    </iframe>
  </div>
</div>
```

After the integration of the video search feature of YouTube, the changed page will look like the following screenshot:

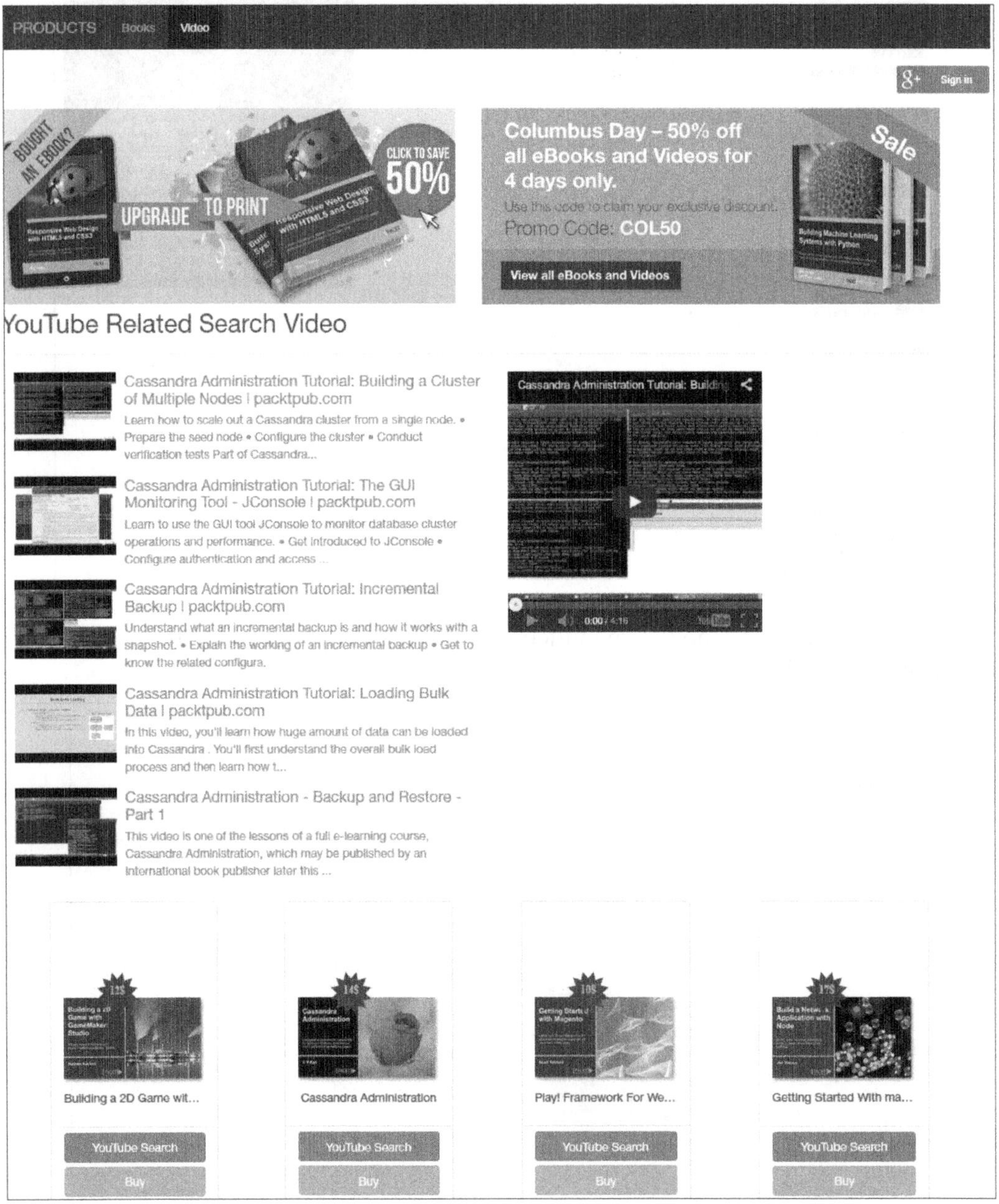

Summary

In this chapter, we have learned about the YouTube API. We have seen how to create a Google client API to use the YouTube data. We have also seen how to use jQuery AJAX and promise to make a request to YouTube videos. Also, we have explored the YouTube provided IFrame API to embed videos in our page. In the next chapter, we will integrate a payment system into our web application.

8

Integrating E-Commerce or Shopping Applications with Your Website

In this chapter, you will learn how to integrate a third-party e-commerce or shopping API to your web application. You will also learn how to integrate the PayPal pay feature into the products. We will also explore and get introduced to the Shopify application.

Creating a shopping cart

In this section, we will develop an **Add to Cart** feature in our application. A real shopping cart has many features, but for the purpose of our application, we will develop a minimal shopping cart. The features that we are going to develop in this section are as follows:

- Adding a product to the cart
- Displaying the minimal view of the cart
- Displaying the cart details in a table

Adding a product to the cart

A new button is added to every product template; this button is labeled as **Add To Cart**. The modified jQuery template is listed as follows:

```
<script id="aProductTemplate" type="text/x-jquery-tmpl">
    <div class="ts-product panel panel-default">
        <div class="panel-head">
```

```
            <div class="fb-like" data-href="${url}" data-
layout="button_count" data-action="like" data-show-faces="true" data-
share="true">
            </div>
        </div>
        <div class="panel-body">
            <span class="glyphicon glyphicon-certificate ts-cost-
icon">
                <label>${cost}$</label>
            </span>
            <img class="img-responsive" src="${url}">
            <h5>${title}</h5>
        </div>
        <div class="panel-footer">
            <button type="button" class="btn btn-danger btn-block
packt-youtube-button" data-bookTitle="${title}">YouTube Search</
button>
            <button type="button" class="btn btn-info btn-block add-
to-cart" data-bookTitle="${title}" data-cost="${cost}">
                <span class="glyphicon glyphicon-shopping-cart">
                </span>
                Add To Cart
            </button>
            <button type="button" class="btn btn-info btn-block twit-
me" data-bookTitle="${title}" data-imgURI="${url}">Tweet</button>
            <div class="g-plus-button">
                <div class="g-plusone" data-width="180" data-
href="${url}"></div>
            </div>
        </div>
    </div>
  </script>
```

The attributes used in the button are listed as follows:

- `data-cost`: This attribute contains the cost of the product
- `data-bookTitle`: This attribute contains the name of the book

The modified product with the new **Add To Cart** button will look like the following screenshot:

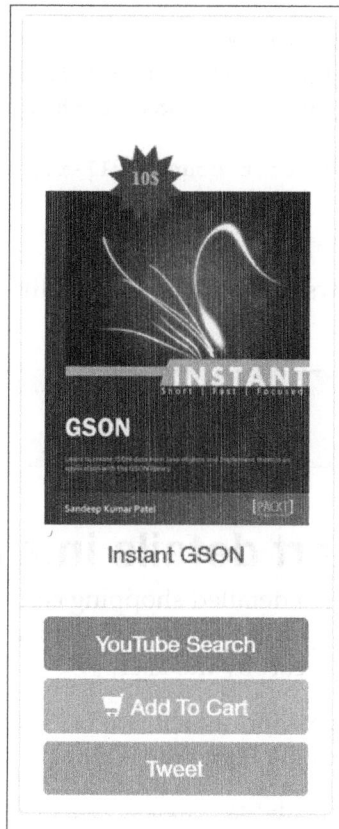

Displaying the minimal view of the cart

In this section, we will develop the minimal view of a shopping cart. A minimal view is very useful for an end user, as it shows the summary of response in an instant. A minimal view in our application has the following features:

- **Counter**: This component shows the number of products added at present by the user. The default count is 0.

- **Click event**: This event is attached to the button and displays the details of the cart in a table.

The HTML markup for the minimal cart view is listed as follows. The Bootstrap 3 classes, glyphicon and glyphicon-shopping-cart, are used to produce a cart icon for the cart:

```
<div class="packt-my-cart-min">
   <button type="button" class="btn btn-info btn-block btn-cart">
       <span class="glyphicon glyphicon-shopping-cart pull-left cart-
icon">MyCart</span>
       <span class="badge cart-count pull-right">0</span>
   </button>
</div>
```

The following screenshot shows the minimal view of the shopping cart for our application:

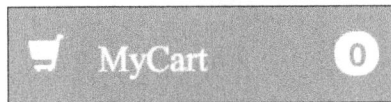

Displaying the cart details in a table

In this section, we will develop a detailed shopping cart view. When a user clicks on the minimal cart view, a pop-up window appears with a table containing the entire product list that is added to the cart by the user.

The HTML code for the pop-up window with modal is listed as follows. The modal has the style class derived from the Bootstrap 3 library:

```
<div class="modal fade" id="my-cart">
    <div class="modal-dialog">
        <div class="modal-content">
            <div class="modal-header">
                <button type="button" class="close" data-
dismiss="modal" aria-hidden="true">&times;</button>
                <h4 class="modal-title">My Cart Detail</h4>
            </div>
            <div class="modal-body">
                </div>
            <div class="modal-footer">
                <button type="button" class="btn btn-default" data-
dismiss="modal">Close</button>
            </div>
        </div>
    </div>
</div>
```

The preceding HTML markup has used Bootstrap 3 CSS classes to build the basic structure of the modal. These classes are listed as follows:

- `modal`: This class indicates the start point of a modal markup
- `modal-dialog`: This class adds styling similar to a dialog box
- `modal-content`: This class indicates the content area of the dialog
- `modal-header`: This class styles the header of the modal
- `modal-footer`: This class indicates the footer area of a modal

The jQuery template for the detailed table of the cart is listed as follows:

```
<script id="myCartTemplate" type="text/x-jquery-tmpl">
<table class="table table-responsive ">
    <thead>
        <tr class="active">
            <th colspan="3">My Cart Details</th>
        </tr>
        <tr class="active">
            <th>Sr No</th>
            <th>Item Name</th>
            <th>Price(USD)</th>
        </tr>
    </thead>
    <tbody>
        {{each ITEMS}}
        <tr>
            <td>1</td>
            <td>${title}</td>
            <td>${cost}</td>
        </tr>
        {{/each}}

    </tbody>
    <tfoot>
        <tr class="active">
            <th>Total</th>
            <th></th>
            <th>${TOTALCOST} USD</th>
        </tr>
    </tfoot>
</table>
<div class="row">
```

```
    <button type="button" class="btn btn-danger btn-block pay-button"
data-cartAmount="${TOTALCOST}">
        Pay With Paypal
    </button>
</div>
</script>
```

In the preceding code, we have used Bootstrap 3's utility classes for the tables and buttons. Details of these classes are listed as follows:

- To style the table, we have used the following classes:
  - `table`: This class is used for basic styling such as padding and for inserting the horizontal divider
  - `table-responsive`: This class is used to make the table responsive
  - `active`: This class is for the color that appears when you hover over a particular row or cell

- To style the button, we have used the following classes:
  - `btn`: This class is used for the basic styling of the button
  - `btn-danger`: This class is used for the background color of the button
  - `btn-block`: This class is used for the size of the button with 100 percent width

The jQuery code to create and update the shopping cart is listed as follows:

```
Product:function(title,cost){
        this.title = title;
        this.cost = cost;
    },

    MY_CART:[],

    addToMyCart: function(product){
        var cartCount = $('.cart-count');
        $('.packt-app').on('click','.add-to-cart',function(e){
            var target = $(e.target),
                title = $(target).attr('data-bookTitle'),
                cost = parseInt($(target).attr('data-cost'),10),
                product = new PACKT_PRODUCT_APP.Product(title, cost),
                isExist = PACKT_PRODUCT_APP.isExist(product.title);
                if(!isExist){
                    PACKT_PRODUCT_APP.MY_CART.push(product);
                }else{
```

```
                    alert("Item already Exist In you cart.");
                }
            cartCount.html(PACKT_PRODUCT_APP.MY_CART.length);
        });
    },

    getTotalCost : function(){
        var sum =0;
        $.each(PACKT_PRODUCT_APP.MY_CART,function(index, product){
            sum += product.cost;
        });
        return sum;
    },
/*This method checks whether an item is already present inside the
cart or not*/
    isExist: function(title){
        var isExist =false;
        $.each(PACKT_PRODUCT_APP.MY_CART,function(index, product){
            if(title === product.title){
                isExist = true;
            }
        });
        return isExist;
    },
/*This method has listener for the cart button click and display the
modal*/
    showMyCart : function(){
        $('.packt-app').on('click','.btn-cart',function(e){
            var data ={
                "ITEMS":PACKT_PRODUCT_APP.MY_CART,
                "TOTALCOST":PACKT_PRODUCT_APP.getTotalCost()
                },
                cartTemplate = $('#myCartTemplate').tmpl(data);
                $('#my-cart .modal-body').html(cartTemplate);
            $('#my-cart').modal('show');
        });
    }
```

All these methods are present inside the PACKT_PRODUCT_APP object. When this modal pop-up window comes up to the screen, it looks like the following screenshot. It has a table listing all the products present inside the cart with the total billed amount and a button for the PayPal payment.

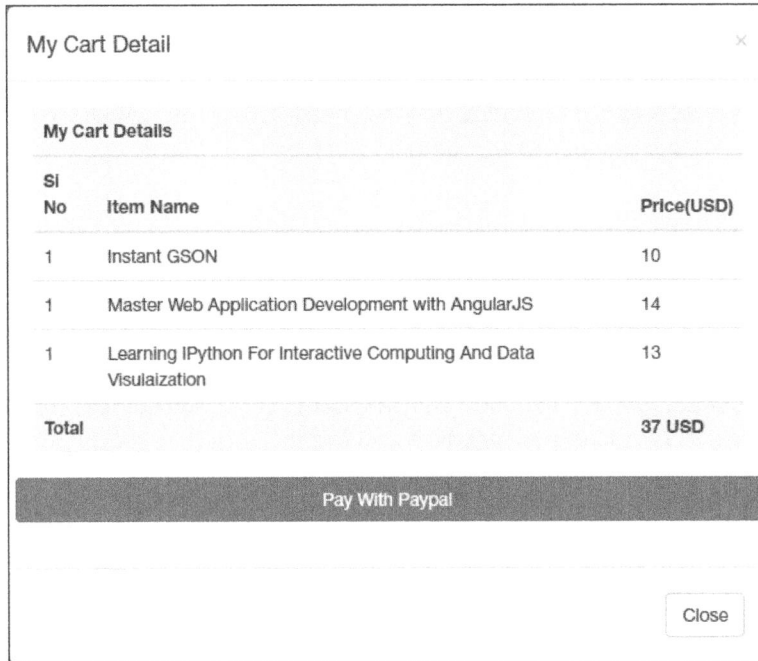

My Cart Detail		×
My Cart Details		
Sl No	**Item Name**	**Price(USD)**
1	Instant GSON	10
1	Master Web Application Development with AngularJS	14
1	Learning IPython For Interactive Computing And Data Visulaization	13
Total		**37 USD**
	Pay With Paypal	
		Close

Configuring the PayPal Developer API

In this section, we will configure the PayPal Developer API in our application for the payment process. To access the PayPal API, we need to create a client application in the Developer's Console. The developer link for the console is https://developer. paypal.com. The following screenshot shows the Developer Console to create a new PayPal application:

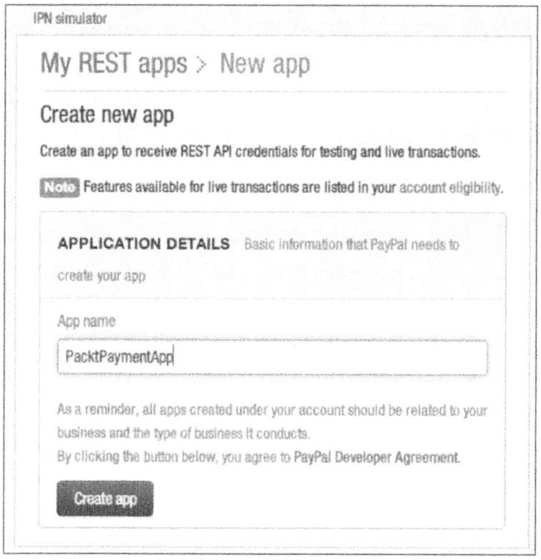

For our application, we have created a PayPal client application named
`PacktPaymentApp`. Once the client application is created successfully, it will
be listed in the dashboard along with its details. The following screenshot
shows the details of our client application registered in PayPal:

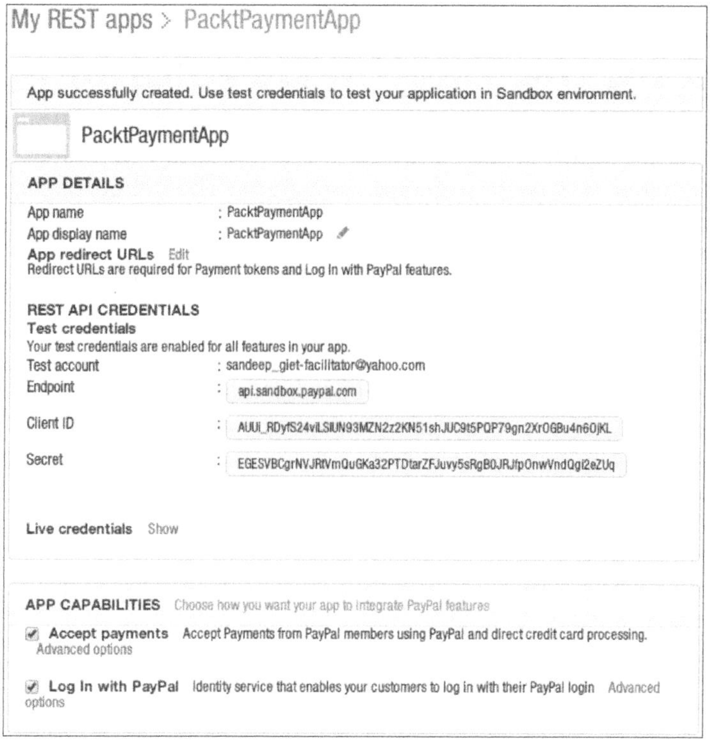

On the **APP DETAILS** page, we can get the client's ID and a secret key for use. We can also configure the return URL for the application. A return URL is the location where the client application will return on success. The following screenshot shows the form to configure the return URL:

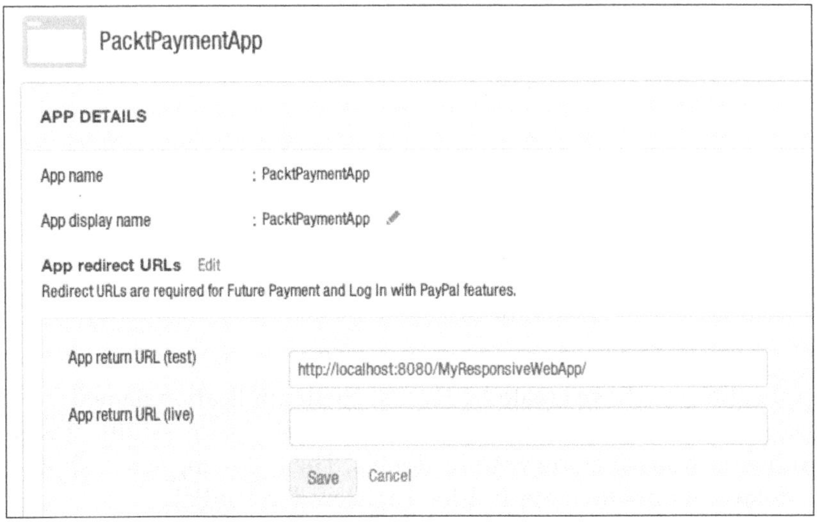

Integrating the PayPal Developer API

In this section, we will integrate the PayPal SDK into our application. The PayPal SDK has two JAR files to be included in the project. It can be downloaded from `https://github.com/paypal/rest-api-sdk-java`. The details of the two JAR files that are to be included in the project are as follows:

- `paypal-core-1.6.0.jar`: This JAR file has all the core classes for the PayPal payment
- `rest-api-sdk-0.9.0.jar`: This JAR file consists of all the classes that are required to convert it into a REST-based access

The following screenshot shows the JAR files added to the classpath of our project:

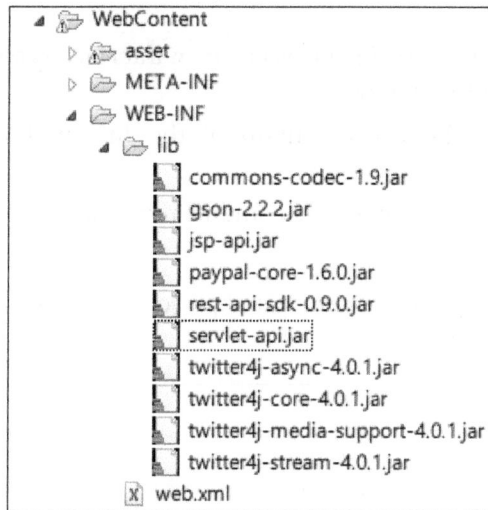

```
▲ 📂 WebContent
   ▷ 📂 asset
   ▷ 📂 META-INF
   ▲ 📂 WEB-INF
      ▲ 📂 lib
            📄 commons-codec-1.9.jar
            📄 gson-2.2.2.jar
            📄 jsp-api.jar
            📄 paypal-core-1.6.0.jar
            📄 rest-api-sdk-0.9.0.jar
            📄 servlet-api.jar
            📄 twitter4j-async-4.0.1.jar
            📄 twitter4j-core-4.0.1.jar
            📄 twitter4j-media-support-4.0.1.jar
            📄 twitter4j-stream-4.0.1.jar
      🗙 web.xml
```

For the integration of the PayPal payment in the application, we have created some Java classes for the shopping cart payment. The `sdk_config.properties` file has all the settings required by PayPal's client application to run. The following code shows the contents of the `sdk_config.properties` file:

```
#Connection Information
http.ConnectionTimeOut=5000
http.Retry=1
http.ReadTimeOut=30000
http.MaxConnection=100
#HTTP Proxy configuration
#If you are using proxy set http.UseProxy to true and replace the
following values with your proxy parameters
http.ProxyPort=8080
http.ProxyHost=127.0.0.1
http.UseProxy=false
http.ProxyUserName=null
http.ProxyPassword=null
#Set this property to true if you are using the PayPal SDK within a
Google App Engine java app
http.GoogleAppEngine = false
#Service Configuration
service.EndPoint=https://api.sandbox.paypal.com
#Live EndPoint
#service.EndPoint=https://api.paypal.com
#Credentials
clientID=EBWKjlELKMYqRNQ6sYvFo64FtaRLRR5BdHEESmha49TM
clientSecret=EO422dn3gQLgDbuwqTjzrFgFtaRLRR5BdHEESmha49TM
```

We have created the following Java files to integrate the PayPal payment into our application:

- `PaypalAppConfig`: This Java class is of an interface type and contains the client API and a secret key
- `PaypalUtil`: This Java class contains all the static methods to be used by the servlet for the PayPal payment
- `PaypalServlet`: This Java class contains the code for the PayPal payment request process

The following screenshot shows the updated project structure with the new PayPal implemented classes:

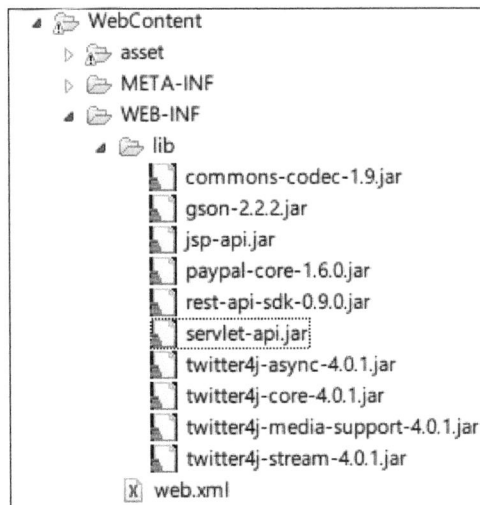

The following code shows the contents of the `PaypalAppConfig.java` file:

```
package com.packt.social.client;
public interface PaypalAppConfig {
    final static String PAYPAL_CLIENT_ID = "AUUi_
RDyfS24viLSIUN93MZN2z2KN51shJUC9t5PQP79gn2XrOGBu4n6OjKL";
    final static String PAYPAL_CLIENT_SECRET =
"EGESVBCgrNVJRtVmQuGKa32PTDtarZFJuvy5sRgB0JRJfpOnwVndQgi2eZUq";
}
```

The following code shows the contents of the `PaypalUtil.java` file:

```
package com.packt.social.client;

import java.util.ArrayList;
```

```
import java.util.List;
import com.packt.product.obj.Product;
import com.paypal.api.payments.Amount;
import com.paypal.api.payments.Item;
import com.paypal.api.payments.ItemList;
import com.paypal.api.payments.Payer;
import com.paypal.api.payments.Payment;
import com.paypal.api.payments.RedirectUrls;
import com.paypal.api.payments.Transaction;
import com.paypal.core.rest.OAuthTokenCredential;
import com.paypal.core.rest.PayPalRESTException;

public class PaypalUtil {

    /**
     * Creates an Total Amount for List of Products
     * @param listOfProd
     * @return
     */
    public static Amount createAmount(List<Product> listOfProd){
        Amount totalAmount = new Amount();
        int sumOfCost =0;
        for(Product aproduct : listOfProd){
            sumOfCost += aproduct.getCost();
        }
        totalAmount.setCurrency("USD");
        totalAmount.setTotal(String.valueOf(sumOfCost));
        return totalAmount;
    }


    /**
     * Creates a Access Token
     * @return
     */
    public static String getAccessToken(){
        String accessToken =null;
        try {
            accessToken = new OAuthTokenCredential(PaypalAppCo
nfig.PAYPAL_CLIENT_ID, PaypalAppConfig.PAYPAL_CLIENT_SECRET).
getAccessToken();
        } catch (PayPalRESTException e) {
            e.printStackTrace();
        }
        return accessToken;
```

```
    }

    /**
     * Creates a Payment method
     * @return
     */
    public static Payer getPayerMethod(){
        Payer payer = new Payer();
        payer.setPaymentMethod("paypal");
        return payer;
    }

    /**
     * Creates aList of Item form List of Product
     * @param saleProductList
     * @return
     */
    public static List<Item> createItemList(ArrayList<Product>
saleProductList){
        ArrayList<Item> items = new ArrayList<Item>();
        for(Product aProduct : saleProductList){
            Item item = new Item();
            item.setName(aProduct.getTitle());
            item.setPrice(String.valueOf(aProduct.getCost()));
            //We have taken USD and quantity as 1 for our application.
            //You can configure it dynamically while doing your
application
            item.setCurrency("USD");
            item.setQuantity("1");
            items.add(item);
        }
        return items;
    }

    /**
     * Creates a transaction list
     * @param amount
     * @param listItem
     * @return
     */
    public static List<Transaction> getTransactionList(Amount
amount,List<Item> listItem){
        List<Transaction> transactions = new ArrayList<Transaction>();
        Transaction transaction = new Transaction();
```

```
        ItemList itemList = new ItemList();
        itemList.setItems(listItem);
        transaction.setItemList(itemList);
        transaction.setDescription("creating a PayPal Payment
MyResponsiveWebApp for Amount "+amount);
        transaction.setAmount(amount);
        transactions.add(transaction);
        return transactions ;
    }


    /**
     * Creates a Payment Object
     * @param payer
     * @param transactions
     * @param redirectUrls
     * @return
     */
    public static Payment createPayment(Payer payer, List<Transaction>
transactions,RedirectUrls redirectUrls){
        Payment payment = new Payment();
        payment.setIntent("sale");
        payment.setPayer(payer);
        payment.setTransactions(transactions);
        payment.setRedirectUrls(redirectUrls);
        return payment;
    }


    /**
     * Creates a pair of Redirect URL
     * @return
     */
    public static RedirectUrls getRedirectURL(){
        RedirectUrls redirectUrls = new RedirectUrls();
        redirectUrls.setCancelUrl("http://localhost:8080/MyResponsiveW
ebApp?cancel=true");
        redirectUrls.setReturnUrl("http://localhost:8080/MyResponsiveW
ebApp?success=true");
        return redirectUrls ;
    }
}
```

The following code shows the contents of the `PaypalServlet.java` file:

```java
package com.packt.product.data;

import java.io.IOException;
import java.io.PrintWriter;
import java.lang.reflect.Type;
import java.util.ArrayList;
import java.util.HashMap;
import java.util.List;
import java.util.Map;
import javax.servlet.ServletException;
import javax.servlet.annotation.WebServlet;
import javax.servlet.http.HttpServlet;
import javax.servlet.http.HttpServletRequest;
import javax.servlet.http.HttpServletResponse;
import com.google.gson.Gson;
import com.google.gson.reflect.TypeToken;
import com.packt.product.obj.Product;
import com.packt.social.client.PaypalUtil;
import com.paypal.api.payments.Amount;
import com.paypal.api.payments.Item;
import com.paypal.api.payments.Payer;
import com.paypal.api.payments.Payment;
import com.paypal.api.payments.RedirectUrls;
import com.paypal.api.payments.Transaction;
import com.paypal.core.rest.APIContext;
import com.paypal.core.rest.PayPalRESTException;

@WebServlet("/PaypalServlet")
public class PaypalServlet extends HttpServlet {
    private static final long serialVersionUID = 1L;
    public PaypalServlet() {
        super();
    }
    protected void doPost(HttpServletRequest request,
HttpServletResponse response) throws ServletException, IOException {
        String saleJsonString = request.getParameter("saleData");
        Type listType = new TypeToken<ArrayList<Product>>() {
        }.getType();
        ArrayList<Product> saleProductList = new Gson().fromJson(
                saleJsonString, listType);
        List<Item> itemsForSale = PaypalUtil.createItemList(saleProdu
ctList);
        String accessToken = null;
```

```
        try {
            accessToken = PaypalUtil.getAccessToken();
            Amount amountToPay = PaypalUtil.
createAmount(saleProductList);
            Payer payer = PaypalUtil.getPayerMethod();
            List<Transaction> transactions = PaypalUtil.
getTransactionList(
                    amountToPay, itemsForSale);
            RedirectUrls redirectUrls = PaypalUtil.getRedirectURL();
            Payment payment = PaypalUtil.createPayment(payer,
transactions,
                    redirectUrls);
            Map<String, String> sdkConfig = new HashMap<String,
String>();
            sdkConfig.put("mode", "sandbox");
            APIContext apiContext = new APIContext(accessToken);
            apiContext.setConfigurationMap(sdkConfig);
            Payment createdPayment = payment.create(apiContext);
            String paypalResJsonString = createdPayment.toJSON();
            response.setContentType("application/json");
            PrintWriter out = response.getWriter();
            out.write(paypalResJsonString);
        } catch (PayPalRESTException e) {
            e.printStackTrace();
        }
    }
}
```

The PayPal payment flow is explained in the following figure:

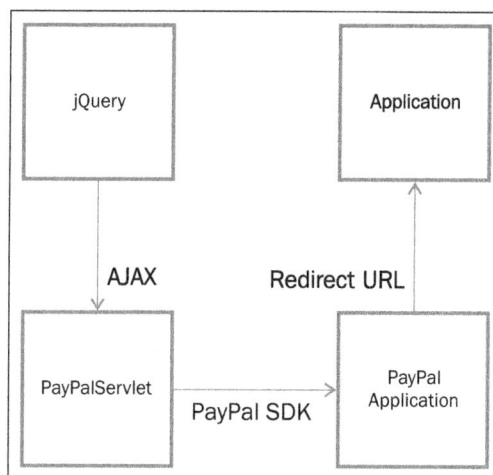

The jQuery script code to attach an event and make an AJAX call to the servlet is listed as follows:

```
processPayPalPay : function(){
        $('.packt-app').on('click','.pay-button',function(e){
            var ajaxRequest=$.ajax({
                    url:"PaypalServlet",
                    dataType :"json",
                    data:{"saleData":JSON.stringify(PACKT_PRODUCT_APP.
MY_CART)},
                    method:"POST"
                });
            ajaxRequest.done(function(data){
                //approval_url redirect the user to PayPal for
approval
                window.open(data.links[1].href,"_self");
            });
        });
    }
```

After clicking on the PayPal payment option, the AJAX call gets triggered to the servlet. The following screenshot shows the request parameter that goes along with the AJAX call:

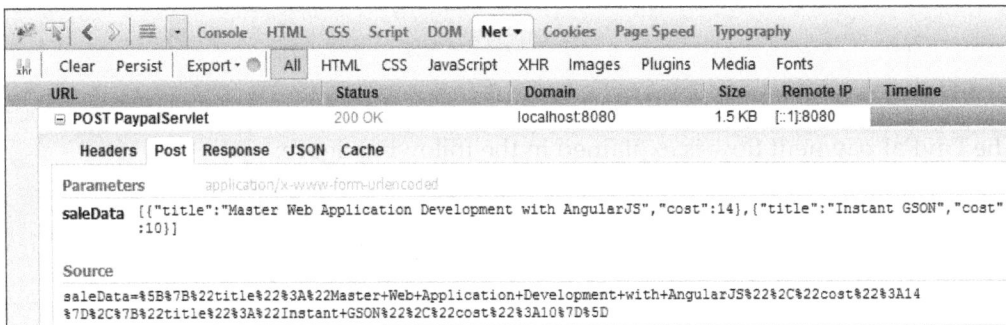

A successful processing returns a JSON response. The JSON response looks like the following code:

```
{
  "id": "PAY-85X50102CT245630YKOBXJMQ",
  "create_time": "2014-05-26T17:06:58Z",
  "update_time": "2014-05-26T17:06:58Z",
  "intent": "sale",
  "payer": {
    "payment_method": "PayPal",
```

```
      "payer_info": {
        "shipping_address": {}
      }
    },
    "transactions": [
      {
        "amount": {
          "currency": "USD",
          "total": "24.00",
          "details": {
            "subtotal": "24.00"
          }
        },
        "description": "creating a PayPal Payment MyResponsiveWebApp for
Amount {\n  \"currency\": \"USD\",\n  \"total\": \"24\"\n}",
        "item_list": {
          "items": [
            {
              "quantity": "1",
              "name": "Instant GSON",
              "price": "10.00",
              "currency": "USD"
            },
            {
              "quantity": "1",
              "name": "Master Web Application Development with
AngularJS",
              "price": "14.00",
              "currency": "USD"
            }
          ]
        }
      }
    ],
    "state": "created",
    "links": [
      {
        "href": "https://api.sandbox.PayPal.com/v1/payments/payment/PAY-
85X50102CT245630YKOBXJMQ",
        "rel": "self",
        "method": "GET"
      },
      {
        "href": "https://www.sandbox.PayPal.com/cgi-bin/webscr?cmd\
u003d_express-checkout\u0026token\u003dEC-4FJ20307KN251643F",
        "rel": "approval_url",
        "method": "REDIRECT"
```

```
    },
    {
      "href": "https://api.sandbox.PayPal.com/v1/payments/payment/PAY-
85X50102CT245630YKOBXJMQ/execute",
      "rel": "execute",
      "method": "POST"
    }
  ]
}
```

From the preceding JSON responses, we can take the `approval_url` link and use it to redirect the user to complete the payment process. The following screenshot shows how the current window is redirected to the PayPal page for an approval of the payment from the user's side. A user can log in to the PayPal site to approve the payment.

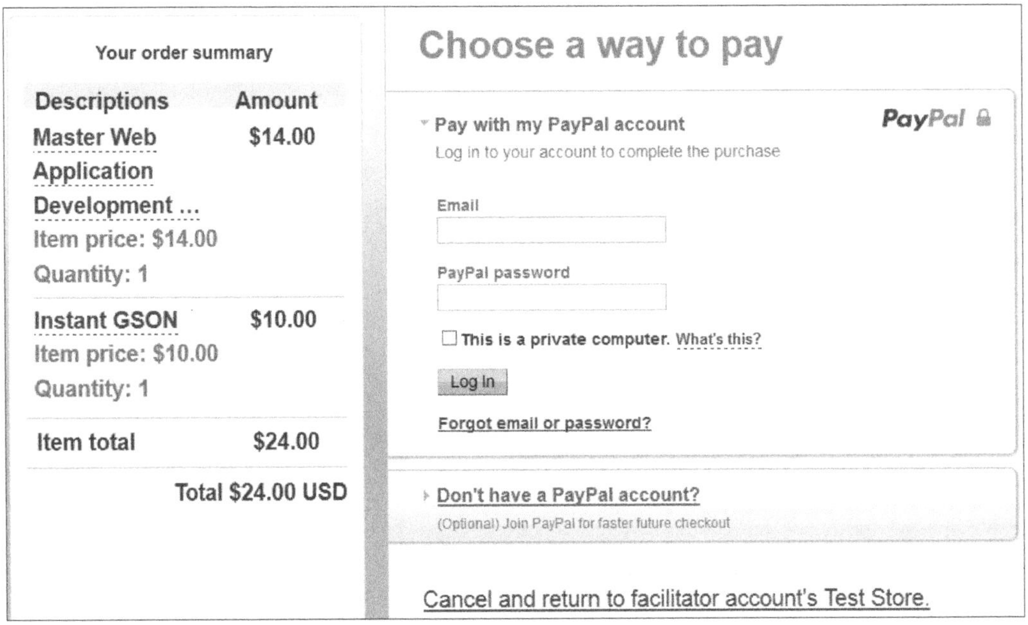

After a successful payment has been made by the user, the site redirects to
`http://localhost:8080/MyResponsiveWebApp/?cancel=success&token=EC-09P460143X2598615` along with a token number. The following screenshot shows
the address bar of the browser that contains the new URL that we configured in the
`PaypalUtil.java` method:

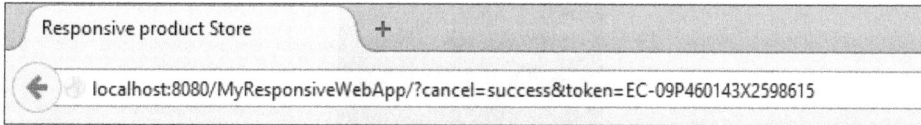

Configuring the Shopify API

In this section, we will provide you with a quick introduction to the **Shopify API**.
Shopify provides a platform to build your own online store. We can create a new
Shopify application using `https://app.shopify.com/services/partners/dev_shops/new`, and we need to sign up for a new account to access this URL.
The following screenshot shows the form to create a new Shopify store:

Integrating the Shopify API

After the store has been successfully created, we can see the **Dashboard** toolbar on the left-hand side of the screen. The following screenshot shows the toolbar of the application that we created:

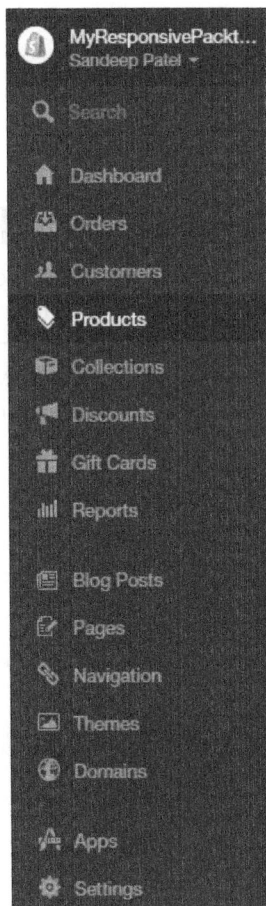

The best thing about Shopify is that it has all the features made available to the admin user by its admin pages. This reduces the code development efforts that users might need to put in. We can access the admin page for our application using `https://myresponsivepacktshop.myshopify.com/admin`. We can add a product using the **Products** tab. The following screenshot shows the form to add a product:

Once the product is added, it will be listed in the products list. The following screenshot shows the product that was mentioned earlier added to our list:

We can also customize the theme and add new features, or create a new application based on the project's requirement. In this chapter, we are not covering all the details about Shopify, as the chapter's main aim is to provide the readers with details about integrating payments into their application.

Summary

In this chapter, we learned how to implement key features such as the implementation of a shopping cart with a minimal and detailed view and how to configure the PayPal payment API. We also briefly explored the Shopify API and its configuration. In the next chapter, we will learn to develop Google's Currency Converter API along with the web application.

9
Integrating the Google Currency Converter with Your Web Application

In this chapter, you will learn how to integrate the Currency Converter API into your web application. You will also learn how to build the Google Currency Converter API using a JAR file and integrate it into your shopping cart to change the currency type.

The Google Currency Converter API

Google provides a Currency Conversion API for Java-based projects. This API is really helpful to get equivalent currency amounts within custom applications. The link for this project is `https://code.google.com/p/currency-converter-api/`. The following screenshot shows the project page in Google Code:

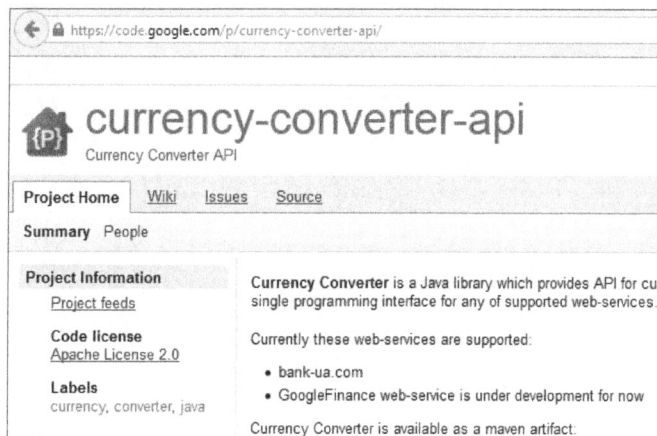

The source code for this project is available at `http://currency-converter-api.googlecode.com/svn/trunk/`. The following screenshot shows the source page of Currency Converter:

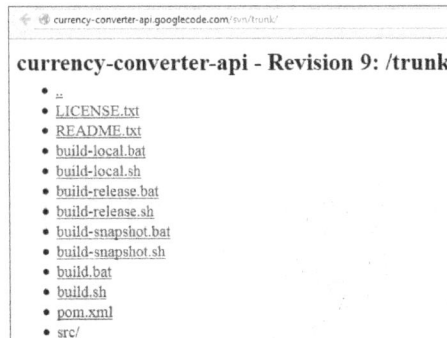

The source code can be copied to your local filesystem using SVN checkout. Before you check out, you need to install SVN on your system. The command for SVN checkout is shown in the following screenshot:

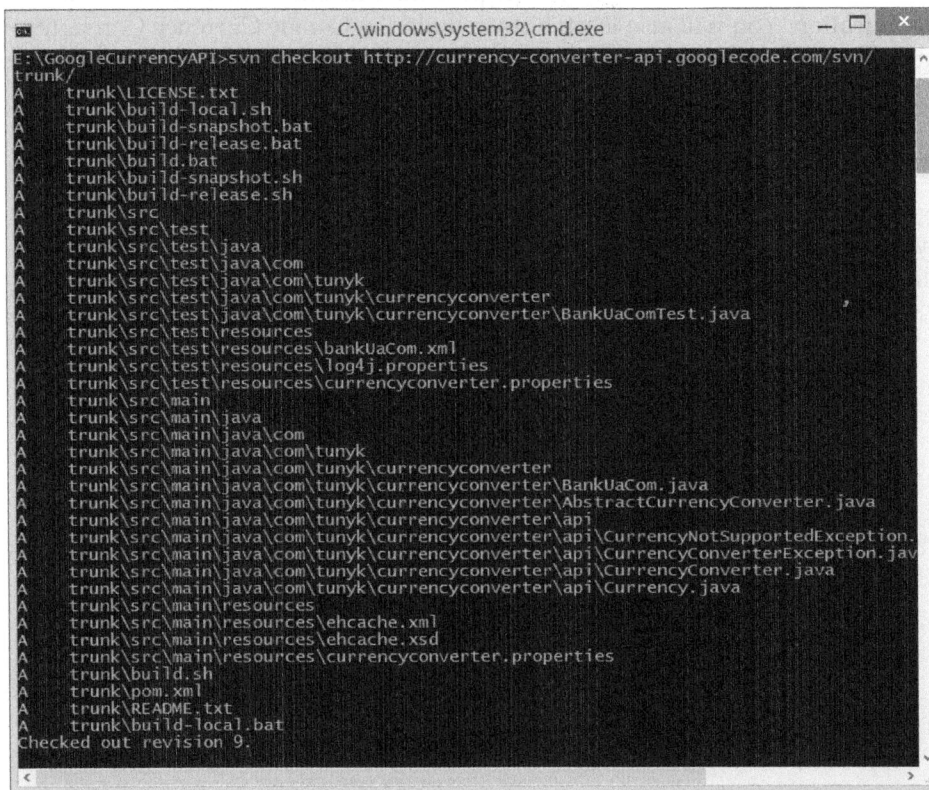

To get a JAR file from this source, we need to configure Maven in the development system; then, we can run a Maven installation. Maven is a tool that can now be used to build and manage any Java-based project. Maven is based on the concept of a **Project Object Model (POM)**. To find out more about Maven, go to `http://maven.apache.org/what-is-maven.html`.

The following screenshot shows the command prompt running the `mvn` installation for the currency project:

Maven's base command is `mvn`, and it takes a number of switch options to perform different application-related tasks. Some of these options are listed as follows:

- `clean`: This option cleans the files and directories generated by Maven during its build
- `install`: This option installs the `built` artifact into the local repository
- `deploy`: This option deploys the `built` artifact to the remote repository
- `compile`: This option compiles Java sources

The `mvn clean install` command will generate the required `currency-converter-api-1.0.jar` JAR file. We can also use the `pom.xml` dependency markup to install and build the JAR file. The following code shows the POM dependency code for a Maven-type project:

```
<dependency>
  <groupId>com.tunyk.currencyconverter</groupId>
  <artifactId>currency-converter-api</artifactId>
  <version>1.0</version>
</dependency>
```

Configuring the Google Currency Converter API

In this section, we will configure the currency JAR file in our application. There are four dependency JAR files that are required to be added in order to configure the currency JAR file. The required JAR files are `ehcache`, `log4j`, `slf4j`, and `slf4j log`. The following figure shows the versions of these JAR files that have been used in this chapter:

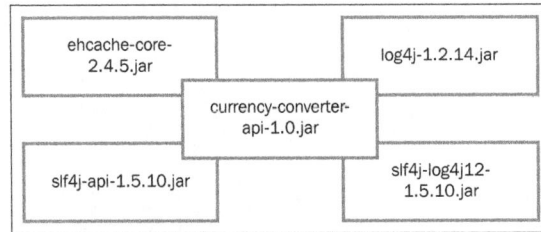

The API documentation for this library can be found at `http://currency-converter-api.googlecode.com/svn/apidocs/index.html`.

Integrating the Currency Converter API

In this section, we will integrate the Currency Converter JAR libraries into our web application. In the previous section, we generated the libraries needed for the configuration. All these JAR files must be added to the classpath of the project. To bundle these libraries with the web application, we added them to the `lib` folder present in the `WEB-INF` directory. The following screenshot shows the JAR files present inside the `lib` folder:

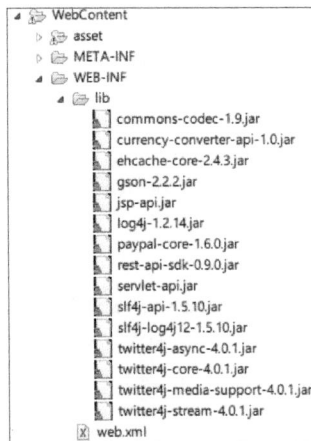

Developing our currency converter

In our application, we will provide a feature for currency conversion in the shopping cart. This will help the end user to compare the total cost with other currencies. For this reason, we will create a jQuery template that has a drop-down menu that contains a list of the currencies supported by the API. When a user selects one of the currencies, he or she makes an AJAX call to find the equivalent value of the total amount of the shopping cart in that currency type. To build this converter component, we have to go through the following steps:

1. Building the currency list dropdown.
2. Processing the conversion request.

Building the currency list dropdown

In this section, we will develop a dropdown with all the currencies supported by the Google Currency API. This API has a `com.tunyk.currencyconverter.api.Currency` enum with the list of currencies as constants. We have built a servlet named `AllCurrencyListServlet.java` that is called when the page loads to retrieve the list of currencies as a JSON array. The code for `AllCurrencyListServlet` is as follows:

```java
package com.packt.product.data;

import java.io.IOException;
import java.io.PrintWriter;
import javax.servlet.ServletException;
import javax.servlet.annotation.WebServlet;
import javax.servlet.http.HttpServlet;
import javax.servlet.http.HttpServletRequest;
import javax.servlet.http.HttpServletResponse;
import com.packt.social.client.GoogleCurrencyUtil;

@WebServlet("/AllCurrencyListServlet")
public class AllCurrencyListServlet extends HttpServlet {

    private static final long serialVersionUID = 1L;
    public AllCurrencyListServlet() {
        super();
    }
```

```
    protected void doGet(HttpServletRequest request,
HttpServletResponse response) throws ServletException, IOException {
        String currencyListJsonString = GoogleCurrencyUtil.
getCurrencyList();
        response.setContentType("application/json");
        PrintWriter out = response.getWriter();
        out.write(currencyListJsonString);
    }
}
```

In the previous servlet, we called a method, getCurrencyList(), from the GoogleCurrencyUtil.java class. This method uses the GSON library to convert the currency's enum values to the JSON array. The code for this method is as follows:

```
package com.packt.social.client;

import java.util.Arrays;
import java.util.List;
import com.google.gson.Gson;
import com.tunyk.currencyconverter.BankUaCom;
import com.tunyk.currencyconverter.api.Currency;
import com.tunyk.currencyconverter.api.CurrencyConverter;
import com.tunyk.currencyconverter.api.CurrencyConverterException;

public class GoogleCurrencyUtil {
    /**
     * Returns Currency list as JSON String
     * @return
     */
    public static String getCurrencyList(){
        List<Currency> list = Arrays.asList(Currency.values());
        Gson gson = new Gson();
        String json = gson.toJson(list);
        return json;
    }
}
```

The following code snippet represents the jQuery template of the currency converter:

```
<script id="currencyConverterTemplate" type="text/x-jquery-tmpl">
<div class="row converter-container">
    <div class="col-xs-7">
        <h4 class="pull-left">Convert Currency To</h4>
```

```
    </div>
    <div class="col-xs-3 col-xs-pull-3">
        <select id="currencyConverter" class="form-control">
            {{each currency}}
                <option>${$value}</option>
{{/each}}
        </select>
    </div>
    <div class="col-xs-2">
        <h4 id="equivalent-currency" class="text-success pull-left">
        </h4>
    </div>
</div>
</div>
</script>
```

The following screenshot shows the currency converter dropdown populated with all the supported currencies:

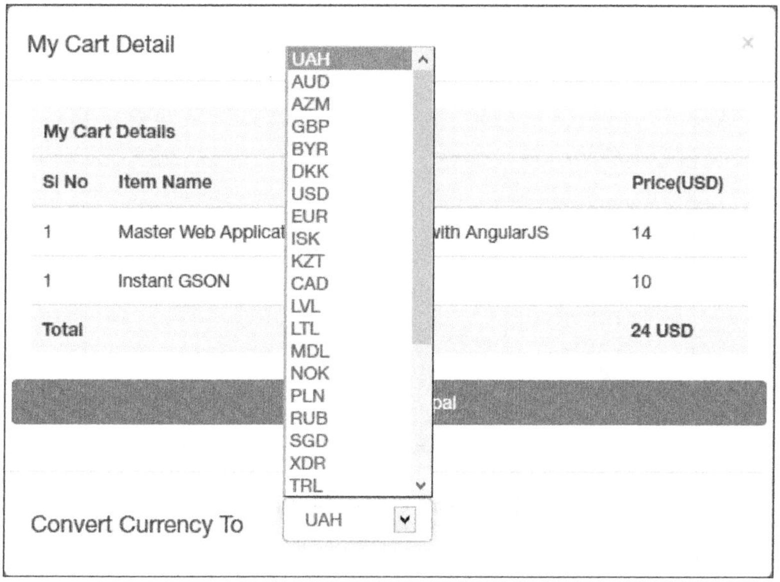

The following screenshot shows the response from the servlet call to get all the currency types as a JSON array:

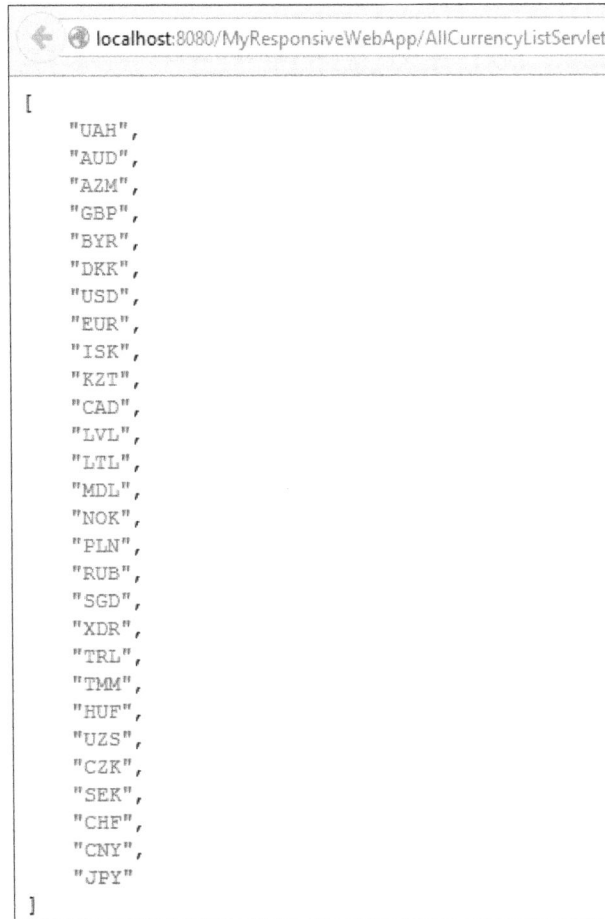

The jQuery script code to download and compile the template is as follows:

```
getAllCurrencyList: function(){
        var ajaxRequest=$.ajax({
            url:"/AllCurrencyListServlet"
        });
        ajaxRequest.done(function(data){
            var aConverterTemplate = $('#currencyConverterTemplate').
tmpl( {"currency":data});
            $('#my-cart .modal-footer').html(aConverterTemplate)
        });
    }
```

In the previous code, the `getAllCurrencyList()` method makes an AJAX request to the `AllCurrencyListServlet` servlet to load the currency list. Once the response arrives, the converter template is compiled and linked with the response data to build the markup for the converter's dropdown.

Processing the conversion request

In this section, we will develop the real request that is passed to the servlet for processing. A jQuery event listener is attached to the change event on the currency dropdown, which is shown as follows:

```
changeCurrencyValue : function(){

        $('.packt-app').on('change','#currencyConverter',function(e){
            var target = e.target,
                selectedValue = $(target).val(),
                totalCost = PACKT_PRODUCT_APP.getTotalCost(),
                promisedCurrency = PACKT_PRODUCT_APP.requestCurrencyVa
lue(totalCost,selectedValue);
                promisedCurrency.done(function(data){
                    $('#equivalent-currency').html(data.value);
                });
        });
    },
    requestCurrencyValue : function(amount,currencyType){

        var ajaxRequest=$.ajax({
            url:"/ConvertCurrencyServlet",
            method:"POST",
            data:{
                "amount":amount,
                "currencyType":currencyType
            }
        });
        return ajaxRequest.promise();
    }
```

In the preceding code, an AJAX request is made to `ConvertCurrencyServlet` as a `post` method using a parameter. The following screenshot shows the request parameters that get posted to the server when a user selects a currency type from the dropdown.

The `amount` parameter represents the total value of the cart in USD, and the `currencyType` parameter represents the user-selected currency type.

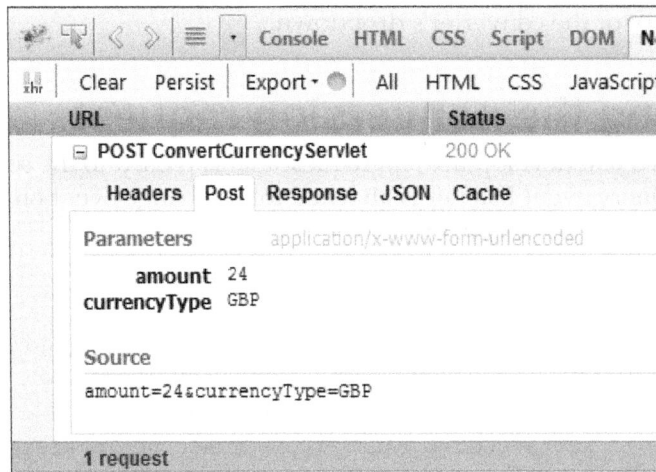

The code for the `ConvertCurrencyServlet` servlet is as follows:

```java
package com.packt.product.data;

import java.io.IOException;
import java.io.PrintWriter;
import javax.servlet.ServletException;
import javax.servlet.annotation.WebServlet;
import javax.servlet.http.HttpServlet;
import javax.servlet.http.HttpServletRequest;
import javax.servlet.http.HttpServletResponse;
import com.google.gson.JsonObject;
import com.packt.social.client.GoogleCurrencyUtil;
import com.tunyk.currencyconverter.api.Currency;

@WebServlet("/ConvertCurrencyServlet")
public class ConvertCurrencyServlet extends HttpServlet {
    private static final long serialVersionUID = 1L;

    public ConvertCurrencyServlet() {
        super();
    }
    protected void doPost(HttpServletRequest request,
HttpServletResponse response) throws ServletException, IOException {
```

```
        String amount = request.getParameter("amount");
        String targetCurrency = request.getParameter("currencyType");
        Float floatAmount = GoogleCurrencyUtil.
convertStringToFloat(amount);
        Currency currencyType = GoogleCurrencyUtil.getCurrencyType(ta
rgetCurrency);
        float currencyListJsonString = GoogleCurrencyUtil.convertCurre
ncy(floatAmount,currencyType);
        response.setContentType("application/json");
        PrintWriter out = response.getWriter();
        JsonObject jsonObject = new JsonObject();
        jsonObject.addProperty("value", Float.toString(currencyListJso
nString)+" "+targetCurrency);
        out.write(jsonObject.toString());
    }
}
```

In the preceding servlet, we used the `GoogleCurrencyUtil` methods to perform some repetitive tasks. The code for these methods is as follows:

```
package com.packt.social.client;

import com.tunyk.currencyconverter.BankUaCom;
import com.tunyk.currencyconverter.api.Currency;
import com.tunyk.currencyconverter.api.CurrencyConverter;
import com.tunyk.currencyconverter.api.CurrencyConverterException;

public class GoogleCurrencyUtil {

    /**
     * ConverCurrency to Float
     * @param amount
     * @param currency
     * @return
     */
    public static float convertCurrency(Float amount,Currency
currency){
        CurrencyConverter currencyConverter = null;
        Float otherCurrencyValue = null;
        try {
            currencyConverter = new BankUaCom(Currency.USD, currency);
            otherCurrencyValue = currencyConverter.
convertCurrency(amount);
        } catch (CurrencyConverterException e) {
            e.printStackTrace();
```

```
        }

            return otherCurrencyValue;
        }


        /**
         * Return an Equivalent Enum Currency type for
         * a String type currency
         * @param currencyType
         * @return
         */
        public static Currency getCurrencyType(String currencyType){
            return Currency.valueOf(currencyType);

        }
        /**
         * Convert String to Float
         * @param amount
         * @return
         */
        public static Float convertStringToFloat(String amount){
            return Float.valueOf(amount);

        }
    }
```

The response of the servlet is a JSON string with a property name value that contains the equivalent currency value. The following screenshot shows the Firebug console with a response from the server:

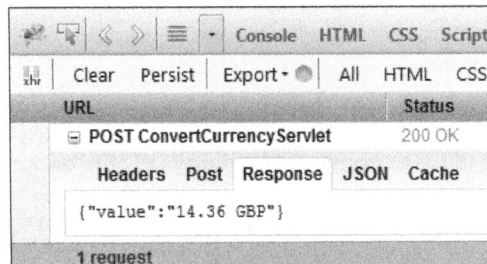

Once the response arrives at the browser, the AJAX success handler gets executed and the equivalent currency type is displayed in a pop-up window. The following screenshot shows the pop-up window with a converted currency value:

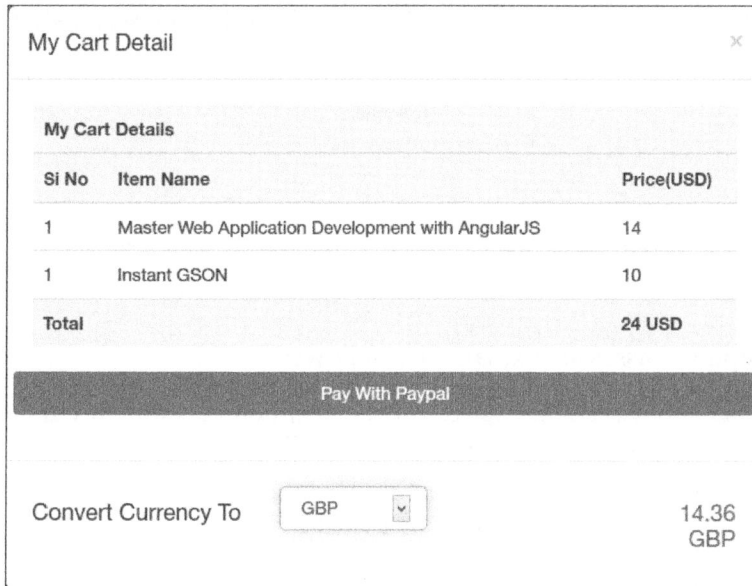

The following screenshot shows the HTML markup in the Firebug console for the currency converter:

Exceptions

In this section, we will learn about the different exceptions that are supported by this API. It has two exception classes, namely `CurrencyConverterException` and `CurrencyNotSupportedException`, as shown in the following screenshot:

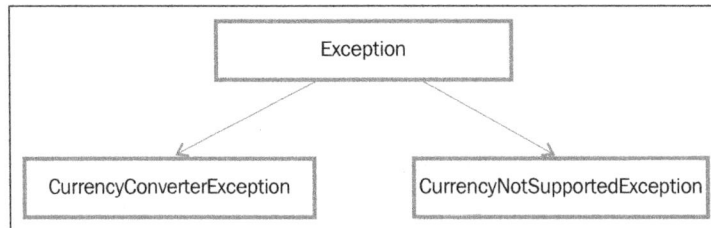

The two exception classes are explained as follows:

- `CurrencyConverterException`: This exception generally occurs when an improper input is given to a conversion API
- `CurrencyNotSupportedException`: This exception occurs when the targeted currency type is not supported by the API

We can find the list of currency types supported by the API at `http://currency-converter-api.googlecode.com/svn/apidocs/com/tunyk/currencyconverter/api/Currency.html`.

Summary

In this chapter, we learned how to configure the Google Currency Converter API, make AJAX requests to these API services, and integrate the API with a web application as a feature to help the end user check the equivalent currency value of the cart at that period of time. In the next chapter, we will be introduced to a list of online and offline tools to test responsive applications.

10
Debugging and Testing

In this chapter, we will learn how to debug a responsive web application. We will also look at a list of available tools to test responsive pages. The following list contains some of the tools that we will get introduced to:

- Dimensions Toolkit
- Designmodo Responsive Test
- Opera Mobile emulator
- Responsinator
- Viewport Resizer
- L-Square Responsive Design Inspector
- FireBreak
- More Display Resolutions 1.0
- The BrowserStack Responsive tool
- MobileTest
- TestSize
- Am I Responsive
- Responsive Design Checker
- Responsive UI Testing Tool (RUIT)
- Responsive Test

Implementing the debugging mechanism

In this section, we will list some of the available offline and online tools that can help a web developer during development.

Dimensions Toolkit

Dimensions Toolkit is available in both online and offline as a Chrome extension. It can be found at the link `http://www.dimensionstoolkit.com`. The main features of this tool include auto refresh such as live reload, resizable dimensions, and custom breakpoints. It also has default breakpoints of 320px, 480px, 768px, and 1024px set. To create a new test in the online version, go to the link `http://www.dimensionstoolkit.com/a`. The following screenshot shows the new test window in the online version:

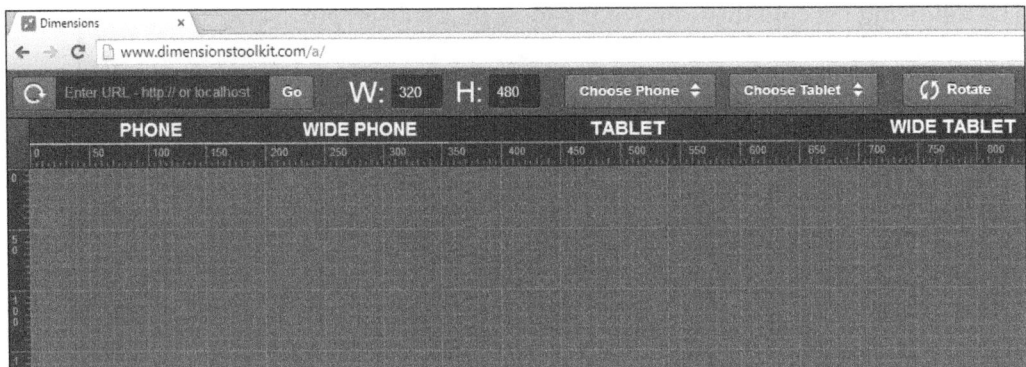

The Designmodo Responsive Test tool

The Designmodo Responsive Test tool is an online tool from the Designmodo team. It can be found at the link `http://designmodo.com/responsive-test`. This tool provides a draggable container interface to change the layout width. It is also equipped with predefined device presets such as MacBook Air 13/11 inch screen size and so on. The following screenshot shows the testing grid for this tool:

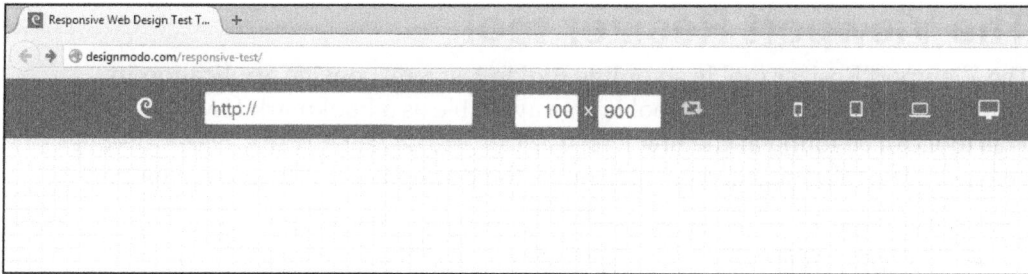

The Opera Mobile emulator tool

The Opera Mobile Emulator tool is a desktop application developed by The Opera Foundation, Inc. It has many customization features such as resolution, screen size, and display type for emulating a test environment. We have already learned about this tool in *Chapter 2*, *Creating a Responsive Layout for a Web Application*.

The Responsinator tool

Responsinator is an online tool that provides a quick view of a web application with a simulated screen size. The most important benefit of this tool is you can create a customized version of an application. This tool can be found at the link `http://www.responsinator.com`. The following screenshot shows the home testing screen for the Responsinator tool:

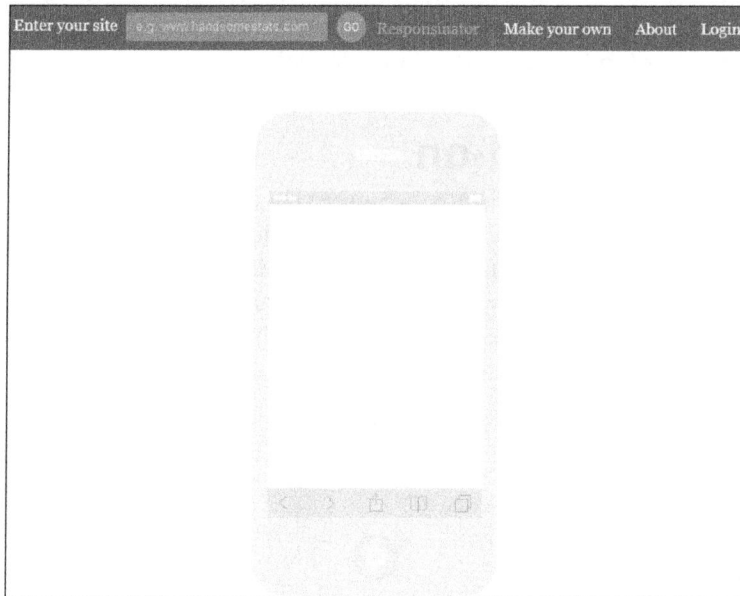

The Viewport Resizer tool

The Viewport Resizer tool is an online tool to test a responsive application in different viewport sizes. This tool is also available as a bookmark for offline use. This tool can be found at the link `http://lab.maltewassermann.com/viewport-resizer`. The following screenshot shows the testing bar for different viewports:

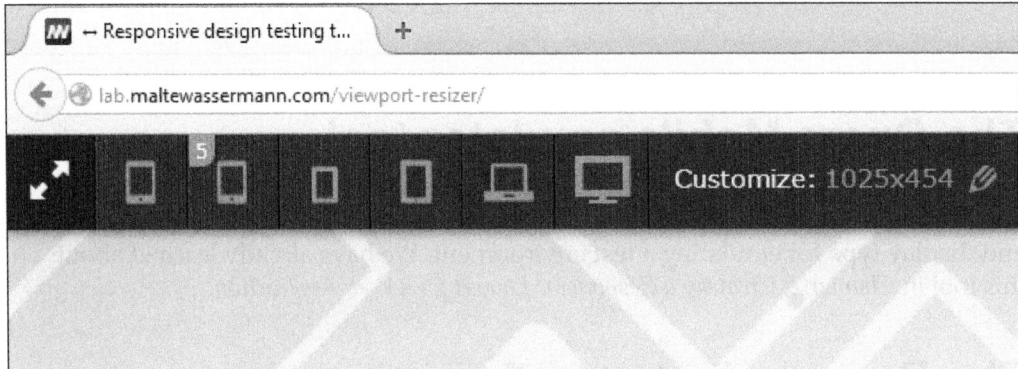

The L-Square Responsive Design Inspector tool

The L-Square Responsive Design Inspector tool is used as a Firefox add-on to measure the size of the screen. It has horizontal and vertical rulers across the screen for measurement. This add-on can be found at the link `https://addons.mozilla.org/en-US/firefox/addon/l-square` for installation.

The FireBreak add-on

The FireBreak add-on is for the Firefox browser. This tool is used to inspect break points in responsive applications. After the installation of this add-on, you can see a small section on the top-right of the browser showing the current pixel size of the window. On resizing the window, the pixel value changes instantaneously showing the current size of the screen. The following screenshot shows the FireBreak add-on at the top of the window:

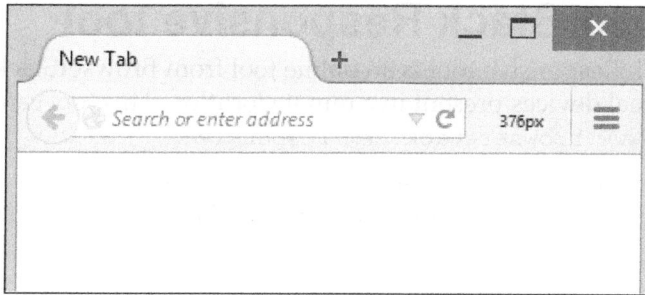

The More Display Resolutions 1.0 add-on

The More Display Resolutions 1.0 add-on is for the Firefox browser. It has a draggable interface that is used to resize the screen's container. It also has the power to take a screenshot of the application in the different sizes of the screen. This add-on can be found at the link `https://addons.mozilla.org/en-US/firefox/addon/more-display-resolutions`. The following screenshot shows the More Display Resolutions 1.0 add-on with different preset screen sizes:

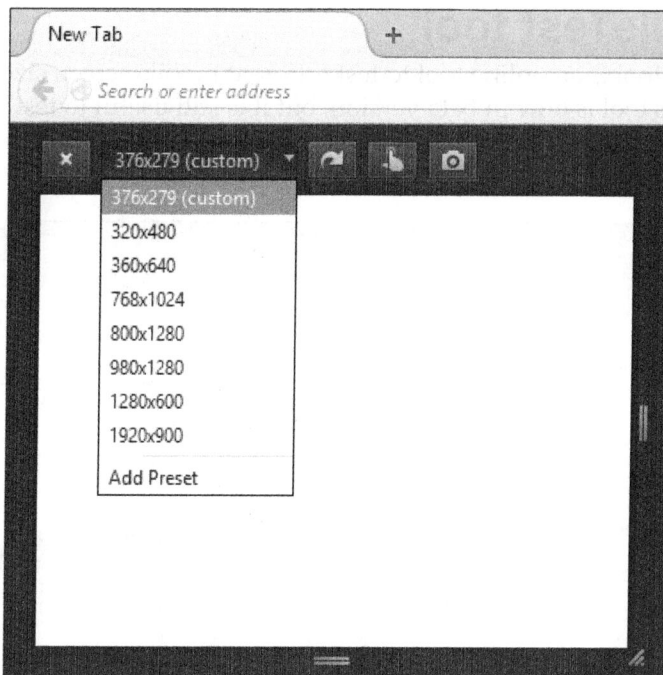

The BrowserStack Responsive tool

The BrowserStack Responsive tool is an online tool from BrowserStack. This tool is connected with real devices present in a remote location. This tool can be found at the link `http://www.browserstack.com/responsive`.

The MobileTest tool

The MobileTest tool is an online tool to test different mobile screen sizes for a web application. This tool is now in beta version, but it is still useful to test the application on mobile devices. This tool can be found at the link `http://mobiletest.me`. The following screenshot shows the home page of this tool:

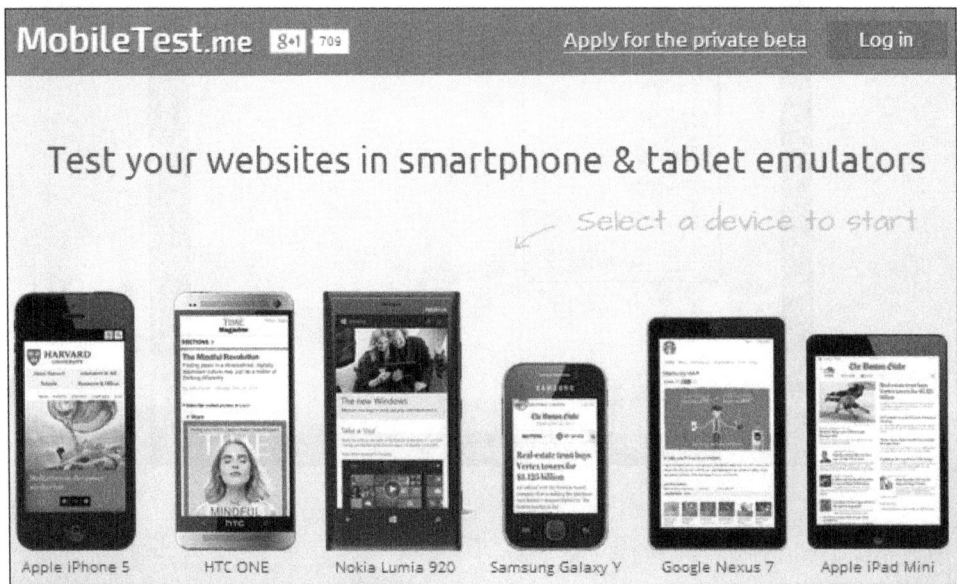

The TestSize tool

The TestSize tool is an online tool to test an application for different screen sizes. This can be found at the link `http://testsize.com`. The following screenshot shows the home page of this tool:

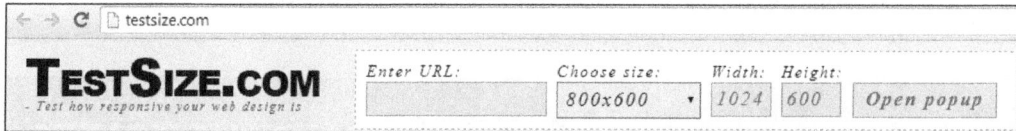

The Am I Responsive tool

The Am I Responsive tool is an online tool to test responsive web applications. This tool is found at the link `http://ami.responsivedesign.is`. The following screenshot shows the home page of this new tool:

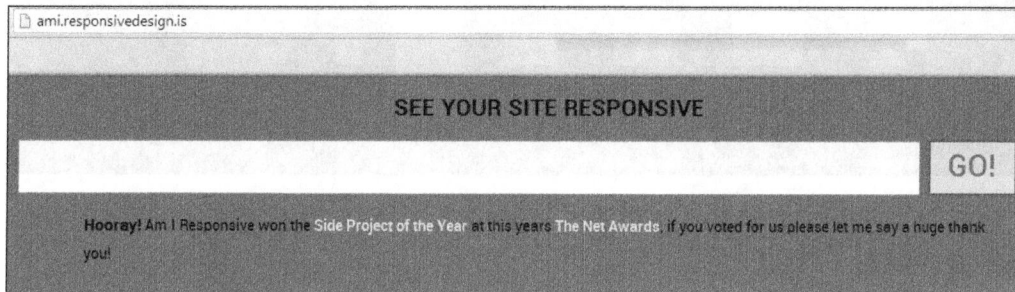

The Responsive Design Checker tool

The Responsive Design Checker tool is an online tool to test responsive design. The sizes are present in inches. It can be found at the link `http://responsivedesignchecker.com`. The following screenshot shows the home page asking for the URL of the targeted web application:

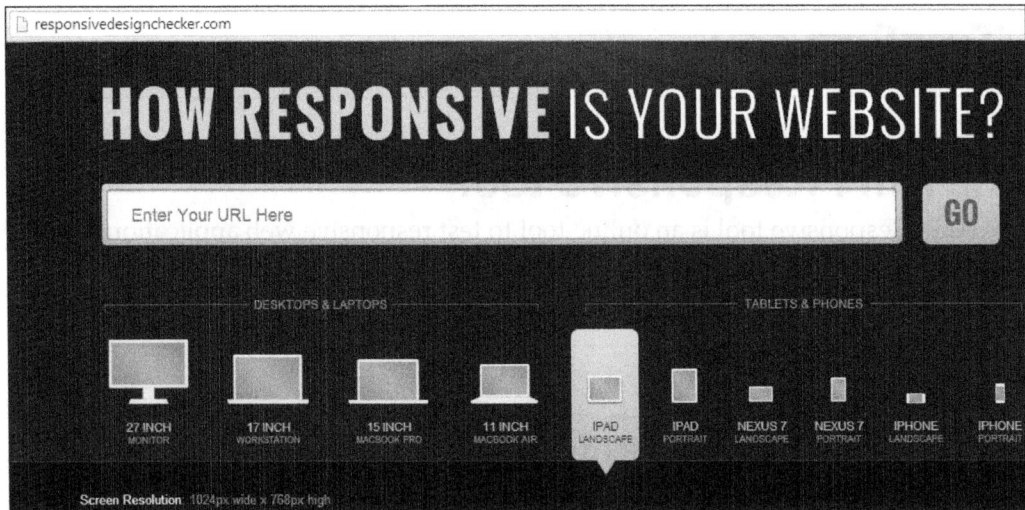

The RUIT tool

The RUIT tool is an online tool for responsive applications. This tool is available at `http://ruit.mytechlabs.com`. The following screenshot shows the home page of this tool:

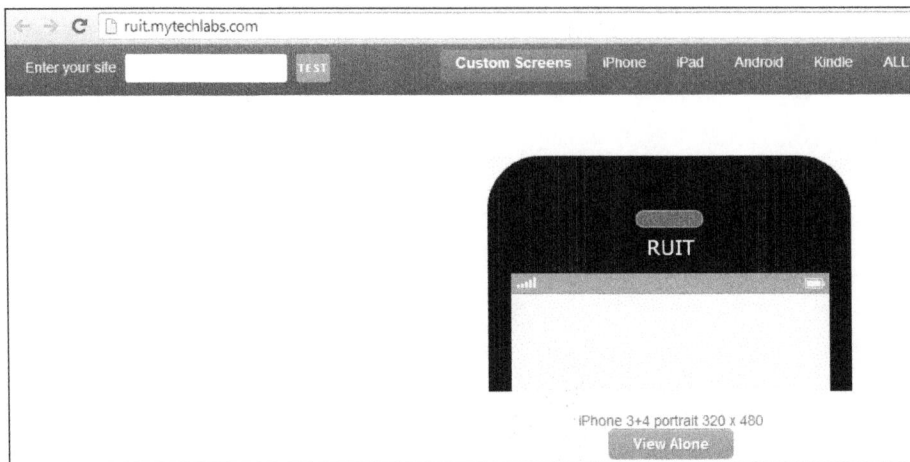

The Responsive Test online tool

The Responsive Test tool is an online tool to test responsive applications.
It is available at http://responsivetest.com. The following screenshot
shows the home page of this tool:

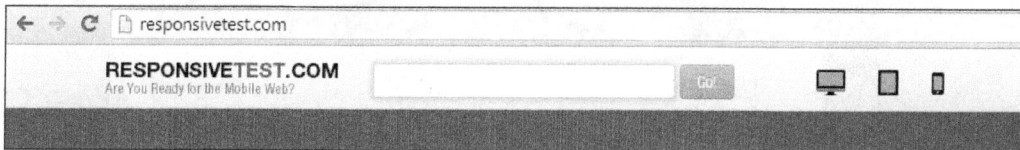

Testing the app as a whole

In this section, we will use some of the previously listed tools for our developed
application. Also, we will check how our developed application looks in different
screen sizes.

The following screenshot shows the Resolution 1.0 test screen for our
responsive application:

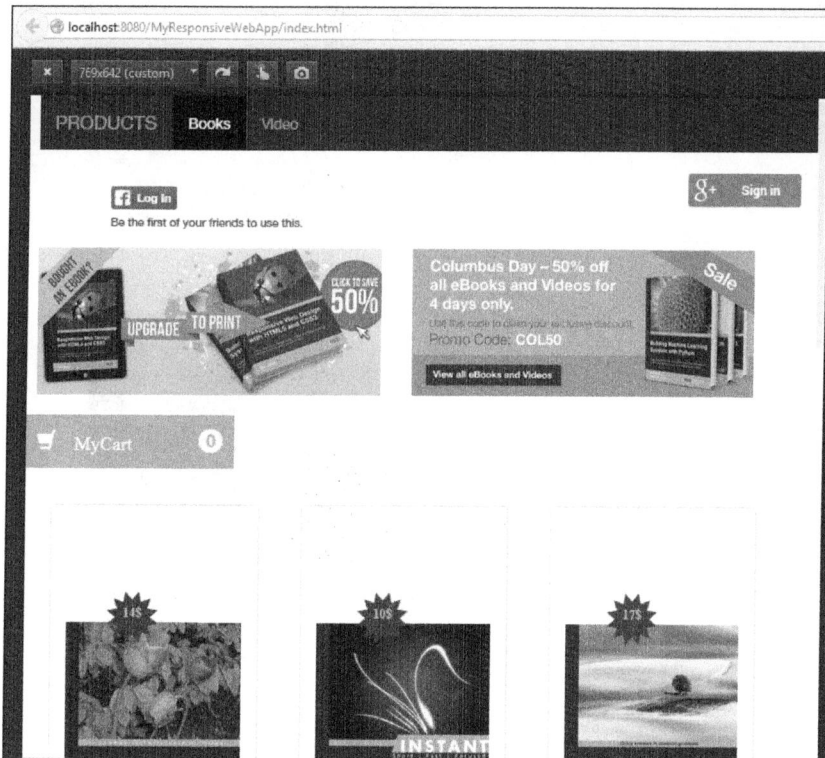

The following screenshot shows the iPad view taken from the Responsive Test online tool:

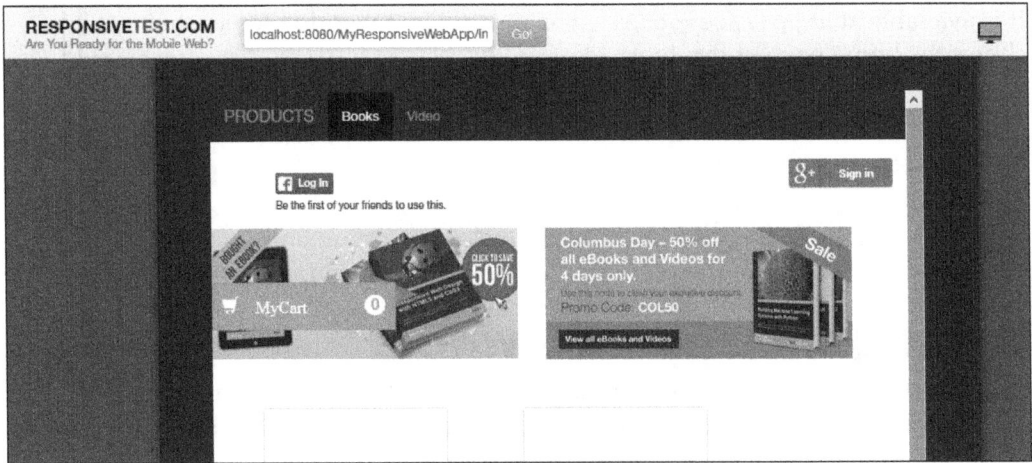

The following screenshot shows the iPhone screen from the Responsinator tool. You can see that the following screen is showing a single product in each row:

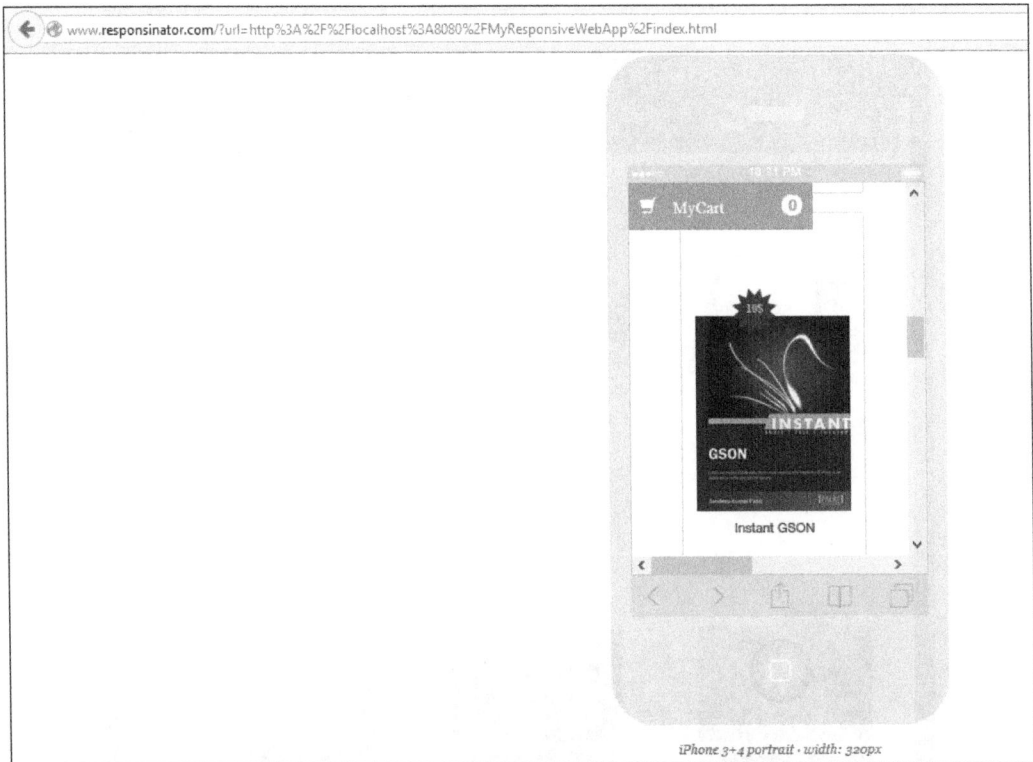

The following screenshot is taken from the Designmodo online tool for Samsung Galaxy Tab 10.1:

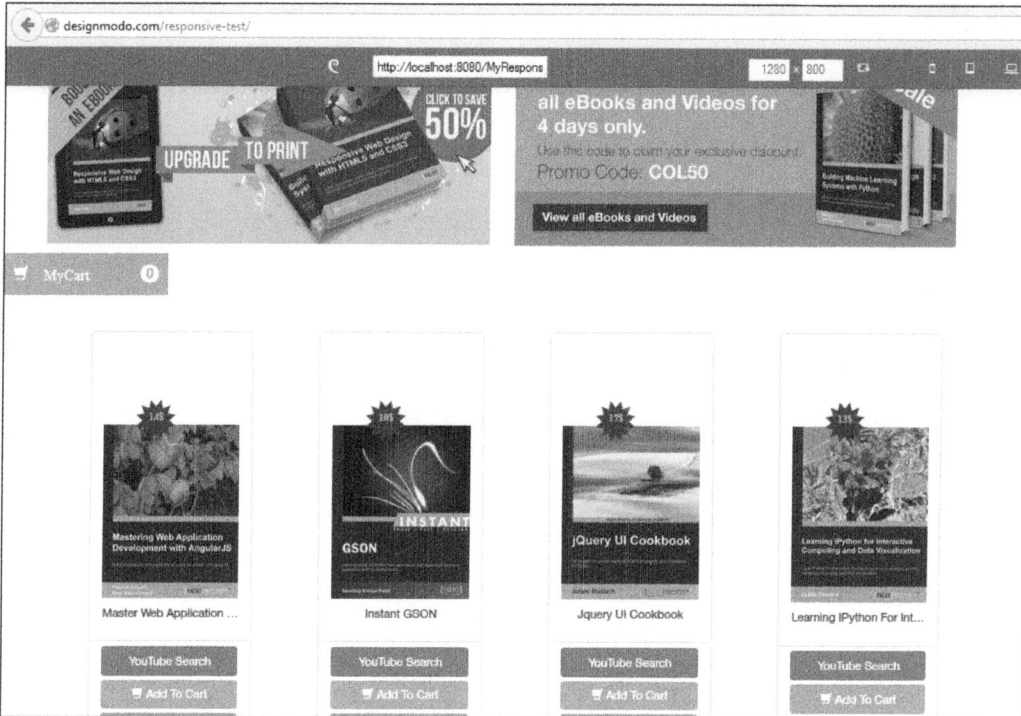

So, from the previous screenshots taken from different tools, we can conclude that the application is responsive on various devices with different screen sizes.

Summary

In this chapter, we listed some of the tools that can help during development to test a responsive application. We also explored some tools available for debugging and testing the responsiveness of our developed application.

Index

S

T

U

unordered list (ul) 33
URL field, Product class 54
User Agent String field,
　　Opera Mobile emulator 46
User Interface field,
　　Opera Mobile emulator 46

V

Viewport Resizer tool
　about 212
　features 212
　URL 212

W

web application
　Twitter4J, configuring 82
　wireframe, creating for 27, 28
Window Scale field,
　　Opera Mobile emulator 46
wireframe
　creating, for web application 27, 28

X

xfbml parameter, init() method 123

Y

YouTube API
　about 151
　configuring 151-154
　enabling, for application 153
　methods, accessing 153
YouTube button markup 156, 157
YouTube Data API Version 3.0 154
YouTube-related search video
　integrating 154
YouTube search
　asynchronous search 158-161
　fields parameter 156
　part parameter 156
　performing 154, 155
　query parameter 158
　results, rendering 162-165
　URL 155
　URL, for searching Cassandra
　　Administration 158
　YouTube button markup 156, 157
YouTube video
　embedding 165-168

[PACKT] open source *
PUBLISHING community experience distilled

Thank you for buying
Developing Responsive Web Applications with AJAX and jQuery

About Packt Publishing

Packt, pronounced 'packed', published its first book "*Mastering phpMyAdmin for Effective MySQL Management*" in April 2004 and subsequently continued to specialize in publishing highly focused books on specific technologies and solutions.

Our books and publications share the experiences of your fellow IT professionals in adapting and customizing today's systems, applications, and frameworks. Our solution based books give you the knowledge and power to customize the software and technologies you're using to get the job done. Packt books are more specific and less general than the IT books you have seen in the past. Our unique business model allows us to bring you more focused information, giving you more of what you need to know, and less of what you don't.

Packt is a modern, yet unique publishing company, which focuses on producing quality, cutting-edge books for communities of developers, administrators, and newbies alike. For more information, please visit our website: www.packtpub.com.

About Packt Open Source

In 2010, Packt launched two new brands, Packt Open Source and Packt Enterprise, in order to continue its focus on specialization. This book is part of the Packt Open Source brand, home to books published on software built around Open Source licenses, and offering information to anybody from advanced developers to budding web designers. The Open Source brand also runs Packt's Open Source Royalty Scheme, by which Packt gives a royalty to each Open Source project about whose software a book is sold.

Writing for Packt

We welcome all inquiries from people who are interested in authoring. Book proposals should be sent to author@packtpub.com. If your book idea is still at an early stage and you would like to discuss it first before writing a formal book proposal, contact us; one of our commissioning editors will get in touch with you.

We're not just looking for published authors; if you have strong technical skills but no writing experience, our experienced editors can help you develop a writing career, or simply get some additional reward for your expertise.

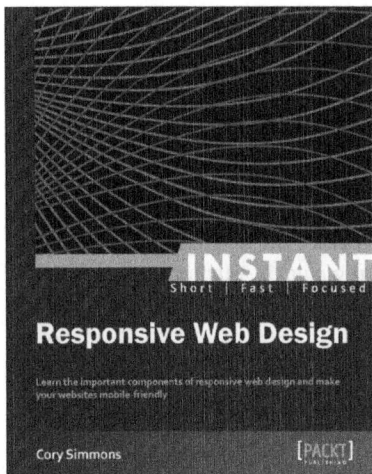

Instant Responsive Web Design

ISBN: 978-1-84969-925-9   Paperback: 70 pages

Learn the important components of responsive web design and make your websites mobile-friendly

1. Learn something new in an Instant!
    A short, fast, focused guide delivering
    immediate results.

2. Learn how to make your websites beautiful on
    any device.

3. Understand the differences between various
    responsive philosophies.

4. Expand your skill set with the quickly growing
    mobile-first approach.

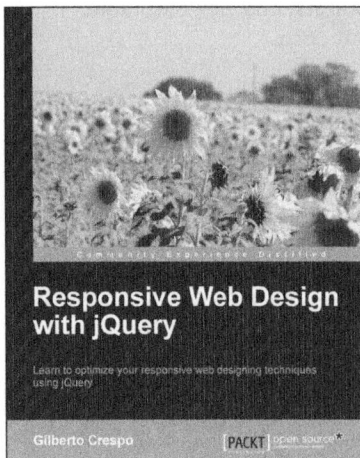

Responsive Web Design with jQuery

ISBN: 978-1-78216-360-2   Paperback: 256 pages

Learn to optimize your responsive web designing techniques using jQuery

1. Learn to swiftly design responsive websites by
    harnessing the power of jQuery.

2. Get your responsive site ready to meet the
    device-agnostic world.

3. Display highlighted content in a carousel and
    implement touch gestures to control them.

4. Understand the mobile-first philosophy and
    put its concept into practice.

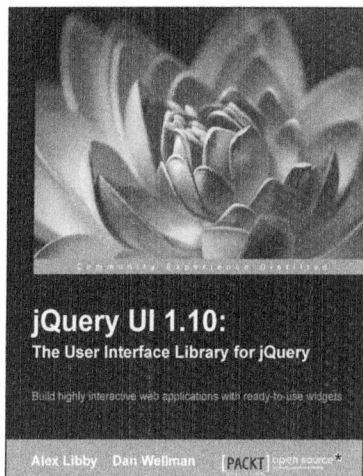

CPSIA information can be obtained
at www.ICGtesting.com
Printed in the USA
FSOW03n1445131214
3878FS